The Environment for Entrepreneurship

The Environment for Entrepreneurship

Edited by
Calvin A. Kent
Baylor University

LexingtonBooks
D.C. Heath and Company
Lexington, Massachusetts
Toronto

Library of Congress Cataloging in Publication Data

Main entry under title:
    The Environment for Entrepreneurship.

    Expanded versions of a series of lectures given during 1982–83 at the
Center for Private Enterprise and Entrepreneurship, Baylor University.
    Includes index.
    Contents: The rediscovery of the entrepreneur/Calvin A. Kent — The
entrepreneurial event/Albert Shapero — The entrepreneurial process/Israel
M. Kirzner — [etc.]
    1. Entrepreneur — Addresses, essays, lectures. I. Kent, Calvin A.
HB615.E65   1984   338′04   83–48736
ISBN 0–669–07507–8 (alk. paper)

Published simultaneously in Canada

Printed in the United States of America

International Standard Book Number: 0–669–07507–8

Library of Congress Catalog Card Number: 83–48736

*This book is dedicated to
Grandpa Homer,
Tina, and Anna:
entrepreneurs of the
past and future.*

Contents

Tables ix

Preface and Acknowledgments xi

Chapter 1 The Rediscovery of the Entrepreneur
Calvin A. Kent 1

Chapter 2 The Entrepreneurial Event   Albert Shapero 21

Chapter 3 The Entrepreneurial Process   Israel M. Kirzner 41

Chapter 4 The Fiscal Environment for Entrepreneurship
Michael J. Boskin 59

Chapter 5 Taxation and the Entrepreneurial Environment
Calvin A. Kent 69

Chapter 6 Regulation and the Entrepreneurial Environment
Kenneth W. Chilton 91

Chapter 7 Patents and the Entrepreneurial Environment
William E. Schuyler, Jr. 117

Chapter 8 The European Environment for Entrepreneurship
Madsen Pirie 155

Chapter 9 The New Entrepreneurs   Calvin A. Kent 173

Index 183

About the Contributors 189

About the Editor 191

Tables

4-1	U.S. Resources Devoted to Research and Development	61
4-2	Patents Issued	62
4-3	U.S. Employment and Unemployment Rates	63
4-4	New Business Formations and Failures	67
6-1	A Decade-by-Decade Comparison of Major Regulatory Legislation	92
6-2	NFIB Survey of the Importance of Government Regulation and Red Tape as a Small-Business Issue, 1974–1983	102
8-1	United Kingdom's Medical Health Service vs. U.S. Medical Industry	159

Preface and Acknowledgments

This book is the result of a series of lectures delivered during the academic year of 1982–1983 at the Center for Private Enterprise and Entrepreneurship, Hankamer School of Business, Baylor University, Waco, Texas. These lectures were made possible by a grant from the Association for Private Enterprise Education which was funded by the Dr. Scholl Foundation of Chicago. This book contains expanded versions of those lectures prepared by the authors, plus additional contributions by the editor, focusing upon the common theme of the environment of entrepreneurship.

There are many people to whom thanks should go for the success of the lecture series and the production of this book, but special thanks go to Nita Sue Kent, who not only edited the contributions, but also reworked them into a comprehensive whole. Martha Horn coordinated both the lectures and the manuscript preparation. Lisa Fowler, Jennifer Harden, and Diane Milam without complaint prepared the manuscript through its many revisions.

The views expressed here are not those of the Association for Private Enterprise Education, the Dr. Scholl Foundation, or Baylor University. Each individual author is to be held fully accountable for his own sins of omission and commission.

1 The Rediscovery of the Entrepreneur

Calvin A. Kent

There appears to be a well-defined but quiet revolution developing in the United States, Western Europe, and throughout the world. This revolution may have as great an impact on the lives of people in the twenty-first century as the industrial revolution had on the lives of those in the nineteenth. This revolution centers on the reemergence of the entrepreneur and the recognition that entrepreneurs are the prime generators of economic progress.

In his book, *Megatrends*, John Naisbitt refers to what he calls the "entrepreneurial explosion," which he views as one of the major trends that will shape America's destiny in the years to come. He perceives that "in the business world people are seeking self reliance and self help by becoming independent of large corporations through entrepreneurship, self employment, and work in small business."[1] In the past thirty years the number of new businesses has risen from 93,000 to 600,000 per year. In the last five years the rate of incorporation has risen 63 percent. Self-employment increased by 25 percent between 1972 and 1979. After decades of antipathy toward business in general and entrepreneurship in particular, a new attitude has arisen in the United States, summarized in Naisbitt's expression, "what's good for small business is good for America." The reason for this recognition, he says, is to be found in recent studies that "have convinced government and business observers that small businesses, not big corporations, are responsible for most of the new jobs created and most of the nation's economic growth and that they are more productive and innovative as well."[2]

A similar appraisal for the United Kingdom was reached by Graham Bannock in his book *The Economics of Small Firms: Return from the Wilderness*.[3] He notes that at the beginning of this century the majority of Britons worked in small firms, but now the chief employers are large corporations and the government. He tells us that until the mid-1970s industrial concentration was viewed as a necessary condition for economic progress. It was felt that no factory could hope to compete in the world market unless it achieved the technical efficiencies believed to be associated with mass production, marketing, and distribution. In Europe and in the United States, government policy was directed either explicitly or implicitly toward economic concentration through mergers both domestic and foreign.

It was the economic events of the 1970s that demonstrated that this was the path toward failure. Western Europe and the United States entered into a prolonged period in which prices and unemployment rose at rates that were economically unacceptable and politically dangerous. In entrepreneurship, surprisingly, the political right and left seem to have found a common cause. The political right supports entrepreneurs because of their perceived contribution to innovation and economic growth, and the political left supports entrepreneurship because of belief the that new ventures will create jobs and allow for a reduced concentration of industrial and political power. The failures of planned societies in the Communist bloc and underdeveloped world to perform as they have promised have led to a reevaluation of the role of new ventures and free markets as vehicles for stimulating economic growth and development. In the years to come material progress will be conditioned by the extent and direction of entrepreneurial activity.

What Is an Entrepreneur?

Unfortunately, there is no consensus among scholars as to what constitutes entrepreneurship or the entrepreneurial event. In his classic essay, "Hunting the Heffalump," Peter Kilby reviews the definitional debate, but concludes that maybe it is more important to search for the results of entrepreneurial action and what causes those results than to quibble over definitions.[4]

Disregarding Kilby's advice, Hebert and Link have completed an extensive tracing of the concept of the entrepreneur throughout the history of economic thought.[5] To Richard Cantillon, an eighteenth-century Irish banker who operated in Paris, the entrepreneur was primarily a bearer of uninsurable risk. Because of this risk-taking propensity, the entrepreneur became the balancing figure in the market, reacting to price movements that signalled shortages and surpluses. The idea of entrepreneur as risk taker was later carried forward in America in the writings of Frank Knight.[6] This view of the entrepreneur as a risk is partially correct but misleading. As Edwin Harwood demonstrates there are many individuals and groups who assume uninsurable risks, but who do not perform the entrepreneurial function.[7] The preoccupation with the entrepreneur as a risk bearer to whom the return of profit is due has caused economists to ignore or misinterpret the role of entrepreneurship in economic growth and development until recently.

The Frenchman J.V. Say first used the term *entrepreneur* as we know it. Say made an important distinction between the entrepreneur and the capitalist. The capitalist or financier was one who supplied money and took a financial risk. This did not necessarily make the capitalist an entrepreneur, although the same individual could perform both the entrepreneurial and the capitalist function. Say saw the entrepreneur as one who brought together the factors of production in such a way that new wealth was created. Say's entrepreneur combined the features of both risk taker and manager. Say felt the number of entrepreneurs was limited because very few had the talents of superintendence and administration as well as the proclivity to bear risk that entrepreneurship requires.

The concept of entrepreneurship has become distorted in British and American economic thought. This is not surprising considering the treatment the entrepreneur received in the works of Adam Smith, the early British economist. While Smith did believe that entrepreneurs had to possess a certain inventive genius, he basically confused the entrepreneurial and capitalist roles. Subsequent English-speaking writers have continued this confusion and invariably have not investigated entrepreneurship as a separate phenomenon. This neglect caused Binks and Coyne to conclude that, "in mainstream Anglo-American economic thought the entrepreneur has been largely ignored."[8] Kilby noted the tendency to treat "profit as a single undifferentiated income flow delegating entrepreneurship to management, a very special variety of skilled labor."[9]

By far the clearest understanding of the entrepreneurial process was given to us by Joseph Schumpeter, who saw the entrepreneur as an innovator. Entrepreneurial innovation occurred in any of five cases.

1. The introduction of a new good or of a new quality of good
2. The introduction of a new method of production
3. The opening of a new market
4. The conquest of a new source of supply of raw materials
5. The carrying out of new organization of any industry

The entrepreneurial function, then, was one of creating disequilibrium. It was one that went beyond discovery and included implementation and commercialization.[10]

> Schumpeter's economic leaders are individuals motivated by an atavistic will to power who occur randomly in any ethnically homogenous population. Their special characteristics are an intuitional capacity to see things in a way that afterwards proves correct, energy of will and mind to overcome fixed habits of thought, and the capacity to withstand social opposition.[11]

An even more current view of the entrepreneur that builds on Schumpeter's has been most eloquently advanced by Israel M. Kirzner, a definition fully developed in his essay in this volume and applied to the question of economic growth. Kirzner sees the entrepreneur as one who perceives what others have not seen and acts upon that perception. The marketplace is constantly sending signals—to those alert enough to perceive them—about equilibrium conditions which if acted upon can lead to profit. Kirzner's entrepreneur is more than just a risk taker and innovator. He or she is the one who sees the future that no one else has seen, and if this perception is correct, brings about a reordering of resources to produce greater consumer satisfaction or technological efficiency. Kirzner's work is also laudable in its stress on the importance of incentives as the spur for entrepreneurial action and the inhibiting effect the environment may have upon those incentives.[12]

Harwood has described the following characteristics of entrepreneurs: 1) taking of initiative, 2) assumption of considerable autonomy in the organization and management of resources, 3) sharing in the asset risk, 4) participation in an uncertain monetary profit, and 5) innovation in more than a marginal or incremental way.[13]

Albro Martin reminds readers of what an entrepreneur is not.

1. A person who owns an enterprise or gives the orders is not necessarily an entrepreneur. The Arthur D. Cole definition of entrepreneurship, especially because it was adopted widely, did a disservice to the understanding of entrepreneurship because it failed to distinguish between the innovator and the administrator.
2. A person who assumes the risk of his or her capital is not necessarily an entrepreneur but may be only an investor. However, one who risks his or her reputation or a position in a large corporate organization as a result of an innovation with which he or she is closely identified, fulfills some of the preconditions of entrepreneurship.
3. A creative person in the literary, artistic, or dramatic sense is not necessarily an entrepreneur. The entrepreneur does not innovate by creating ideas, but by recognizing their value and exploiting them.[14]

The entrepreneur is more than self-employed. Those who start businesses solely as an alternative to wage employment do not participate in the entrepreneurial event. Entrepreneurship requires the element of growth that leads to innovation, job creation, and economic expansion.

The Importance of Entrepreneurship

The resurgence of interest in small business in general and in entrepreneurship in particular can be traced to certain benefits that are widely believed to be associated with the growth and establishment of small firms.[15] It must be reemphasized not all small firms are entrepreneurships, but most entrepreneurship begins in small firms. It is generally accepted by the authors in this volume that actions which encourage the formation of small firms will also improve the entrepreneurial environment and create more of the benefits associated with new-venture initiation. What are some of these alleged benefits?

Growth and Jobs

It has almost become rote for those who advocate the virtues of small business to cite its contribution to the generation of jobs. This enthusiasm has been based on studies done at MIT by David Birch and his associates.[16] His 1979 study indicated that businesses with fewer than five hundred employees generated 86.7 percent of the private-sector jobs, with the majority coming from companies of less than twenty employees. This study indicated that 66 percent of all new jobs in the economy during the sixties and early seventies came from small firms less than five years old.

The White House Commission on Small Business indicated that the nations's one thousand largest corporations generated less than one-half of one percent of all of the new jobs created in the economy between 1969 and 1976, and concluded, "if we are to achieve anything approaching a healthy level of employment for Americans in the 1980's, the leverage for public policy lies in spurring entrepreneurship and existing small companies."[17] The assumption here is that an improved environment for small business will lead to the generation of new jobs necessary to absorb not only those currently unemployed but new entrants into the labor market and those seeking to upgrade their positions.

In recent years the validity of this conclusion has been questioned by studies conducted at the Brookings Institution.[18] Further contrary evidence has been offered by a study limited to California.[19] The Small Business Administration has reviewed these counterarguments and now feels that the answer to the question of how many new jobs are actually contributed by small as opposed to large businesses is "more complex than suspected."[20] These studies found lower estimates for the number of jobs created by small business when enterprises were counted separately from establishments. Establishments are small businesses owned and operated by a single individual, whereas enterprises may be small businesses owned by larger corporations. Fifteen percent of all small-business employment occurs in establishments that are actually owned by larger corporations. In addition, not all small firms generate new jobs. It was found that somewhere between 12 and 15 percent of all small firms generate the new jobs created in the small-firms sector. Birch, in a later study (1981), concluded that the very vigorous growth of a few new ventures which are highly entrepreneurial and clustered in a few industries accounts for a significant percentage of all new jobs in the economy.[21] Studies done for the United Kingdom produced similar results: smaller firms contributed a net increase in employment while larger, more established firms provided few if any new employment opportunities.[22]

It appears indisputable, however, that entrepreneurial firms contribute a disproportionate share of new jobs. In addition, new ventures provide the entry-level jobs so necessary as training experience for the unskilled. These ventures may also be viewed as subsidizing larger firms by developing the work force and preparing workers to move into positions demanding discipline and education.[23]

Innovation

Since the writings of Schumpeter, entrepreneurship has been viewed as an innovative force as opposed to larger businesses, which may have a vested interest in keeping new innovations off the market to protect their investments in existing technology. As Schumpeter notes, "you do not ask the owner of the stage line to build the railroad." Small businesses facing no such constraint are free, if not compelled, to develop new products and bring them to the market.[24]

A National Science Foundation study indicated that each dollar spent by small firms on research and development produced four times more innovation than the same dollar when spent by larger enterprises.[25] The U.S. Office of Management and the Budget credits more than half of the technological advances in this century to individual inventors or small companies. Among these are xerography, air conditioning, the Polaroid process, cellophane, insulin, penicillin, helicopters, and ballpoint pens.[26]

O.J. Krasner attempts to distinguish between contributions to innovation by larger firms and entrepreneurships.[27] He accepts Prager and Omenn's contention that

> The overall innovative process encompasses a spectrum of activity from basic research to the commercial application and marketing. For the innovative process to be productive, the generation of knowledge and the translation of that knowledge into commercial products and services must be linked.[28]

Krasner on one hand finds evidence to support the idea that large organizations are more successful than entrepreneurships in product innovations that are essentially improvements. This means large organizations are more likely to innovate in terms of devising new ways of producing already existing products or to make improvements in the products they already bring to market. Such innovations present no threat to the established firm as it improves its competitive advantage, either in terms of product cost or desirability.

On the other hand, research indicates entrepreneurs are more likely to make "leapfrog" innovations, which involve the development of entirely new processes and products. These type of leapfrog innovations create a discontinuity in the operations of existing firms and are likely to be shunned by them. Entrepreneurs who have nothing to lose by the introduction of new products or technologies and do not have large amounts invested in existing capital are most likely to produce the more significant forward steps in the development of entirely new products and processes.

Bannock supports this view in the United Kingdom.

> The principal economic importance of small firms lies in their responsiveness to change and since change is what is required if economic growth is to be resumed, it is desirable that more rather than fewer resources should be channeled into small business. Being small and individually owned and managed by fewer people they are more flexible than larger firms. . . . [N]ew small firms are the prime initiators of new industries and new markets. As new firms start up and others fail they are testing out new products, processes and forms of organization without committing large amounts of resources and without causing disruption if they fail.[29]

During a period in which R&D expenditures as a percent of the U.S. GNP are decreasing and in which foreign nations are outperforming the United States in the development of new technology, the encouragement of the entrepreneurial sector would seem to be an appropriate policy.

Impact on Communities

In chapter 2, Albert Shapero contends that a community is better off if its employment base is diversified among many small entrepreneurial firms, rather than dependent upon one large major industry. His conclusion is supported by the White House Commission on Small Business, which cites studies that found communities with small-business bases had higher income levels, more stable economic growth, and a higher level of civic participation by industry leaders. These towns were characterized by more abundant retail facilities, a higher level of home ownership, fewer slums, better sanitation standards, and higher expenditures for education, recreation, and religious activities.[30]

Another study showed that when small firms in Wisconsin were merged with larger firms, the impact on communities was to cut off local suppliers, advertising agencies, and banks, with less concern for community problems and a lower rate of community participation by managers. It appears obvious that a community dependent upon one firm will be highly susceptible to the vicissitudes of the industry. A more diversified economic base of entrepreneurial firms leads to more stability and a higher quality of community life.[31]

Consequences of Business Failure

When large business entities are faced with collapse, almost irresistable pressure begins to develop upon state and national governments to do something to assist. The recent bail-outs of Lockheed and Chrysler are testimonies to this point. The consequences of allowing these large firms to go under in terms of the numbers of jobs lost, the financial impact on shareholders and pension funds, the balance sheets of banks, the impact on suppliers, and the loss of state and local tax revenues mean these cries cannot be ignored. The results are potential drains upon the public treasury and demands for protection against foreign competition until the failing firm's house is again put in order. The failure of a small firm does not produce such widespread or dire consequences. As Bannock has noted, "the failure of a single small firm, or for that matter, the starting up of a new one has no measurable affect upon the economy, however, and no political repercussions. It is the part of a seamless bank of economic change."[32]

Economic Integration of "Outsiders"

Only recently have scholars come to recognize that entrepreneurship is perhaps the most effective way of integrating those who feel disposessed and alienated into the economy. Despite the low rates of entrepreneurship among the minorities and women, venture initiation may in the future provide the best opportunities for improved standards of living and upward mobility for these groups. In declaring October 2–8, 1983, "Minority Enterprise Development Week," President Reagan stated:

> [T]he success of minority business enterprise demonstrates that hard work and individual determination can serve as a powerful engine for social mobility and economic progress. Our challenge today is to enhance the ability of minority Americans to participate more fully in the market economy and to achieve greater economic interdependence.[33]

Minority-owned businesses account for only 5 percent of total businesses in the United States.[34] Women-owned businesses are about four to five times more prevalent.[35]

Preliminary estimates show striking improvements in both areas. The Small Business Administration (SBA) statistics reveal a significant rate of increase in minority business growth from 1977 to 1981, a rate that has exceeded that for the growth of business for the nation as a whole. For women-owned businesses, the growth rate has been even more spectacular. The number of such firms increased by one-third over this same period. Although women are now moving into nontraditional businesses such as mining, manufacturing, finance, insurance, and real estate, their efforts still tend to be concentrated in the services and retail trades.

In addition to providing the mechanism to integrate minorities and women into the economic system, entrepreneurship apparently has been successful in functioning similarly for many of those who became disillusioned with American institutions in the 1960s and 1970s. John Naisbitt explains how this happened.

> But much of that anticorporate feeling went underground during the 1970s as graduates went to work—where else?—in big business. Many of us thought that was the end of it; another generation of idealists wised up to the real world. The baby boomers were not just another generation of idealists, though. Their numbers made them a megageneration, an army that was not easily absorbed in society. And the 1970s, when their ranks hit the job front, were not exactly booming times. Consequently, some baby boomers were forced into self-employment, even entrepreneurship, by a weak job market. Others who had cherished independence in the 1960s and given it up for high-paying corporate jobs in the 1970s were, all the while, saving, learning, and plotting their escape into entrepreneurship. In the late 1970s it all exploded into an entrepreneurial boom.[36]

Entrepreneurial Economics

It is in vogue today among economists to talk about demand and supply-side economics. These terms provide a useful framework in which to investigate entrepreneurial economics. Although the distinction between these two schools of thought often breaks down, they do represent two views of the entrepreneurial process.

In it simplest form supply-side entrepreneurial economics considers the number of entrepreneurs who will be available at any point in time to any nation or social group. It views the supply of entrepreneurs as being highly dependent on psychological and sociological factors. Economic motivation such as profit may be of secondary importance in causing one to become an entrepreneur. The literature on the psychology of the entrepreneur has been evaluated by Brockhaus.[37] Entrepreneurs have been analyzed as having a different psychological makeup than managers and others in the economy. Psychological variables that distinguish entrepreneurs are the need for achievement, beliefs about the locus of control, risk-taking propensity, and other personal values.

In addition there are environmental or sociological factors that will affect the supply of entrepreneurs, such as dissatisfaction with previous work, role models, and displacement. My own recent research and that of my colleagues indicates that entrepreneurs do tend to have a different set of lifetime and educational experiences than do individuals who become managers.[38]

There does appear to be impressive evidence that psychologically entrepreneurs are not the same as those who choose management or wage employment.

Economists appear in general to have been guilty of ignoring supply-side considerations in entrepreneurial economics. Kilby notes, "the economist who operates in the mainstream of his discipline assumes that the supply of entrepreneurial services is highly elastic and the failures in entrepreneurship are attributable to maladjustments in the external environment."[39] In recent years this has been because of economists' general preoccupation with Keynesian demand-side macroeconomics. For nearly four decades after the Great Depression and the publication of Keynes's general theory, economists have been primarily concerned with aggregate demand.[40] In Keynes's model, aggregate demand or total spending is viewed as the result of consumption spending by households, investment spending by businesses, governmental spending by political entities, and net spending in the foreign sector (the difference between exports and imports). The great contribution of Keynesian economics is the realization that aggregate demand might be insufficient to produce full employment of all resources. In the Keynesian analysis there was no reason to expect, as earlier economists had, that automatic forces operating in the economy would ensure full employment following a period of adjustment.

From the standpoint of entrepreneurial economics, the great deficiency of Keynesian analysis is its assumption that if aggregate demand is high enough, sufficient incentives will be present in the economy to bring forth enough entrepreneurs to produce a level of investment great enough to ensure economic growth and a steady flow of innovation. Keynes, and to a greater degree his disciples, felt that private investment may not be sufficient to ensure full employment and massive infusions of government spending will be necessary if jobs are to be created for all those willing and able to work.[41] This is the essence of demand-side entrepreneurial economics. Entrepreneurship will be forthcoming so long as total spending is maintained at a sufficiently high level either in the private or public sector to produce full employment.

The chapters in this book are based on the premise that neither the supply-side nor the demand-side explanation of entrepreneurship is sufficient to explain the level of entrepreneurial activity at any given time. The environment for entrepreneurship must also be considered, along with demand and supply-side considerations, as a principal determinant of entrepreneurship. As Binks and Coyne have commented, "it is evident that entrepreneurial skills may be more widely distributed in any population than is immediately apparent, but it requires a sympathetic economic environment to nurture and harness those skills in the creation of enterprises."[42] The focus of the chapters that follow is on government policies as they affect the environment for entrepreneurship. There is an implicit assumption here that if certain policies are followed, the number of individuals willing to take the risks associated with innovation and new product development will expand. It is not assumed that the only consideration worth studying in the process of entrepreneurship is the environment created by governmental action. It is assumed that no matter what psychological factors characterize a population or what the level of total spending may be, the amount of new product development and venture initiation will be conditioned by the external environment for entrepreneurship. What follows is a summary of each chapter.

The Entrepreneurial Event

Albert Shapero notes the growing national attention being focused on entrepreneurship because of a changing cultural climate that places a higher priority on individual achievement and initiative. To him the entrepreneurial event is the result of two decisions: the decision of an individual to change his life path and the decision to start a new business. The decision to change one's life path comes as a result of personal displacement, often the result of negative forces such as desertion, loss of job, or frustration.

Not all displaced individuals become entrepreneurs, however. Venture initiation must be seen as both feasible and desirable. This recognition is conditioned by the culture in which the entrepreneur finds himself. Individuals who have had close past association with entrepreneurs, or who had an entrepreneur parent, are more likely to start their own businesses than others. The perceived availability of financing is also important. Psychological factors play a role since entrepreneurs tend to be individuals with a high desire for independence along with a significant tolerance for risk.

Educational experience is also important in creating willingness to assume entrepreneurial risk. Shapero sees U.S. education in the past as having been antientrepreneurial producing individuals better suited for the bureaucracies of big government and big corporations than for venture initiation.

Shapero recommends that cities and areas that wish to become entrepreneurial incubators should not pander to divisions of large corporations but should work on developing a diversified industrial base of small, high-growth ventures. Government policies on the whole have retarded the entrepreneurial event, even when these policies have had encouraging entrepreneurship as their express purpose.

The Entrepreneurial Process

It is Israel Kirzner's contention that economists have invariably either ignored the entrepreneurial process or assumed that it has always existed and functions smoothly. Kirzner sees the entrepreneurial process as having two meanings. The first concerns entrepreneurial competition, which is a short-term phenomenon forcing prices to the equilibrium level. The second is concerned with entrepreneurial discovery, whereby inventions become innovations and long-term economic growth results. According to Kirzner, economic growth takes place when today's bounds, created by limited resources, are exceeded by expanding the resource base through new technology or the discovery of resources and technical knowledge already in existence but which were not being applied.

It is this expanded awareness of existing opportunities that the entrepreneur grasps. The entrepreneur sees what others have missed and acts on the opportunities that have gone unnoticed and unexploited. The existence of profit and the security of property rights is central to the entrepreneurial process. Also essential is freedom of entry, which allows prospective entrepreneurs to freely exploit their perceptions of unexploited opportunities.

The Fiscal Environment for Entrepreneurship

Nowhere do governments and entrepreneurs interact more closely than in the area of governmental fiscal policy, according to Michael Boskin. Boskin includes in the entrepreneurial process not only those who initiate new business, but also those who develop new processes and policies, along with scientists and others who generate the ideas that ultimately come to the marketplace as new products or technology.

The recent history of the United States has not produced a favorable fiscal environment for entrepreneurship. The results of this hostile environment are declining research and development expenditures as a percentage of national income, a decrease in the number of new patents issued, and a reduction in the number of students training as scientists, technicians, and engineers.

Boskin feels that inflation does more than just debasing the monetary unit. Inflation creates an additional element of uncertainty in the already risky process of entrepreneurship, thus discouraging venture capitalists and financial institutions from making money available for new-venture formation. Corporate income tax is also seen as a menace to capital formation. Boskin advocates instead a single integrated tax on all business earnings whereby profits are taxed only to shareholders rather than double taxed under both personal and corporate levies. He also suggests that a tax levied solely on consumption would increase the amount saved and invested in the economy. The fiscal environment for entrepreneurship would also be improved if the confidence of the innovating and investing public were restored in the credibility of government to employ stable fiscal and monetary policies.

Taxation and the Entrepreneurial Environment

In chapter 5 I investigate recent developments in U.S. tax policy as it has affected the entrepreneurial sector of the economy. It was the intention of supply-side economics when proposed by President Reagan to improve the climate for saving and investment, which would lead to increased productivity and expansion in new venture initiation. In 1981 the Economic Recovery Tax Act (ERTA) was passed, granting significant tax decreases to both businesses and individuals. Less than a year later many of the benefits gained under that legislation were repealed by the Tax Equity and Fiscal Responsibility Act (TEFRA). Significant changes have also been made in Social Security taxes and in the treatment of small corporations that elect to be taxed under Subchapter S.

Many of the advantages granted under recent tax legislation will not be of benefit to some new ventures, because those firms often have no taxable income against which tax credits can be applied. In addition, the labor-intensive nature of most emerging enterprises means that the increases in payroll taxes resulting under the new Social Security legislation will reduce their competitive status relative to the more capital-intensive larger corporations who are their rivals.

Large corporations may manipulate their corporate tax liability by using losses or credits in some divisions to offset the taxes or profits earned in others. Small businesses lack this flexibility. A tax system designed to encourage entrepreneurship recognizes this difference. It is the contention of this chapter that many of the tax changes were designed to spur investment, not specifically to help small businesses. As a result large businesses may have fared better than the entrepreneurial sector.

Among the tax changes discussed here are the new rules for Subchapter S corporations, the reduction in capital gains, the Accelerated Cost Recovery System (ACRS), the credits for research and development expenditures, the simplification of the Last In, First Out (LIFO) inventory accounting, the increases in Social Security levies, and changes in the Unified Estate and Gift Tax. On the whole the tax environment for entrepreneurship may have improved slightly, but needs to be even more favorable if new ventures are to have adequate access to capital and to compete with established firms not only for investment dollars but also for markets.

Regulation in the Entrepreneurial Environment

Kenneth Chilton analyzes the impact on entrepreneurs of the rush to regulation that began with the environmental movement in the late 1960s and spread in the 1970s to encompass worker health, consumer safety, equal employment opportunities, regulation of securities, and a host of other social concerns. Chilton views this growth in regulation as a major impediment to entrepreneurship and innovation, but does see hopeful signs that the regulatory environment may be changing for the better. Chilton finds three pervasive and perverse effects on the entrepreneurial environment that have resulted from regulation. The first is the government-induced economies of scale that have pushed per-unit cost up for small businesses to a greater degree than for large established firms. In addition, governmental regulation has significantly increased labor costs. More labor intensive than large companies, small firms have been disproportionately affected by labor-market regulation. If all this were not bad enough, the phenomenal paper report burden associated with these regulations frustrates entrepreneurs as they attempt to comply with ever-expanding and increasingly complex agency edicts. Larger firms can hire more specialized staff to deal with this morass of paperwork.

Chilton also finds that recent regulation has limited the entrepreneur's access to capital, the most important ingredient in business survival. Programs enacted by the Small Business Administration are viewed as failures. The Securities and Exchange Commission regulation of new stock issues is also criticized as not being sensitive to the problems of smaller firms. Other governmental regulations create barriers to entry and have excluded entrepreneurs from pursuing profits in new and growing industries.

But Chilton is not totally pessimistic. He feels that the public attitude toward entrepreneurship has changed for the better with congressional passage of the Federal Regulatory Flexibility Act, the Equal Access to Justice Act, and Paperwork Reduction Act. The executive branch has also instituted reform. While President Reagan's regulatory task force is found to have been largely ineffective, several agencies either willingly or unwillingly have demonstrated a more sympathetic view.

Chilton's underlying message is that entrepreneurs should look to the government not for protection, but merely to create an open and flexible market environment in which they should prosper. Chilton warns against the small-business and entrepreneurial psychology that condemns governmental intervention yet actively pursues it when it is in their interest to do so.

Patents and the Environment for Entrepreneurship

William Schuyler relates the U.S. patent system to the process of innovation and new product development. Under the U.S. Constitution, patents and trademarks are intellectual property and like other personal property may be used, licensed, sold, assigned, or given away at the discretion of the owner. Under patent law there is a trade-off of rights and responsibilities between the owner and the general public. The public benefits from the patent system since it provides incentives to invent, to develop new ideas, and to inform the public about the state of the arts as they pertain to certain technologies. In addition, patents give an incentive to investors who are looking for some guarantee before risking their financial capital on a new idea.

Though patents are an essential ingredient in the process of entrepreneurship and innovation, many successful firms have developed without patent protection. One of the most current controversial areas concerns computer software. The level of entrepreneurship and new product innovation in this area is currently unexcelled in the United States, but pertinent patent law is only slowly evolving. Even more important as an aid to the entrepreneur are trademarks. Unlike patents, these do not expire and often prove to be more effective incentives to develop and market new products. Names like Kodak®, Kleenex®, and Xerox® are more important than are their patents.

The patent system serves different industries and different innovations in different ways. Well-established firms in the market need patent protection much less than do new entrants. Also, in industries where the time from invention to commercialization is long, patents are more necessary than when such time is short.

There are problems associated with the patent system. The cost of obtaining a patent is extremely high; there are legal fees necessary in obtaining a patent search by a competent lawyer. In addition the patent holder may be faced with extensive costs if it is necessary to take legal action to enforce the patent right. Since many patents are invalidated when brought to trial, inventors face a sizable financial risk when they seek to enforce their patents. The length of time necessary to conclude patent litigation is also a major barrier to new invention.

Patent policy has changed significantly in recent years. The most important of these changes is the patent reexamination statute. Reexamination provides a quick, simple way for ascertaining the validity of already issued patents without going to litigation. The move to a single court system for patent cases has begun. Previously there has been little uniformity in judicial decisions made at lower levels by federal courts. The establishment of a court of appeals for the federal circuit combining the judges of the Customs courts and the Patents Appeal courts will bring a better understanding of the intricacies of patent law. In addition, there has been an increased use of arbitration as a technique to settle patent issues. Schuyler concludes with further agenda for reform of the patent system including upgrading of the examination process, extension of the patent term after litigation is completed, and the establishment of incontestable patents.

The European Environment for Entrepreneurship

In chapter 8 Madsen Pirie explores what he views as a budding transformation of Europe's environment for entrepreneurship. He contends that the European environment is bad, but it is getting better. He cites as evidence of an improved environment the growth of free zones in Belgium and the United Kingdom, which will demonstrate the virtues of freeing industry from the burdens of excessive taxation and regulation. The trend toward privatization of public enterprise in Europe is equally important in contributing to an improved entrepreneurial environment. Public enterprises are being dismantled and sold to private producers, financed with private rather than public capital; and their services are sold in the marketplace at market-clearing prices instead of at fixed prices in markets controlled by the government.

Pirie sees the following main sources of impediment for entrepreneurial activity in Europe: governmental regulation and taxes, unions, bureaucrats, and the climate of public opinion that has tended in the past to value public service over business initiation. He asserts that this environment can be changed because "governments can be pushed around, unions can be bludgeoned, and bureaucrats can be sidestepped," and details how this has been accomplished.

One of the more intriguing ideas in Mr. Pirie's chapter is the suggestion for special incentives for new businesses called *portable enterprise zones*. These portable enterprise zones would not have geographic boundaries, but instead would encompass the small-business sector of the economy, and would be exempt from taxes and regulations until the businesses matured. Pirie concludes with nine steps toward the privatization of government functions. The European experience indicates that all nine steps can successfully return all or part of public enterprise to private hands. As this is done, new opportunities emerge for entrepreneurs. More important, privatization is a way of diminishing governmental control of the individual's decisions, an important step toward a more free society.

The New Entrepreneurs

If one theme is constant in this book it is that governmental policy can, but usually does not, improve the entrepreneurial environment. The concluding chapter looks at entrepreneurship in the environment created by command economies. The Soviet Union, the People's Republic of China, and Hungary are used as case studies because each demonstrates a different degree of central control and direction of economic life. These case studies verify that the entrepreneurial impulse cannot be destroyed, but only misdirected.

In the command economies what has emerged is a new class of entrepreneurs. In the Soviet Union the activities of this class are often illegal but essential, particularly in the production of food. The thriving black market and the existence of parallel production in socialist enterprises with its attendant corruption is testimony to the efficacy of markets in producing both efficiency and innovation. Recent reforms in the People's Republic of China have added a degree of freedom and increased efficiency to the agricultural sector. At least on paper this trend is to spread from the farms to the industrialized sector. Hungary is the showplace of socialism. The semiprivate enterprises which are legal, along with the small retail shops, constitute the free sector of the Hungarian economy. In each group output and efficiency have increased as restrictions have diminished. In all three nations the extent to which the economy can become decentralized and a more favorable entrepreneurial environment be created is severely limited by totalitarian states that cannot risk loss of control over production and the distribution of income.

Entrepreneurial effort in the United States has also been misdirected by the taxes and regulations discussed in earlier chapters. The way to profit is not by producing new goods or developing new technologies, but by discovering some way to avoid the taxes and regulations now in place. As a result of these restrictions, a phenomenal amount of effort goes into paperwork. To this is added the short-run, bottom-line mentality of managers, which also discourages long-run innovation and risk taking. Revival of the traditional process of innovation and venture initiation is essential for national growth, if not national survival.

Notes

1. John Naisbitt, *Megatrends* (New York: Warner Books, 1982), pp. 145–149.

2. Ibid., p. 146.

3. Graham Bannock, *The Economics of Small Firms: Return from the Wilderness* (Oxford: Basil Blackwell, 1981), pp. 8–9.

4. Peter Kilby, "Hunting the Heffalump," in Peter Kilby, *Entrepreneurship and Economic Development* (New York: Free Press, 1971), pp. 1–43.

5. Robert F. Hebert and Albert N. Link, *The Entrepreneur* (New York: Praeger Publishers, 1982), pp. 1–72.

6. Frank H. Knight, *Risk, Uncertainty, and Profit,* Series of Reprints of Scarce Tracts in Economic and Political Science, No. 16 (London: London School of Economics and Political Science, 1948), pp. 264–313.

7. Edwin Harwood, "The Sociology of Entrepreneurship," in Calvin

A. Kent, et al., *The Encyclopedia of Entrepreneurship* (Englewood Cliffs, N.J.: Prentice-Hall, 1982), pp. 91–98.

8. Martin Binks and John Coyne, *The Birth of Enterprise* (London: Institute of Economic Affairs, 1983), p. 13.

9. Kilby, "Hunting the Heffalump," p. 2.

10. Joseph Schumpeter, *The Theory of Economic Development* (Cambridge, Mass.: Harvard University Press, 1936), p. 66.

11. Kilby, "Hunting the Heffalump," p. 7.

12. Israel M. Kirzner, *Competition and Entrepreneurship* (Chicago: University of Chicago Press, 1973); and *Perception, Opportunity and Profit* (Chicago: University of Chicago Press, 1979).

13. Edwin Harwood, "The Sociology of Entrepreneurship," in Calvin A. Kent, et al. *The Encyclopedia of Entrepreneurship,* p. 98.

14. Albro Martin, "Additional Aspects of Entrepreneurial History," in Calvin A. Kent, et al., *The Encyclopedia of Entrepreneurship*, p. 16.

15. For a comprehensive review see Karl H. Vesper, *Entrepreneurship and National Policy* (Chicago: Heller Institute for Small Business, 1983), pp. 10–37.

16. David L. Birch, *The Job Generation Process* (Cambridge, Mass.: MIT Program for Neighborhood and Regional Change, 1979); and David L. Birch and Susan McCracken, "The Small Business Share of Job Creation, Lessons Learned from the Use of Longitudinal File," Report on Research Prepared for the Office of Advocacy (Washington, D.C.: Small Business Administration, November, 1982).

17. White House Commission on Small Business, *America's Small Business Economy: Agenda for Action* (Washington, D.C.: April 1980), p. 20.

18. Katherine Armington and Marjorie Odle, "Small Business: How Many Jobs?" *Brookings Review* (Winter 1982); and Katherine Armington and Marjorie Odle, "Sources of Employment Growth: A New Look at Small Business," *Economic Development Commentary* (1982).

19. Michael B. Teitz, Amy Glasmeier, and Douglas Svensson, "Small Business and Employment Growth in California," Working Paper No. 348, University of California, Berkeley, Institute of Urban and Regional Development, March 1981.

20. Small Business Administration, *The State of Small Business, A Report to the President, 1983,* (Washington, D.C.: March 1983), p. 62.

21. David L. Birch, "Who Creates Jobs?" *The Public Interest* (Fall 1981), p. 8.

22. Binks and Coyne, *The Birth of Enterprise,* p. 41.

23. Vesper, *Entrepreneurship and National Policy,* p. 18.

24. Schumpeter, *The Theory of Economic Development,* pp. 62–94.

25. National Science Foundation, "Science Indicators," (Washington, D.C.: 1979).

26. Technological Innovations," Environment and Management Report to the Panel on Invention and Innovation to the Secretary of Commerce, (Washington, D.C.: January 1967), p. 18.

27. O.J. Krasner, "The Role of Entrepreneurs in Innovation," in Calvin A. Kent, et al. *The Encyclopedia of Entrepreneurship,* pp. 277–283.

28. D.J. Prager and D.S. Omenn, "Research Innovation and University-Industry Linkages," *Science* (January 1980), p. 207.

29. Bannock, *The Economics of Small Firms* pp. 8–9.

30. C. Wright Mills and Melville J. Ullmer, *Small Business and Civil Welfare,* Report of the Smaller Plants Corporation to the Special Committee to Study Problems in American Small Business (Washington, D.C.: February 13, 1946).

31. Jon G. Udell, "Social and Economic Consequences of the Merger Movement in Wisconsin," (Madison, Wisconsin: University of Wisconsin, Graduate School of Business, May 1969).

32. Bannock, *The Economics of Small Firms,* p. 9.

33. U.S. Office of the President, "Minority Enterprise Development Week 1983: A Proclamation," (August 1983).

34. The Small Business Administration, *The State of Small Business, 1983,* p. 302.

35. Small Business Administration, *The State of Small Business, 1983,* p. 315.

36. Naisbitt, *Megatrends,* pp. 149.

37. Robert H. Brockhaus, "The Psychology of the Entrepreneur," in Calvin A. Kent, et al., *The Encyclopedia of Entrepreneurship*, pp. 39–55.

38. Calvin A. Kent, Donald Sexton, Philip Van Auken, and Dean Young, "Lifetime Experiences of Managers and Entrepreneurs: A Comparative Analysis," (Waco, Texas: Baylor University, Center for Private Enterprise and Entrepreneurship, August 1982).

39. Kilby, "Hunting the Heffalump," p. 3.

40. John Maynard Keynes, *General Theory of Employment, Interest, and Money* (New York: Harcourt, Brace and World, 1936).

41. Alvin H. Hansen, *Business Cycles and National Income* (New York: Norton and Co., 1964).

42. Binks and Coyne, *The Birth of Enterprise,* p. 75.

2 The Entrepreneurial Event

Albert Shapero

There is a large and growing worldwide interest in entrepreneurship. Governments, corporate mangements, the media, and even professors, who five years ago would have yawned at its mention, are now vitally concerned with entrepreneurship: what it is, what makes it work, and how to elicit more of whatever it is in a country, company, or community. There has, of course, always been a popular fascination with entrepreneurship. What is new is the sudden discovery by the "movers and shakers" of society and by trendsetting intellectuals of a very pervasive and profoundly human process.

The recent plethora of discussions on entrepreneurship represent the confluence of diverse currents of thought generated by a combination of human frustrations and hopes in a very unsettled world. The discussion has been fed by recent studies of the role of new and small businesses compared with large, old ones as generators of jobs and innovations,[1] by an uneasy feeling of being held hostage by large organizations, by a shift of values represented first by youth in the 1960s and 1970s, and by a worldwide hunger for hope, creativity, and new ideas.

Perhaps the most powerful component in the new interest in entrepreneurship arises out of the apparent intractability of a very depressing world economy. The economists are in disarray (agreeing only that no noneconomist shall be allowed to say anything about the subject), and offer little hope. Consequently, there has been a desperate, almost shrill welcome given to reports that new businesses are responsible for a fantastic number of new jobs relative to old businesses and that small, new, technical companies are responsible on the basis of their size and employment for more major innovations than are old, established companies. The logic goes that if we could only get more entrepreneurship, particularly the high-technology variety, all would be economically well again.

Unfortunately, the data upon which studies of the relationships among jobs, innovations, and company age and size are based do not bear close scrutiny. One of the major data sources, for example, has been Dun & Bradstreet, whose information is voluntarily supplied by its subjects and is used as the basis for credit ratings, which raises doubts as to the completeness or accuracy of the reporting.[2] Nevertheless, the conclusions of the studies can be defended logically. Small, new companies are more likely to generate new jobs and more innovations than large companies. Large companies strive for productivity, which means more output with less input, including labor. What is a risky innovation to a large corporation is a golden opportunity to a small company. For example, a large company will establish a minimum anticipated market as a threshold for entry into the marketplace of 4 million cases per year, while a small company might see 100,000 cases per year as a bonanza. When a small company proves the market and develops it to a point where it meets large-company criteria, it becomes attractive acquisition. Small companies do tend to innovate. Large companies tend to acquire.

Though it is not clearly articulated, there is spreading unease about the power of large institutions and investments. No matter how incompetent or venal the management, we feel we cannot let a large corporation fail. No matter what it costs a community in terms of money and pride, we do not want a local corporate division to pick up and leave. No matter how it defaults on a contract, we do not want a large defense contractor to pay the legal price. Perceptive corporate managements are beginning to realize that they are trapped by very large capital investments that make them hostage to yesterday's technology and products. It is interesting to note that some steel-company managements are seeking ways to design and function with small-scale units.[3]

Small businesses, however, are not threatening. A small business is local and personal. Its business decisions consider the community in which it is located, for that is the home of its owners and managers. A corporate division with corporate headquarters in New York or Tokyo and incorporated in Delaware or Aruba is far more impersonal, evaluating a proposed decision in terms of the cost of labor in Mexico, the price of gold in London, or the chances of acquiring the United Astrology Corporation.

One of the consequences of the so-called "flower children" years is a general shift in the values held in society. A value is a concept of the desirable, and our concepts of what is desirable have shifted. We are far more concerned with self-expression and self-realization than were our forebears. We are far less responsive to notions of company loyalty, brand loyalty, and party loyalty. We have experienced at least two generations of affluent people in the Western world, who act like rich and privileged people have always acted. We and our children expect government and businesses to respond to us just as the rich always have. We want service. We want personal treatment. We want gratification now and not later.

The shift in values is expressed in the phrase, "I don't want to be a cipher in someone's organization!" We are witnessing a significant growth in new-business formations among the generation who were growing up in the 1960s and 1970s. Former hippies have turned entrepreneur: a host of building contractors, remodelers, artisans, tofu producers, solar energy companies and the like have sprung up, happy to accept credit cards or, better yet, cash in payment for goods and services. The phenomenon is worldwide, and in the United States and France such counterculture entrepreneurs have their own small-business publications, such as *In Business*.

A final impetus toward entrepreneurship is hunger for creativity, for new ideas, innovations; something to offer us futures and hope, and entrepreneurship seems to be a way to achieve these.

For all these reasons there is a fascination with entrepreneurship, a growing interest in what it is and how to make it happen so that we can reap its perceived benefits. To suggest some answers, I will discuss the entrepreneurship process—who starts businesses under what conditions—and explore ways in which the environment interacts with that process in terms of how the environment influences the generation of entrepreneurship, how it affects the survival and growth of entrepreneurial events, and how, in turn, entrepreneurship affects the environment.

The Company Formation Process

In 1983 in the United States there will be between 800,000 (as estimated by Dun & Bradstreet) and 1 million (my estimate) new-company formations. These formations occur despite recession, high interest rates, inflation, uncertain economic prognoses, and the advice of worried relatives and dear friends. Each of the company formations is the end result of one very personal human process and the beginning of another. Though each company formation is a unique event, examination of the data of company formations in different economic sectors suggests a general pattern to the process and certain common characteristics no matter where it occurs. Though the pattern is highly complex and involves many variables, it is recognizable and describable. However, it is important to understand that the company-formation process is what psychologists refer to as *overdetermined*, that is, no single factor can account for the outcome of the process. It is describable and recognizable, but it is not amenable to simple manipulation.[4]

Rather than review the various definitions of the terms *entrepreneur* and *entrepreneurship*, I have chosen to define the unit of interest as the *entrepreneurial event*. Focus on the event avoids the question of whether an individual who has carried out one entrepreneurial act in his or her lifetime is or is not an entrepreneur. It permits one to consider the one-time entrepreneur and the part-time entrepreneur as well as the repetitive entrepreneur, and to consider a large variety and number of activities that are considered entrepreneurial without being tied to the special features of a particular kind of individual. The event becomes the dependent variable while the individuals or groups that generate the event become the independent variables, as do the social, economic, political, cultural, and other situational variables as they affect company formation.

Operationally, each entrepreneurial event is denoted by

1. *Initiative taking*—an individual or group takes the initiative;
2. *Bringing together resources* in organizational form to accomplish some objective (or reorganizing the resources in an existing organization);
3. *Management* of the organization by those who took the initiative;
4. *Relative autonomy*—relative freedom to dispose of and distribute resources; and
5. *Risk-taking*—the organization's success or failure is shared by the initiators/managers.

Though innovation is widely associated with entrepreneurship, it is not included here as part of the definition of the entrepreneurial event. The entrepreneurial event itself is the innovation, and there is no necessity to tie the event to new technology.

As defined here, every entrepreneurial event is denoted by all of these characteristics, and it can include the one-time entrepreneur, the hawker, the promoter, intracorporate events, some civic activities, and events in countries with socialist or planned economies. Many events partake of some but not all of the definitional elements. Many managers take initiative, innovate in the technological sense, and even bring together resources, but if they do not personally share the risk of success or failure, or if they do not manage the organization with a considerable degree of autonomy, they might be considered entrepreneurial or entrepreneurlike, but they have not generated a genuine entrepreneurial event.

Each company formation or entrepreneurial event is the result of two decisions: the decision to change from a given life path, and the decision to start a company. To make a major change in a life path is not a trivial affair, and it is seldom done casually. All of us are held on course by a myriad of forces: family situation, job responsibilities, and the simple, powerful force of inertia. It takes a great deal of force in a new direction (or a summation of a host of small forces) to change from a given life path. The second decision, to start a company, is one choice among the thousands of new life paths one might have chosen, raising the question, "Why this particular path rather than one of the others?"

The decision to change one's life path comes about as the result of personal displacement, usually through negative forces. Despite the fact that most people say that they would like to be in business for themselves, I have only encountered one person among the hundreds I have interviewed who had a deliberate, step-by-step plan for starting a company and carried it out. There is a great gap between desire and action, and few take the initiative to translate a personal goal into planned action. There is nothing like a personal dislocation to galvanize one into action. A tremendous number of of company formations occur among refugees, people who have been fired, women experiencing the 'empty nest syndrome', and people who are insulted or frustrated on their jobs. Of course, not all displacements are negative. Companies are started by people who are between jobs; by men called back to the military reserves whose careers have been disrupted; by parolees; by individuals who have just completed an additional degree. And there are the positive incentives of a friend who says "Let's do it!", the customer who says, "I'll give you a contract," the unexpected windfall of an inheritance or a winning lottery ticket.

Having been displaced, however, why does anyone decide to start a company? After all, the conventional wisdom is that 90 percent of all new companies fail in the first year, times are terrible, and that entrepreneurs have to work one hundred hours a week. Why should anyone choose this peculiar thing? The choice of a particular life path is the product of two perceptions: the perception that a particular path is desirable, and the perception that the path is feasible. Unless one perceives that a particular path is both desirable and feasible there is little chance that it will be considered at all or chosen if considered. Of course, the two perceptions are not completely separate. If something is perceived as very desirable, we may revise our estimates of its feasibility and vice versa.

Perceptions of desirability have to do with values. A value is defined as a concept of the desirable.[5] Values are conceptions of the desirable, explicit or implicit, distinctive of an individual or characteristic of a group, that influence choices. Our perceptions of what is desirable are the result of our placement in a matrix of culture, socioeconomic structure, family, education, peers, and influential persons. The broader culture in which we find ourselves conveys to its members what is considered desirable. Thus, a mother might want her son to be a doctor rather than a factory worker since she percives the doctor as having a higher value in our culture.

Culture

The culture that places a high value on being in business, on entrepreneurship, and the kinds of behavior associated with such activities such as initiative taking, risk taking, innovation, and independence, is more likely to spawn company formation than a culture that does not value these things. The United States, with its frontier tradition and emphasis on individual opportunity has a favorable value system for entrepreneurship. Being in business for yourself is perceived here as something to be desired, and associated behaviors are valued highly. It is not surprising that the annual rate of U.S. company formations is high. In Italy if a man of education starts a company he drops socially. People wonder why a man of culture would do such a gross thing as to enter into trade. My perception during my year in Italy was that the Italian rate of company formation is very low.

Within a national culture there are many subcultures (regional, ethnic, and religious) that shape the individual's value system. The Smoeland region in Sweden is known for entrepreneurship. Similarly, the people from Cork are considered the most entrepreneurial in Ireland, the people from the Brabant in the Netherlands, and my Texas students seemed more likely than my Ohio students to think seriously about starting a business. There are many familiar ethnic and religious differences with regard to how entrepreneurship is valued. Many ethnic and religious groups show a high incidence of entrepreneurship. Some cultures that value entrepreneurship are the Ibos in Africa; Gujeratis, Jains, and Parsis in India; the overseas Chinese in southeast Asia; Antioquenos in Columbia; Jews; Lebanese; the people from Pyongan in North Korea; and Mennonites and Mormons in the United States.

Family

The influence of family values in determining whether or not one perceives entrepreneurship as desirable is a dominant one, and, though a family exists within a particular culture, there are variations among families. One way to gauge the effect of family on the value attributed to entrepreneurship is to examine the data on the parents of company formers. Studies of company formations in a variety of industries and locations in the United States place the percentage of company formers found to have fathers or mothers who were independent (company owners, free professionals, independent artisans, or farmers) between 50 to 58 percent.[6] This compares with a census count of less than 12 percent of the U.S. population listed as self-employed. In a northern Italian study, the percentage of entrepreneurs with independent parents was 56 percent. In Carroll's study of Filipino manufacturing entrepreneurs, the percentage was 74 percent; in Marris and Somerset's study of Kenyan entrepreneurs, 80 percent; in Harris's study of Nigerian entrepreneurs, almost 89 percent; and in Jones and Sakong's study of Korean entrepreneurship, almost 80 percent.

The data follow the same pattern in study after study and in culture after culture. Of Lipman's Bogotan entrepreneurs, 61 percent had independent fathers; Roubidoux's Quebeçois, 68 percent; Sayigh's Lebanese entrepreneurs, 74 percent; Hammeed's Sudanese industrial entrepreneurs, 70 percent; and Finney's Gorokans of New Guinea show a high incidence of fathers who could be interpreted to be relatively independent in terms of tribal position. Borland (1974) found that the variable most positively associated with a business student's declared expectation or desire to start a company was whether the student's father had been an independent businessman, farmer, professional, or artisan.[7]

Other Influences

Other influences on an individual's value system include peers and influential others, those with whom the individual identifies. Influential others include teachers, mentors, respected public figures, and writers. Perception of feasiblity is another factor. An individual must be able to realistically imagine himself or herself going through the action of starting and operating a company for the act to be seen as feasible. Perceptions of feasibility come about as an amalgam of knowledge, resources, and the assurances that come from respected individuals or from observing the actions of others like oneself.

Know-how gained from personal experience in a particular business or from formal education contributes to an individual's perception of the feasibility of starting a particular business. Relevant know-how comes in different forms. Individuals tend to start businesses in the fields in which they have worked. People work in small businesses or in small corporate divisions are more likely to start business than those who work in a large firm, because they gain familiarity with the whole business process, which makes starting a business seem much more feasible. Individuals who have had customer contact are found more frequently among those who start businesses than those who have not; familiarity with the marketplace adds to perceptions of feasibility.

Obviously, the availability of resources is also a powerful influence on one's perceptions of the feasibility of starting a company. The relevant resources include financial resources in the form of personal savings, credit, and equity capital; but also include equipment, tools, materials, and labor. Entrepreneurs work long hours because they are substituting their own labor for that of others; this is known as sweat equity. The personal labor of the entrepreneur is a substitute for money.

Perhaps the most powerful influence on perceptions of the feasibility of forming a company comes from the observance of others. To see someone like yourself do something makes it much more likely that you can imagine yourself doing the same thing. Once Roger Bannister broke the four-minute mile, that apparent barrier was surpassed by others within months. It is no accident that such a high proportion of entrepreneurs have parents who are independent, worked for small businesses, had peers who started businesses, or are members of regional, ethnic, or religious groups identified with entrepreneurship. This is not a classical case of role modeling. It is rather a case of seeing someone like yourself who did it who is no better than you are. Hundreds of interviews have elicited statements such as, ''By gosh! If he can do it, anyone can do it" or "I did everything the boss did except take home the profits."

Summarizing the Company Formation Process

The company-formation process begins with a situation in which an individual or group of individuals is forced from or decides to change to a new life path. The situations are as varied as life itself, but more people respond to negative displacements than positive ones. A particular situation, however, elicits different responses from different individuals. Among a group of refugees, one person might respond to the situation with resignation while another undertakes the formation of a company. The choice of response is a product of an individual's perceptions of the desirability and feasibility of various alternatives, and those perceptions are influenced by the individual's cultural antecedents, family, peers, education, and experiences.

The company formation process is demonstrated by the fact that many successful entrepreneurs have tried and failed at least once. Henry Ford failed completely twice. The individual who has failed in an entrepreneurial venture has suffered a major displacement, but has learned a great deal about the desirability and feasibility of being an entrepreneur. Commonly, three years after a failure the entrepreneur is ready for another venture, and this time there is a higher level of know-how and a different perception of the desirability of being in business for oneself.

I have said nothing of the psychology of entrepreneurs. It is not by oversight. The more I study entrepreneurs, the more I am impressed by the great variety of kinds of people who are entrepreneurs, and the more I find it difficult to be satisfied with simple psychological profiles. Entrepreneurs are not born, they are developed. The great majority of people are capable of being made more entrepreneurial.

If I had to pick the dominating motivation of the entrepreneur, it is independence. Ask a complaining entrepreneur how much money would make him opt to be a manager, and 50 percent will reject the thought out-of-hand while the majority of the remainder will name some ridiculous figure like five to one-hundred times their current earnings. Entrepreneurs are characterized by a strong internal locus of control, that is, they see themselves as being in control of their own lives. Entrepreneurs are also characterized by a high tolerance for ambiguity. An entrepreneur can issue checks on Friday and spend the weekend scurrying around to find money to cover the checks. Entrepreneurs are denoted by high energy levels. Many of these characteristics, however, are learned behaviors.[8]

Environment

Ten years ago one of my best doctoral students completed doctoral research comparing the responses of private individuals of wealth in two cities, Austin and Waco, Texas, to investment opportunities represented by a set of new and very young companies. The set of investment opportunities had been carefully developed from real cases and included both technical and nontechnical businesses.[9] The idea was to see if there was a significant difference in the investment responses of the two communities with a view to shedding light on the very different growth patterns of the two cities. Both communities are in the same general sociocultural environment and share the same state laws, taxes, and regulations. Though both cities had approximately the same population at one point, Austin had grown rapidly and Waco had lost population.

Of course, many factors can explain the differences in growth including the fact that Austin, as state capital, benefited from the marked growth in state government. Nevertheless, it seemed reasonable to consider local investment propensities as being a significant influence on local economic development and population growth. The research did find a marked difference in the investment responses obtained in the two communities. The Austin respondents were far more ready to include others in their deals, imposed far less onerous conditions, and were far more in contact with investors in other communities than those in Waco.

In a second situation, I was told by different citizens of Midland, Texas, that they estimate that about one-fourth the professionals in Midland-Odessa area had started businesses in recent years. Their comments were underlined by the fact that the president of the local community college had quit to go into the oil and gas business. Much of what happened in that West Texas region reflects the recent boom in oil and gas, but a major factor is the favorable climate for entrepreneurship in that community.

Both situations illustrate the effects of elements of the overall environment on entrepreneurship. The first situation suggests something about the effects of the financial environment on entrepreneurship. The second situation suggests something about a general community outlook that reflects a very positive social view of risk taking. Both situations illustrate the effect of environment on entrepreneurship.

Environment and the Company Formation Process

Entrepreneurship comes about through the interaction between a specific situation and a specific individual or group of individuals. The situations we encounter in life include the uncontrollable actions of others (such as someone in China inventing something that will make an entire industry obsolete) and, to a very limited extent, the things that we do. Our votes do count. Some are in a position to start wars or affect the economy through manipulation of immense personal wealth or power. In general, however, the situations we encounter are impossible to predict with any accuracy, and difficult to control once they occur. This is true for both individuals and communities. It is only by hindsight that we know exactly how to have anticipated or dealt with what has happened. The situations that lead to entrepreneurial formations, such as political upheavals, layoffs, or frustration on the job, are one-time opportunities that communities cannot easily choose to create.

The way individuals perceive the events that occur and the ways they respond to them is primarily a by-product of their past and present cultural and social environment, ethnic and regional affiliations, family, peers, formal education, and life experiences. A community *can* consciously and deliberately do much to affect relevant parts of its social and cultural environment with regard to entrepreneurship. We can do something about changing attitudes within a community, the way we educate our children, the way we choose to regard risk and innovation. Within the larger constraints of world economics and politics, communities and individuals can choose to do something about their perceptions of what should be done.

Historical Bias against Entrepreneurship

Perhaps the most formidable barrier to entrepreneurship in most countries is a deep-seated cultural bias against commerce and trade, particularly among social elites and intellectuals. It is a bias that can be affected through our educational system. The bias is rooted in social and religious outlooks that date back very far in history. Almost all religions have honored asceticism as opposed to the self-indulgence implied in efforts to achieve material gains. The charging of interest on money was treated as a sin or crime for centuries, and medieval Italian bankers developed elaborate protocols for giving gifts of money that the recipient repaid with larger gifts, on time at and a fixed rate. Some Islamic banks today do not charge interest because of their religion, but they do charge healthy fees for services rendered.

In medieval days, warriors gained noble status by reason of their physical strength, skill with arms, and cunning. The intellectuals found their place in the church and dedicated themselves to influencing the nobility and educating the children of the nobility to make moral judgments. Craftsmen, though lesser, were respected. Independent farmers were respected, though it varied by country. Both nobility and intellectuals looked down upon or had contempt for trade, commerce, and the men who took part in them.

In the Western world, not only were businessmen considered crass because they were interested in material gain, but also they tended to disrupt the settled order of things by innovating. Any activities that would give one individual or shopkeeper a greater share of the market was considered disruptive. Trying to get more customers was considered unfair. Advertising was forbidden. Innovation was considered dangerous. Price cutting was antisocial. There was much legislation to control the number of craftsmen in a town. Some of these laws are still active in parts of Europe today. Only outsiders such as Jews, gypsies, or foreigners were tolerated as innovators or price-changers or money lenders.

In many cultures, the social stigma of entrepreneurship has been so powerful that even today the children of the self-made wealthy turn away from commerce to become landed gentry as their price of entry into good society. Carrying on the tradition of the clergy-intellectuals of the Middle Ages, university academics today continue their antipathy to trade, commerce, and entrepreneurship. Perhaps the only entrepreneurship that is looked on favorably is so-called high-technology entrepreneurship, because the high-technologists are seen as educated persons. But even the high technologist does not always receive unlimited approval. In the United States, considered a model of technological entrepreneurship, academics are often fired from universities for engaging in entrepreneurship despite some highly publicized exceptions. Even the business schools share the academic bias, favoring big business over small business if they consider the latter at all.

There are virtually no colleges of business in the United States today, there are only academies of bureaucratic middle management. The 1,180 institutions granting degrees in business and management teach how to fit into and serve the 5,000 largest corporations. The concepts and values taught are those of the corporate bureaucrat or staff professional. Although the typical MBA might vote for a conservative political ticket, his training has prepared him to work equally well in the Department of Energy, General Motors, or a Soviet commissariat.[10]

In a country with a popular culture that regards the entrepreneur highly and that is powerful enough to counterbalance the antipathetic intellectual culture, entrepreneurship can flourish. The United States is a prime example. In the United States the entrepreneur is a folk hero. In the United States it is common for newspapers and popular journals to feature stories of individuals who have started new businesses in a very positive light. Having tried and failed in business is considered better than not having tried at all. It is no accident that Henry Ford failed twice completely and felt free to try again. Thus, despite an intellectual culture that looks down on the entrepreneur and businessman, there are a great number of new-business formations in the United States every year. I know of no other country with a popular culture that takes quite the same positive view of entrepreneurship though there are many subcultures that do.

The Importance of Academic Values

The values held by the academics of a country are critical to any discussion of the elicitation of entrepreneurship in a modern society. It is in academia that the greatest socialization of a country's intellectuals occurs. I would guess that with every enlargement in the numbers and segments of a country's population participating in the benefits of higher education the greater the odds of a prejudice against trade, commerce, and entrepreneurship. Higher education has tremendous leverage in affecting our environment. Institutions of higher education have a virtual monopoly on the preparation of professionals of all kinds. There are the professional teachers and educational administrators. There are the professionals who influence public opinion and values and the policymakers who turn values into legislation. Then there are all of the potential technical entrepreneurs, the engineers and scientists, whose perceptions of entrepreneurship are most readily influenced during the time of their education.

Doing Something to Improve the Environment

In the short run there are many actions to be taken to counteract the consistent denigration of smaller businesses and to enhance their desirability in the perceptions of the young. The first action is to improve the self-images of small-business people. The intellectual value system has become so pervasive that entrepreneurs who love their independence and who would never work for anyone else encourage their children to seek security in large bureaucracies. I cannot understand how entrepreneurs accept the fact that our high school counselors convince our young to opt either for jobs in corporate life or to be mechanics.

Enhancing entrepreneurship begins with the family. If you opt to be an entrepreneur, your children will see it as a feasible if not a desirable option. If your children do not see entrepreneurship as desirable and feasible, ask yourself why that is so. I have been amazed over and over again to find that the first time a son or daughter realized what his or her entrepreneur parents had accomplished was the result of an interview required in my courses. Where is the pride of accomplishment? Where is the positive transmission of the entrepreneurial culture from generation to generation?

Our politicians from both parties all proclaim their appreciation for small business, quoting statistics to the effect that small business accounts for 49 percent of the GNP, 97 percent of the companies, the vast majority of new jobs, and the bulk of innovations. But when it comes to action, less than 1 percent of the actions of politicians go to support small business. States and communities do not support small businesses as they do big corporations. Who has offered small businesses with cash flow problems the help given Chrysler Corporation or International Harvester? When will small-business people begin to demand 49 percent or 97 percent or 75 percent of the attention of government? When will small-business people begin to harass the media every time they depict the small-business community as being made up of kindly morons? (Just think of the small-business people portrayed on television's *Alice, the Jeffersons*, and *All in the Family*.)

At the Community Level

There are very direct ways in which a community can change its environment to enhance entrepreneurship. Consider the company-formation process. More companies are generated out of small businesses than out of large ones. By attracting desirable small businesses instead of corporate divisions, a community can raise the probability of new-company formation as well as acquire the requisite diversity that makes a community invulnerable to unexpected events. The more small businesses in a community, the more likely it is that more will form. Communities have been missing a golden opportunity to attract the best of the country's small businesses with the lure of financial support during this period of cash-flow problems by offering them the kind of financing we offer larger corporations.

Once the company formation process becomes apparent in a community, the more likely it is that new companies will form. Small companies beget more companies, and company formations trigger more company formations. There is often an epidemic quality about the process. It is no accident that we witness flurries of spinouts from major corporations. Each spinout becomes a credible example to the people left behind. Each observed formation serves the same purpose for others in the community. It is a pervasive feeling of entrepreneurship going on "all around" that marks, for example, Midland, Texas, and helps to explain the numbers of company formations found there.

The local economic environment, particularly the way a community's financial people respond to new and different companies, has a critical impact on whether or not new companies will be formed. In several studies comparing growing and stagnating cities, we found a distinct difference in the way local bank-loan officers and investors responded to requests for loans and requests for investments in new and different companies. Lively cities had lively financial people. In the growing, lively cities (and banks) financial people were far more likely to take an active interest in new and different companies than those in cities that were not growing. Lively cities were denoted by an orientation toward success rather than an interest in hedging against failure. There was a distinctly greater readiness to lend or invest in new and different companies coupled with a requirement for far less security in the lively cities. There was a far greater tendency to take an active part in structuring a new business to succeed in the lively cities. In the stagnating cities investors were far more reluctant to lend or invest and had a tendency to structure loans and investments for maximum security in case of failure.

A financial environment can be modified, particularly at the local level. Most local bankers, like most people in any field, tend to stick to the kinds of things with which they are familiar. However, local bankers would really like to be more responsive than they are given credit for, and the attitudes and practices of local financial people can be influenced through awareness and education. Where the local financial community is not amenable to change it may be possible to invite in others from the outside.

At the Political-Legislative-Administrative Levels

The primary effect of the political-legislative-administrative environment on entrepreneurship is negative. Political ideologies are expressed through law and regulation, and they in turn act to prevent entrepreneurship or make it difficult. The clearest examples are found in totalitarian states, especially those in the communist orbit. Where businesses are forbidden by law, entrepreneurship is drastically reduced and pushed underground. The popular press assures us that every communist country has a large, underground entrepreneurial economy; and that in fact these countries cannot function without this second economy.[11] Where entrepreneurs are considered with suspicion or contempt and this attitude is translated into taxes or regulations that severely curtail the possibility for company formation, formations are very few indeed. Many Third World countries fall into this category, but so do highly developed countries like those in Scandinavia.

Unfortunately, efforts to positively influence company formations through modifications of the political-legislative-administrative environment have not proven very effective. The experience of the past several years with interventions ranging from set-aside funds to direct financing has not been very encouraging. For example, despite extensive effort there has been no significant enlargement of the pool of minority business in the United States. The political process has been used with some success to remove legal and administrative barriers to entry (for example, antitrust legislation) and to structure taxes to make investment in new businesses more attractive, but the resulting effects on company formations have yet to be demonstrated. Economists and politicians are constantly pressing for policies and legislation that would provide incentives for investment in new businesses, but there is little evidence that they have affected the rate or volume of new-company formations. To illustrate, we presented an investor with a set of investment situations and asked what the effect of a tax policy permitting rollover of capital gains from one investment to another would have on his decisions. The answer was very revealing. He stated that he favored the policy in general; however, it would not change any of his specific investment decisions!

There is an area that lies between the economic and political elements in the environment. Public bodies can make public resources available to entrepreneurs and potential entrepreneurs. Public bodies can make resources available in the form of various kinds of financing, but public bodies tend to be incompetent financiers of private-sector ventures. The record is replete with the creation of public institutions to finance so-called risky new businesses. Invariably they become more conservative than private investors because of the necessary requirement to defend their decisions before legislatures. Public resources in the form of abandoned military bases, empty schools or municipal buildings, and closed-down plants can be supplied as facilities to entrepreneurs or small companies from other areas. Sometimes the purchasing power of public bodies can be used to help desirable new companies to get established, but here again, the record is not too encouraging. The record of the various set-aside programs for small business and minority business are examples of dismal results.

The Environment and the Survival and Growth of Entrepreneurial Events

The economic and political environments play crucial roles in the survival and growth of new and small businesses. Our current experiences with inflation, high interest rates, and slipping construction and retail sales have brutally reinformed us of our sensitivity to the economic environment. There is a need, however, to make mention of the qualitative and quantitative differences in the effects of the economic environment on new and small businesses. It is obvious that the smaller business has fewer resources, and consequently is far more vulnerable to shifts and disruptions in the environment than are big businesses. The last years have been a testing period for the new and small businesses of our country.

The problem is that in addition to the natural disadvantages they face because of more limited resources, small businesses are artificially disadvantaged by the way our economic institutions and governmental agencies treat them. Smaller businesses are penalized with higher interest rates than such notable credit risks as Chrysler, International Harvester, or Mexico. Federal and state governments rushed to underwrite Chrysler, but ignored the problems of Chrysler's nineteen thousand suppliers. State governments vie to provide large domestic and foreign corporations with low-cost financing backed by tax-supported revenue bonds, training grants, publicly paid for utilities and roads, and a host of other inducements with no thought to the needs of small businesses that have paid local taxes for many years. The effect of most governmental regulation is relatively more severe on smaller businesses, requiring a disproportionately greater amount of labor, management, and money for compliance. The small pharmaceutical company has practically disappeared because of the costs imposed by the testing requirements of the Federal Drug Administration.

It is a compliment to small businesses that so few of them have folded under current conditions; a mere eighteen thousand this year out of the 15 million that continue to function. It is a sterling proof of Shapero's Second Law that says that, "No matter how you design a system, humans make it work anyway." Nevertheless, there is an inherent blindness on the part of those who can do something about it to the effects of their actions on the environment of the smaller businesses. Further, it is important for us all to be concerned with the environment for small business and entrepreneurship because entrepreneurship has a critical role to play in our society's environment and ability to deal creatively with the unknowable future.

The Effects of Entrepreneurship on the Environment

When we talk about economic development we seldom ask ourselves exactly what we mean. When do we become developed? How can we know when are we half-way there? The economists discuss development in relative terms: our GNP is bigger than your GNP, or our unemployment is less than yours. It seems reasonable to suggest that development means the achievement of communities in which the residents find life fulfilling; and fulfillment has something to do with an ability to deal with the unknowable future, with continuity from generation to generation, with the attraction and retention of educated young people, particularly our children; in a word, with dynamism.

Comparisons of cities that have continued to be dynamic over long periods of time with those that have not provide us with clues as to what it is we are striving for in development. The qualities that distinguish dynamic cities from all the rest are *resilience, creativity, initiative taking*, and above all, *diversity*. The ability to absorb whatever happens in the economic, social, and political environment and to bounce back; the ability to generate and to experiment; the ability to do things without waiting for others to take the initiative; and the variety of enterprises that enable the community to assure that no single event can cripple its ability to continue: all these describe the developed state for which we should be striving.

Policy Agenda

Entrepreneurship is vital to the development of dynamic, creative, free societies, and policies should be chosen to help shape an environment that elicits and enhances entrepreneurship. Since it is axiomatic that resources are limited, intelligent policymaking requires that we must first determine whether and where available resources can effectively be used to create an environment that elicits and enhances entrepreneurship.

First, can entrepreneurship be elicited and enhanced? There is really no question that entrepreneurship can be deliberately elicited. My optimism is based on the available body of knowledge and grows in proportion to the growth of the pool of data on entrepreneurship. Studies of entrepreneurship are multiplying, and the data are sufficient for purposes of application if not grand theory. There is substantial agreement among scholars and practitioners that there are policy options that can stimulate entrepreneurship significantly though there is disagreement over what means might be most effective. What follows is a listing of some exemplary policy options.

Education

In the long run, the most effective policies are those aimed at developing an attitudinal climate that sees entrepreneurship as good and welcomes steps to develop the skills that make entrepreneurship possible. Within the broad spectrum of educational institutions, the greatest leverage is obtainable through policy options focused on the university. Policy options that work through the university value and reward systems have the highest probabilty of achieving long-term, lasting effects on what is taught and what is advocated in the classroom, the heart of academic activities. Some examples of possible policy options include the following:

Provision of support for research on entrepreneurship and small business, areas that now receive limited and uneven support.

Provision of doctoral and postdoctoral fellowships focusing on entrepreneurship and small business to enhance research in and the status of the subject.

Systematic support for professional-society activities, journals, and special awards for entrepreneurship research to provide the academic infrastructure required to solidly establish entrepreneurship in the academic world.

Broad expansion of small-business contacts through sponsorship of cooperative education, internships, and educationally related consulting activities.

Broad expansion of entrepreneurship-related continuing education programs, particularly those tailored for professionals.

Broad expansion of continuing education for small-business owners to help improve their performance.

At the secondary-school and vocational education levels there is a need for policies aimed at increasing the level of awareness of entrepreneurship on the part of both teachers and students. The goal of such policies is to show entrepreneurship as a desirable and possible career option. Relevant policy options include efforts in all aspects of education including curriculum offerings, educational materials, workshops, games, short courses for teachers, and the like. For vocational education the goal is to develop students as potential job generators rather than just job takers. It is also very important to influence the school counseling system, which essentially does nothing to direct students toward entrepreneurial careers.

The Financial Community

The attitudes of the local financial community with regard to new and different companies is crucial to the formation and growth of new and young companies and to the attraction of such companies. Policy options to increase the propensity of financial people (bankers and private investors) to invest and make loans in new and different companies can include programs to motivate them in the desired direction and programs to inform and educate the motivated financial people so that they can do the job effectively. The goal of programs aimed at the financial community is to carry out a policy that makes sure that no new or young company is turned away for the wrong reason.

To increase the flow of capital to an area, policy options can be fielded that make use of interregional bank-correspondent relationships, develop relevant insurance-company and pension-investment programs, and that make intelligent use of the placement of government deposits. To increase the relevant flow of capital within an area, policy options can include pooled loan programs in which banks join to share risks, and programs to enhance the networking of investors and commercial banks.

Economic Development Programs

Since small companies are far more likely to spawn entrepreneurial spin-offs than large companies and corporate divisions, it is important to make some effort to attract small companies as part of a community's economic-development activities. A program to attract small companies has much to commend it. There is almost no competition for the smaller firm while 30,000-plus local development organizations are all competing to attract large corporate divisions. The likelihood of success in attracting small companies is higher than with large firms while the economic and political costs are lower. Small companies add to the diversity of a community making it less hostage to events than otherwise. Ten small companies with $1 million of payroll each make a community far less vulnerable to events than does one large corporate division with a $20 million payroll. A multiplicity of companies provides a community with diversity in many dimensions, including decision making.

Policies aimed at providing resources and the kind of infrastructure required by new and small businesses can go far to attract small businesses to a community, make it easier for new companies to start, and enable young companies to survive and grow. Examples of relevant policy options include

Offering small companies the same kinds of incentives offered to corporations to attract them to a community (they make a far greater difference to the overall financial picture of the small company than that of the large transnational corporation).

Providing facilities for new companies.

Providing incentives for commuter airline services (free or very cheap hangar facilities) and other transportation and communication facilities.

Gearing vocational-school offerings to the particular needs of small companies.

Conclusion

Entrepreneurship is the premier expression of resilience, creativity, and initiative taking. Entrepreneurship represents a resilient response to threats or opportunities. Each entrepreneurial event is a creation, and, by definition, entrepreneurship and the resulting formation of new companies provides a community with the diversity that is requisite to its long-term survival as a dynamic entity. Finally, entrepreneurship begets entrepreneurial behavior. The presence of entrepreneurs doing entrepreneurial things creates an environment congenial to innovation, initiative taking, creativity, and resilience, providing a community, a nation, or all human society with what it needs to survive and prosper.

Notes

1. David L. Birch, "Who Creates Jobs?" *The Public Interest* 65 (Fall 1981).

2. National Science Foundation, *Indicators of International Trends in Technological Innovation* (NSF-6884) (Washington, D.C.: 1976).

3. "Inland Steel Strikes Back at Minimills: Since It Can't Beat Them in Making Bars, It'll Join Them," *Industry Week*, Nov. 15, 1982.

4. Albert Shapero, "Some Social Dimensions of Entrepreneurship," in Calvin A. Kent, Donald Sexton, and Karl Vesper, eds., *The Encyclopedia of Entrepreneurship* (Englewood Cliffs, N.J.: Prentice-Hall, 1982).

5. C. Kluckhohn, "Values and Value-Orientations in the Theory of Action: An Exploration in Definition and Classification," in T. Parsons and E. Shils, eds., *Toward a General Theory of Action* (Cambridge, Mass.: Harvard University Press, 1951).

6. Calvin A. Kent, et al., "Managers and Entrepreneurs: Do Lifetime Experiences Matter?" in Karl H. Vesper, ed., *Frontiers of Entrepreneurship Research 1982* (Wellesley, Mass.: Babson College, 1982), pp. 516–526.

7. J.J. Carroll, *The Filipino Manufacturing Entrepreneur: Agent and Product of Change* (Ithaca, N.Y.: Cornell University, 1965); B.R. Finney, *Big Men and Business: Entrepreneurship and Economic Growth in the New Guinea Highlands* (Honolulu: University of Hawaii, 1973); K.A. Hammeed, *Enterprise: Industrial Entrepreneurship in Development* (London: Sage Publications, 1974); J.R. Harris, "Entrepreneurship and Economic Development," in Cain and Eselding, eds., *Business Enterprise and Economic Change* (Kent, Ohio: Kent State University, 1973); L. Jones and Il Sakong, *Government Business, and Entrepreneurship in Economic Development: The Korean Case* (Cambridge, Mass.: Harvard University Press, 1980); A. Lipman, *The Colombian Entrepreneur in Bogota* (Coral Gables, Fla.: University of Miami, 1969); P. Marris and A. Somerset, *African Businessman: A Study of Entrepreneurship and Development in Kenya* (London: Routledge & Kegan Paul, 1971); J. Roubidoux, "Profil Electif D'Entrepreneurs des Enterprises a Success au Quebec," (Unpublished paper, University of Laval, 1975); Y.A Sayigh, *Entrepreneurs in Lebanon* (Cambridge, Mass.: Harvard University Press, 1962); A. Shapero, J. Garcia-Bouza, and A. Ferrari, *Technical Entrepreneurship in Northern Italy* (Milano: IIMT, 1974).

8. Borland, *Locus of Control, Need for Achievement and Entrepreneurship* (Doctoral dissertation, University of Texas, 1974).

9. Cary A. Hoffman, "The Venture Capital Decision Process" (Doctoral Dissertation, University of Texas, 1972).

10. Albert Shapero, "On Business Schools Teaching Business," *INC.* (January 1982).

11. "Living Conveniently on the Left," *Time*, June 23, 1980, p. 50; Eric Bourne, "Pizza Hut Communism Splits East Bloc," *Christian Science Monitor*, Nov. 9, 1982, p. 1; John Wallace, "Capitalism Still Thrives in a Chinese Village," *US News and World Report*, Feb. 2, 1981, p. 63.

3 The Entrepreneurial Process

Israel M. Kirzner

The term *entrepreneurial process* has come to possess two rather distinct, although interrelated, meanings: The two meanings are 1) the process of entrepreneurial competition responsible, in the short run, for the tendencies for the market price of each commodity or input to move toward the respective market-clearing level, for the array of outputs to reflect the pattern of consumer preferences in the light of currently available technological possibilities, and for pure profit opportunities to be ground down to zero; and 2) the process of entrepreneurial discovery, invention, and innovation through which long-run economic growth is stimulated and nourished. The first kind of entrepreneurial process (short-run) is seen as responsible for a continuous tendency toward economic balance and internal economic consistency. The second (long-run) achieves a continual series of steps that together propel the engine of long-run economic growth and development. The second kind of process is the better known than the first, and was perhaps most notably discussed in the work of Joseph Schumpeter.[1] Most of this chapter will be concerned with the entrepreneurial process in a sense closer to the second of these two meanings than to the first. However, it is central to my view that a full understanding of long-term entrepreneurial processes will reveal them to be simply a consistent implication and extension of the short-run processes. Although Schumpeter himself did not see the long-run entrepreneurial process quite in this way, I shall argue that the Schumpeterian process can be illuminated by an understanding of the first (short-run) entrepreneurial processes. And I shall argue further that in attempting to formulate policy that should encourage (or at least release) the long-run processes of entrepreneurial discovery necessary for vigorous growth, it will be highly useful to bear in mind the linkages that prevail between these long-run and short-run processes. In other words, the way to permit long-run entrepreneurial growth processes to take off is to recognize and encourage the kinds of entrepreneurial discoveries that make up the short-run processes.

The Neglect of Entrepreneurship in Growth Economics

Until quite recently growth economics suffered rather seriously from the neglect of the entrepreneurial role. As Harvey Leibenstein has pointed out, it is one of the "curious aspects of the relationship of neoclassical theory to economic development" that "in the conventional theory, entrepreneurs as they are usually perceived play almost no role."[2] This neglect pervaded not only growth economics but economic analysis in general. It would have been too much to expect an analytical framework that, in regard to markets in general, accorded no special significance to entrepreneurial activity—or in fact any scope for such activity—to analyze growth along entrepreneur-theoretic lines.

As a consequence, conventional thinking about the way in which economic growth occurs and about the ways in which it might be enhanced tended to be clouded. Much of the discussion of economic growth and development was, for example, aggregative in tone and approach. The economy was discussed as if it were an integrated economic organism; as if individual decision making by firms, investors, and consumers could be costlessly suppressed insofar as the processes of economic growth were concerned. Certainly no need was recognized for any mutual information among individual participants in the economy.

Moreover, the aggregate economy was seen as rigidly circumscribed by resource scarcity that limited growth possibilities along very definite paths. These scarcity constraints were thought not only to govern the possibilities in hypothetical market economies, but also to delineate optimal growth patterns. Little awareness was displayed that the objectivity of these constraints disappears as soon as it is realized how heavily dependent they are on the assumption that nothing further can or is likely to be discovered concerning new and better ways of using given resources, or concerning the existence of hitherto unsuspected resources.

An important ingredient in economic growth was recognized to be the continual availability of improved technology. But technological advance was seen as occurring in an inexorably impersonal manner and to be somehow effortlessly and automatically available to all parts of an economy. In particular, the opportunities for growth were seen as marked out, given initial technology, by a clearly defined array of intertemporal investment possibilities that existed somehow apart from any need for them to be discovered, and whose very existence dictated the appropriate growth path. There was no suggestion that the set of opportunities likely to be in fact discovered might in some way depend on the institutional framework within which growth was sought.

It is therefore hardly surprising to find that this earlier growth and development literature not only failed to explore the policies and institutional patterns that might stimulate profit-motivated individual market-entrepreneurship; it in fact tended to take it for granted that markets were entirely unnecessary for the achievement of growth, and that the naturally preferred mode for growth was through wise central planning.

An Entrepreneurial View of Economic Development

The view of economic growth and development in this chapter contrasts sharply with that critically described in the preceding section. I will emphasize the *open-endedness* of economic systems. Although I will by no means ignore or deny the prime importance of resource scarcity, both in respect to output at any given date and in regard to the possibilities of increases in output level over time, my emphasis will be on the need and scope for processes of discovery that may in effect render scarcity less overriding in accounting for growth. I will thus be concerned not so much with the ways through which human beings assure that every ounce of perceived output possibility is properly exploited, but rather with the incentives to stimulate the perception of possibilities. It is this perception that is responsible for the open-endedness of the economic process. We never know what real possibilities remain to be discovered; we never know what the real limits are to the elasticity of the resource constraints that circumscribe our existence.

In understanding the processes of entrepreneurial discovery that are crucially important for growth, aggregation is a distinct handicap. Treating the economy as a whole and abstracting from the opportunities created by interpersonal error within the system inevitably diverts analytical attention from discovery processes made necessary and possible by such error. Treating growth simply as a phenomenon best achieved through deliberate planning inevitably clamps economic growth into a framework from which open-ended discovery is excluded. To plan is not to discover; in fact to plan presumes that the framework within which planning takes place is already fully discovered. In contrast, I see the unfolding development of a nation's economy over time as a process made up, to a major extent, of the interaction of innumerable individual acts of mutual discovery. An understanding of the institutional climate within which such spontaneous processes of unpredictable mutual discovery can best flourish is central. Let us first examine somewhat more systematically the way in which entrepreneurial discovery constitutes a unique ingredient in economic growth.

Robinson Crusoe, Entrepreneurship, and Economic Growth

Imagine a "Robinson Crusoe" economy with a low volume of output. We might initially classify the possible reasons for this low level of production (and for Crusoe's consequently low standard of living) in the following manner: (1) Crusoe may command only severely limited resources, thus constraining output to a low level; (2) resources may be available to permit higher levels of output, but these levels are not being attained because of

Crusoe's lack of technical knowledge of how to properly utilize the resources available (3) both the resources able to permit higher output and the knowledge necessary to harness the resources may be available to Crusoe, but the higher output is not forthcoming because of Crusoe's ignorance of the availability of the resources and/or of the availability of the technical knowledge needed to utilize them. In terms of this array of possible reasons, it is clear that a process of economic development raising the quantity and quality of Crusoe's output may be the result of any or all of the following: an increased endowment of resources (including an increased stock of capital goods, presumably as a result of deliberate saving and investment); an increased command over the technical knowledge needed to exploit available resources; or discovery of the resources and the technical knowledge that are already available.

Now this way of putting matters is obviously awkward. Technical knowledge is no less a resource for Crusoe than is steel, or labor, or land. Changes in the endowment of Crusoe's knowledge need not, it may be objected, be treated separately from changes in his endowments of other resources. This deliberately awkward classification has been, in fact, employed strictly in order to accentuate an important but often missed distinction—between the technical knowledge needed to utilize given physical resources on the one hand, and, on the other hand, *the knowledge that resources are in fact available*. Technical knowledge can be treated as a resource; but knowledge of the availability of resources cannot. There is a fundamental difference between the manner in which changes in the stock of technical knowledge may enter into the explanation of economic development, and the manner in which changes in the knowledge of *availability* of resources enter into such explanation.

Economic development based on growth of Crusoe's technical knowledge may be perceived to occur in the same logically understandable manner as development based on expanded physical resources. Expansion of physical resources may, of course, be either planned or unplanned. In the case of unplanned expansion of physical inputs, as for example when unexpected beneficial changes in climate occur, Crusoe enjoys expanded output by simply continuing to exploit available resources to the utmost. In the more important case of planned expansion of inputs, Crusoe may, by deliberately channeling his productive energies to this end, increase the volume and quality of capital goods, thus generating eventual increases in output flows. Economic growth and development, in these cases, follows for Crusoe from the logic of expanded opportunities made possible by the planned or unplanned available volume of resources. Output possibilities are restricted by the scarce available resources; expansion of resources is followed by exploitation of the now-expanded volume of output possibilities.

Growth of Crusoe's technical knowledge, quite similarly, expands the range of productive possibilities. What Crusoe can produce today out of given physical resources with today's technical knowledge, is greater than what he could produce without today's knowledge with the same resources. The expanded technical knowledge may have been at least partly unplanned (as has occurred on numerous occasions during the history of technology) or more likely it may have come about at least partly as a result of deliberate investment in research. Growth in technical knowledge expands the range of production possibilities, thus providing an immediate explanation for growth in output.

The key point is that in such cases development consists in the exploitation of expanded opportunities. The volume of opportunities grows, hence output grows. A very large part of economic analysis depends on the postulate that an optimal opportunity that exists is an opportunity that is immediately grasped. From this perspective, growth in the availability of Crusoe's resources, whether consisting in physical inputs or in technical knowledge, whether as a result of planned investment or the result of fortuitously increased endowment, provides an immediately convincing explanation for growth in output.

Here lies the important distinction, for explanations of development, between growth in technical knowledge on the one hand, and an increased awareness of the availability of resources on the other. For where development occurs as a result of increased awareness of the availability of resources, it occurs *not* because of the availability of new opportunities, but because of expanded awareness of existing opportunities. To understand development that has occurred in this way, it is necessary to escape the economist's assumption that an optimal opportunity that exists is an opportunity immediately grasped. It is necessary to recognize that desirable opportunities may go unnoticed and hence unexploited; it is necessary to understand the entrepreneurial process whereby opportunities that were hitherto existent but unseen become opportunities seen and exploited.

Entrepreneurial discovery of existing opportunities is relevant to an understanding of economic development along two dimensions.

1. At a given point in time output may be less than is possible and desired, because of opportunities that have remained unnoticed. Entrepreneurial discovery of these opportunities makes possible a growth in output.
2. As time goes by, expansion of resources (physical or otherwise, planned or unplanned) expands the range of productive possibilities. For this is to be translated into growth in output, it is not enough that these expanded possibilities exist—they must be perceived. Here too entrepreneurial discovery is an indispensable ingredient in economic development.

**Markets, Entrepreneurship, and Economic Growth:
An Apparent Problem**

The foregoing Crusonian discussion may be applied, with appropriate modification, to a certain problem in the analysis of growth in a market context. A correct allocation of resources is one that commits each unit of resource to its most highly valued use. An expansion of available resources is presumed to generate expanded output value because we take it for granted that decision makers will tend to correctly allocate the increased resources. This applies to increased technical knowledge no less than to expanded physical resources. If an available unit, say of a scarce raw material, can be utilized in production somewhere in a competitive economy, its market price will, we are taught, tend to rise toward the value of its marginal product in its best use, ensuring that its owner will tend to find it wasteful not to deploy it in that use. Similarly, if a scrap of scarce technical knowledge can enhance the productivity of physical resources somewhere in the economy, potential users of this knowledge will bid for it until its market price tends to correspond to its highest marginal usefulness. But the same market process does not directly apply to knowledge of the availability of resources, or, more generally, to knowledge of value.

Let us imagine that a simple, costless operation linking together two items each valued at $1, can transform them into a product worth $12. Clearly this availability of an opportunity for $10 pure entrepreneurial profit indicates that market participants in general have not realized that this profitable transformation is feasible, or that it is profitable. The market lacks knowledge of the resources available to create $10 pure profit. Or we may say that the market lacks the knowledge of the true value of the two items of input: the true joint value of these inputs is $12; the market incorrectly believes it to be only $2. Can we, with respect to this missing knowledge, rely on the general market tendency for items to be valued so as to fully reflect their most important uses? Can we assume a tendency for the market to correctly assign full value to this missing knowledge? There are serious logical difficulties involved in any attempt to answer these questions affirmatively.

To assume a tendency for the market to assign full value to the missing knowledge would require that would-be users of this missing knowledge bid for it. That is, we would have to postulate that competing bidders, eager to capture the $10 profit (available through transforming the $2 inputs into $12 output) are prepared to pay for the information that would make such capture possible. This could force up the price of this knowledge of value until it approximates the full $10 that it is capable of generating. But the truth is that we cannot, in this case, assume (as we were able to assume in the case of technical knowledge) that there will be bidders for the missing knowledge.

A moment's reflection should make this clear. Market participants have in general failed to notice that there is a way to transform $2 worth of input into $12 worth of output. In other words, these market participants are not aware that they are overlooking the $10 opportunity of pure profit. Those aware of the inputs place no higher value upon them than $2. Those aware of the high $12 value of the output are aware of no opportunity to achieve such output at an outlay that would make its production available. It is not that market participants feel they lack specific knowledge capable of yielding $10; rather it is that market participants have no inkling that there is anything to be known. Under these circumstances we have no right to assume that anyone will be bidding for the knowledge of how to convert the $2 worth of input into $12 worth of output or that potential bidders have any idea of the value of such knowledge.

The source of the $10 profit opportunity resides in the undervaluation by the market of the two inputs, in the existence of unperceived value. The true joint value of the two inputs should be $12; the market values them at $2. The value to any individual of the knowledge of this undervaluation should surely be the full value of the pure profit such knowledge can generate the full amount of the undervaluation. But, by hypothesis, the market is not aware of this undervaluation. It follows, therefore, that the market is not aware that any value attaches to knowledge of such undervaluation since no undervaluation is in fact suspected.

Knowledge of the true value of inputs is thus quite different, in this respect, from technical knowledge. Technical knowledge may be valuable, potential bidders may assess its value and as a result seek its possession. The knowledge of the true value of inputs may indeed be said to possess value, but this value is of a kind that, by its nature, precludes the possibility of its being able to motivate market participants to deliberately seek it out. *To imagine its being deliberately sought after, is to imagine away the source of its value.* The knowledge of value is valuable only if it is not known to be valuable. As soon as the market correctly values the knowledge of value, that correctly assessed value shrinks to zero.

If these conundrums surround the notion of the value of the knowledge of value, then it follows that we cannot rely on competitive market bidding to call forth correct knowledge of value—at least in the way in which that competitive bidding can be relied upon to mobilize productive resources. We cannot, apparently, rely on competitive market bidding to ensure that valuable possibilities will be perceived, that the inputs capable of sustaining these possibilities will be correctly valued. And it is here that we recognize the existence of two distinct avenues along which economic development may proceed: through expansion of opportunities arising through increased availability of resources; or through the discovery of hitherto unperceived opportunities. In practice both strands of developmental causation operate in an intertwined manner. In order for resources to expand, newly possible opportunities must first be perceived.

These two lines of development differ in important ways, however. Where development occurs through the expansion of opportunities, it may be the outcome of a deliberate planning process to expand the volume of resources through investment in human resources or in physical capital goods. The possibility of such a deliberate planning process permits economic development to be understood as the smooth unfolding of a designed growth path. But with respect to that line of development which arises from the flow of discovery of existing opportunities, no such smooth unfolding of designed growth can be identified. It is impossible to deliberately plan a series of discoveries. Just as we cannot imagine an opportunity being deliberately overlooked unless because of some significant cost of deliberate search that in fact renders the opportunity less than worthwhile after all, so too we cannot imagine a systematic plan to notice that which has hitherto been overlooked. All this means that economic development requires, as part of its explanation, understanding of the entrepreneurial element and of the way in which this element eludes the analytical tools of standard economic theory.

Allocation, Growth, and Entrepreneurship

A good deal of modern economics is concerned with the forces that determine the allocation of society's resources among alternative production possibilities. There were times, in the past at least, when professional economic discussion seemed to draw a sharp distinction between the allocative function of economic systems on the one hand and the process of economic growth on the other. It was as if economic growth presented a series of problems and tasks to which allocative considerations were totally irrelevant. Thus, for example, economists who expressed full confidence in the capacity of markets to allocate society's resources with reasonable efficiency were quick to deny any similar ability of markets to achieve a desirable rate of growth for the economy.[3] The allocative properties of markets apparently failed to include, as an implication, the capacity to successfully lift the total volume of output over time. To use existing resources efficiently called for deploying these resources to avoid waste. To achieve growth, it was held, called for the fulfillment of a quite different task: the steady increase of the total volume of these resources.

This dichotomy appears flawed in several somewhat subtle respects, though it does, of course, possess a certain superficial plausibility. An increase in the total volume of resources available to society is after all not the same as a more effective social utilization of the resource volume given at a particular date. Indeed, a case can emphatically be made that to increase the total volume of resources calls for qualities—of an entrepreneurial character—unrelated to those required for calculative, optimizing, allocative activity.

The fact that a market can successfully stimulate the efficient allocation of resources is no guarantee that it can perform similarly with respect to the entrepreneurial activity required for growth. If the economists referred to had wished to draw attention to these important distinctions, there would have been far less over which the critic could quibble. Unfortunately this was decidedly not the case. As mentioned earlier, for a long time economists discussing growth virtually ignored entrepreneurship. And, for a world in which entrepreneurship in the discovery of new resources (or in the discovery of new uses for already known and available resources) is seen as having no scope, the distinction between allocation and growth is deeply flawed.

In a world of given resources (with no scope for any addition to these resources that might arise from discovery) it should be obvious that growth necessarily arises from a particular (intertemporal) pattern of resource allocation. In exactly the same way as efficient allocation of resources is required in order to ensure that society's scarce resources are directed to the particular basket of current consumption goods that are judged most urgently required, efficient intertemporal allocation of resources is required in order to express any preference rankings that place higher future levels of well-being above currently higher levels of well-being. Economic growth, in a world of given resources, depends strictly on the rate at which consumption enjoyments are postponed to permit capital resources to be built up or new technological knowledge to be acquired.

There seems little basis for the postulation of any analytical distinction between allocation processes as they relate to alternative current uses of resources on the one hand, and allocation procedures as they relate to alternative temporal production possibilities on the other. It is not at all obvious why a market system acknowledged to achieve effective patterns of resource allocation in the first of these senses should be held incapable of achieving comparably efficient intertemporal allocative patterns.

The sharp dichotomy that seemed to be drawn between economic allocation of resources and economic growth was flawed in a rather more complicated sense as well. It is not merely that economic growth turns out to be merely a special case of the more general allocation problem. As soon as scope for entrepreneurial discovery is acknowledged in the context of economic growth, such scope must be acknowledged in the context of short-run resource allocation as well. So that although it appeared, in a world without entrepreneurship, as if allocation economics necessarily embraced—indeed, swallowed up—the economics of growth, almost the opposite seems to occur as soon as the role of entrepreneurial discovery is recognized. As soon as the economics of growth becomes correctly viewed as being in large part the economics of entrepreneurial discovery, it becomes difficult to see the processes of short-run resource allocation as anything but special cases of the more general discovery processes that constitute economic growth.

From this latter perspective, then, the allocation/growth dichotomy is flawed not so much because it overlooks the allocative aspects of economic growth, but because it tends to reinforce the neglect of the role of entrepreneurship in both short-run and long-run economic processes.

Opportunities, Alertness, and Economic Processes

For an analytical perspective in which entrepreneurship and its role are seen as essential elements, the centrality of allocation is highly questionable. Neither at the level of the analysis of the individual economic decision, nor at that level concerned with understanding how society's resources are allocated, is it possible to proceed without transcending the allocation schema within which economics has so frequently been constrained.[4] Despite the enormously valuable clarity introduced into modern economics by Lord Robbins' formulation (in which economics was rigidly identified as concerned with the consequences of human allocative behavior, and which led to the popular notion of economics as being concerned with the ways in which societies do and should allocate their scarce resources)[5] the truth is that economics can no longer make do with this rather narrow conception of its nature and concerns.

Economists can no longer take it for granted that individual decision makers, or groups, engage in nothing more than allocative decisions against the background of clearly perceived alternatives. Economists must consider that economic processes, and especially market processes, have profound impact upon the way in which individuals perceive the options available to them, while the accuracy and sensitivity of opportunity-perception itself crucially affects the nature of these economic and market processes that they set in motion. In other words, economic analysis must grapple with the inescapable entrepreneurial element in action and in society.

Individual action is not seen as merely the calculation of the optimum position relevant to a given set of data; it is seen as an attempt to grasp opportunities that the human agent judges, as he peers through a fog of uncertainty, to be available. The interaction of decisions in markets is not seen as an instantaneous meshing of plans in which the pattern of calculated optima for the participants is such as to permit all of them to be simultaneously sustained. Rather it is seen as an unrestrained, but by no means haphazard, process in which the opportunities perceived to be available are those that have been overlooked by others. In the face of ceaseless and unpredictable exogenous change, the continual pursuit of as-yet-unperceived opportunities keeps perceptions from straying too far from reality. The role of entrepreneurial alertness in this sequence deserves to be briefly elaborated.

Entrepreneurial theory labors under the burden of what appears to be a serious handicap: the specific outcome selected in any particular entrepreneurial decision cannot, even in principle, be predicted.[6] In contrast, the choice made in the course of allocative decision making is, in microeconomic analysis, viewed as emerging errorlessly and ineluctably from the interaction between the agent's objective function and resource and technological constraints. Economic science can, in the case of the allocative decision, claim to account precisely for the action decided upon. But such can certainly not be claimed for the entrepreneurial decision, in which the agent must determine what he or she believes the relevant environment to be, within which a course of action must be taken.

Economic science is unable to account precisely for the outcome of such entrepreneurial determination. (It should also be pointed out that the purely allocative decision never does occur, and that in fact it is sheer illusion to imagine that economic science can ever provide the kind of precision suggested in microeconomics textbooks.) Yet it is important not to conclude that, simply because the application of the theory of constrained optimization is insufficient to yield precise outcomes, entrepreneurial decision making and the market processes set in motion by such decisions are entirely without guidance.

The truth is that all human decision making is guided by an extremely powerful force—the motivation to see relevant facts as they are.[7] This pervasive pressure to avoid error and to learn from mistakes operates in ways that are far from being fully known. But this powerful instinct is responsible for whatever success humanity has achieved in coping with its environment. To be human is not merely to calculate correctly within an already perceived environment; it is to be able, by peering into a murky present and an even murkier future, to obtain a reasonably useful grasp of one's true situation.

In the market context a correct perception of one's situation calls not only for a perception of physical possibilities and constraints, but also of the possibilities and constraints imposed by the actions, present and prospective, of others. The market process consists of a sequence of entrepreneurial decisions, each of which, being only partially correct in anticipating the decisions of others, leaves room and incentive for further mutual discovery. Were such decisions made haphazardly, there would be no basis for claiming the existence of systematic entrepreneurial market processes. Such systematic processes of entrepreneurial discovery are based on the determined, purposeful alertness of market participants.

Types of Entrepreneurial Activity

There are many opportunities for alert entrepreneurs. Some opportunities are of relevance only for short-run market processes; others hold relevance for long-run processes of growth and development. I will show that despite the validity of such classification, the nature of entrepreneurial decision making is, at bottom, no different in regard to long-run growth contexts than in regard to short-run contexts.

There appear to be three major types of concrete entrepreneurial activity: (1) arbitrage activity; (2) speculative activity; and (3) innovative activity. *Arbitrage* activity consists of acting upon the discovery of a present discrepancy (net of all delivery costs) between the prices at which a given item can be bought and sold. Such activity involves the discovery of error, since those who sold at the low price are simply unaware of those who buy at the higher price, and vice versa. This discovery constitutes a discovery of an opportunity for pure gain. It is surely the incentive provided by such opportunities that is responsible for the powerful tendency for such arbitrage opportunities to continually disappear. Arbitrage calls for no innovation. In its pure form it calls for no risk bearing and no capital, since buying and selling are simultaneous.

Speculative activity is an arbitrage across time. It is engaged in by the entrepreneur who believes that he or she has discovered a discrepancy (net of all relevant carrying costs, and to be revealed through subsequent history) between the prices at which a given item can be bought (today) and sold (in the future). To believe that one has discovered such a price discrepancy is to believe that one has discovered an opportunity for pure gain. There can be no doubt that it is the incentive so provided that inspires entrepreneurs to undertake speculative activity that, if correct, tends to stabilize price over time. Of course such activity is inextricably intertwined with the bearing of uncertainty and also calls for the cooperation of the capitalist (to bridge the time gap involved in the speculation). No innovation is required for the activity of the pure speculator.

Innovative activity consists in the creation (for a future more or less distant) of an output, method of production, or organization not hitherto in use. For such activity to be profitable, it will of course be necessary for the innovator to introduce not just any innovation, but one that displays the very same pattern of intertemporal price discrepancy that is identified with speculative activity. Innovative activity, like speculative activity, retains important parallels with the case of pure arbitrage. Innovation calls for the discovery of an intertemporal opportunity that cannot, even in principle, be said to actually exist before the innovation has been created. To talk of the existence of an undiscovered opportunity for an as-yet-uncreated innovation is merely to engage in metaphor (although it should be pointed out that in important cases the use of such metaphor may be highly instructive).[8]

Nonetheless innovative activity too can bridge a gap between two markets across time, overcoming (what at least from a later perspective can be seen to have been) error, inspired by the opportunity to grasp the pure gain set up by the relevant price discrepancy.

Alertness is a concept sufficiently elastic to cover not only the perception of existing (arbitrage) opportunities, but also the perception of intertemporal speculative opportunities that can only be definitively realized after the lapse of time, and even also the perception of intertemporal opportunities that call for creative and imaginative innovation. Certainly the concrete manifestation of successful speculative (or of innovative) activity may call for substantially different personal and psychological qualities than those needed to engage in pure arbitrage.

Yet the parallelism among the various kinds of entrepreneurial activity remains. All of them consist of taking advantage of price differentials; all are inspired by the pure-profit incentive constituted by the respective price differentials; all are made possible by less competent entrepreneurial activity (the errors of others). In other words all of them involve *knowledge of value*—with all its attendant conundrums discussed earlier. It is the commonality expressed in these parallels, and in this shared link to the elusive knowledge of value, that I wish to emphasize here.

Incentives, Competition, and Freedom of Entry

A feature common to all kinds of entrepreneurial discovery is the incentive of pure profit, arising out of the respective price discrepancies of which the entrepreneurial opportunities consist.[9] It should be emphasized that this is an incentive rather different from the notion of an incentive in the nonentrepreneurial context. In the nonentrepreneurial context incentives are called for to motivate an agent to engage in some *costly* activity. To provide such an incentive is therefore to arrange that the gross payoff from the relevant activity to the agent be seen to be more than sufficient to offset the associated cost sacrifice. To provide an incentive for a laborer to work is to arrange a wage payment that will prove more attractive to the laborer than, for example, the leisure alternative.

In the context of entrepreneurial opportunities, however, the notion of an incentive is quite different. Incentive in this case is for the discovery of an opportunity for net gain. Were the opportunity already perceived, no further incentive would be required to persuade the agent to exploit it. However little we know about the ways in which different entrepreneurs discover what they discover, almost all such discoveries would not be made if there were not the possibility of personally attractive, desirable outcomes.

For the sequence of entrepreneurial discoveries that constitutes the market process, the system of incentives is spiced and sharpened by the awareness that market opportunities are to be found only where they have been overlooked by others. It is here that entrepreneurial incentives and the conditions required for dynamically competitive markets intersect crucially and fruitfully.

It is now fairly well understood that the dynamic competition upon which market systems rely for their effectiveness calls for only one basic prerequisite—freedom of entry.[10] If incumbent firms are aware that others are free to enter whenever they sense an opportunity of profit, this causes incumbents to concentrate on the discovery of yet more effective ways of efficiently serving the consumer. This means that the entrepreneurial discovery of better ways of serving the consumer is spurred both by the incentives provided to nonincumbents by their perception of as-yet-unexploited pure profit opportunities, and by the incentives provided to incumbents by the threat of losses that may ensue from the entry of competing entrepreneurs. I will now consider the rather limited public-policy implications of the insights into the entrepreneurial process developed thus far in this chapter.

The Entrepreneurial Process and Public Policy

The entrepreneurial process is a continual, endless process of discovery. The opportunities for discovery embrace both those consisting of the discovery of errors by others trading (or expected to trade) in markets now or in the future, as well as the discovery of unsuspected resources or technical feasiblities that constitute genuine innovation.

The solution to society's economic problem (identified by F.A. Hayek as that of the coordination and mobilization of scattered scraps of information) calls for a steady series of successful discoveries. Moreover, once the possibility for discovery is introduced, it becomes increasingly apparent that Hayek's coordination problem can, in principle, be extended to cover the opportunities for innovation as well.[11]

> The current price of natural gas and the current level of its consumption may be fully coordinated with one another and with other current prices and market activities (informed by the most up-to-date intelligence). Yet this price may be "too high" and consumption "too low" from the perspective (that may, in several years, be provided by technological or other discoveries) of the possibilities, say of tapping solar energy.[12]

If society has a stake in encouraging the solution to Hayek's coordination problem, this must surely extend also the intertemporal coordination opportunities that can be exploited only by innovative, entrepreneurial breakthroughs. How can society achieve this? What policies can, without incurring unacceptable costs, stimulate or release the potential for discovery that exists in all motivated human beings that make up a society's population?

It should be clear that to stimulate the potential for discovery must be a task rather different from that of stimulating or coaxing out a greater supply of a given scarce resource-service. The potential availability of a given scarce resource is usually treated by economists as capable of being expressed by a supply curve. Such a curve relates various potentially available quantities of the resource to the resource prices capable respectively of eliciting these quantities. To command larger available quantities, such as a supply curve generally reports, it will be necessary to offer more attractive resource prices. With respect to entrepreneurial talent, however, we are not able to discourse in this fashion. The knowledge of value is never an item deliberately sought after. Nor do those possessing the knowledge of value consciously treat it as a deployable or salable resource.

It is simply not useful to treat entrepreneurship in terms of a supply curve. The exercise of specific quantities of entrepreneurship involves no identifiable cost or required amounts. Yet, it is impossible to treat the degree of entrepreneurial discovery prevailing in a society as totally unrelated to public policy. There are two separate ways in which policy may in principle affect the emergence of entrepreneurial discovery. The first relates to policy that may affect the entrepreneurial attitudes and character of a population. The second relates to policy that may, with a population of given entrepreneurial attitude, stimulate it to be more alert to entrepreneurial opportunities. Arthur Seldon has remarked that the qualities that make for entrepreneurial alertness (such as restive temperament, thirst for adventure, ambition, and imagination), may be nurtured or suppressed. "They are presumably similar in Germany on both sides of the Iron Curtain, in Korea North and South of the 38th parallel, on both sides of the China Sea separating the Chinese mainland from the island of Taiwan, but the results are very different according to the institutions created by government."[13]

Other authors emphasize both access to profit opportunities and security of property rights. The opportunity to obtain profit is by itself not yet sufficient for the emergence of entrepreneurial activity. "The entrepreneur must also be reasonably assured that he may keep entrepreneurial profits that he legitimately acquires. Thus certain institutional practices in a market economy will tend to encourage a high level of entrepreneurial activity, especially (1) a free and open economy that permits equal access to entrepreneurial opportunities, (2) guarantees of ownership in property legally acquired, and (3) stability of institutional practices that establish points 1 and 2."[14] Let us see further what these two kinds of policy goals involve, and what, if anything, can be concretely proposed toward their implementation.

Nurturing the Entrepreneurial Spirit

Seldon's references to the Iron Curtain, the 38th parallel, and the China Sea on the one hand express a conviction that the profound institutional differences that relate to the areas separated by these boundaries have much to do with the nurturing or the suppression of the thirst for adventure, ambition, and imagination. On the other hand, these references reflect a willingness to recognize the possibility, at least, that ethnic and geographical factors may be important factors in the determination of the extent to which a population displays an entrepreneurial attitude.

It should be apparent that in regard to the ways in which geographic and ethnic factors do or do not affect entrepreneurial spirit, our knowledge is woefully meager. Moreover, research effort applied to these questions has been extremely limited. Nonetheless a beginning has been made. Interesting work has, for example, been done by Benjamin Gilad in bringing to bear existing studies that point to a relationship between alternative institutional and cultural environments—particularly as these impinge on the freedom of the individual—and human qualities germane to the entrepreneurial attitude.[15] It remains to be seen whether further research in this area strengthens the insights so far suggested, and whether such results offer ideas capable of being translated into meaningful public-policy proposals. It is, nonetheless, worth noting that the conclusions to which Gilad's work points—that economic growth may depend upon the stimulus to the entrepreneurial spirit supplied by an environment of economic freedom—run precisely counter to that implied by earlier economists, who saw economic growth as requiring economic regimentation.[16]

Stimulating Alertness

Research into techniques of stimulating the alertnes of a given group of persons is fragmentary and unsystematic.[17] Many discussions of entrepreneurial alertness have relied on the "plain, unremarkable statement of a fundamental facet of human nature" *that human beings tend to notice that which it is their interest to notice* (italics mine).[18] The social significance of a market system does not reside in the beauty of the allocation pattern under equilibrium conditions. Rather it rests upon the capacity of markets to translate the errors made in the immediate past into opportunities for pure entrepreneurial profit of direct interest to potential entrepreneurs. Features of the institutional landscape that strengthen the linkage between socially significant opportunities and the likelihood and security of associated entrepreneurial gain (such as those proposed by Hebert and Link, note 13 this chapter) clearly improve the chances for entrepreneurial discovery. The linkage between dynamic competition and entrepreneurship is of direct relevance here.The incentives provided by freedom of entrepreneurial entry, as they act on incumbent entrepreneurs and potential entrants are relevant in devising ways in which to stimulate entrepreneurial alertness and discovery.

The Danger of Taking the Entrepreneur for Granted

Perhaps the most important contribution that the recent renewal of professional interest in the entrepreneurial process can make toward public policy is to stimulate a general awareness of the grave dangers that accrue from the error of taking the entrepreneur and his role for granted. No doubt there were eras in the history of the development of economic understanding when this kind of error was relatively less critical. No doubt an understanding of the general pattern of results produced by the entrepreneurial process was more important, for such eras, than an understanding of that process itself. But the error of imagining that there really is nothing for entrepreneurs to do, that economic processes are somehow propelled without the entrepreneurial spirit and genius for discovery, is to fall prey to a way of thinking that can harmfully affect social policy. To take the entrepreneur for granted is to overlook the dangers of regulatory or fiscal or antitrust policies that block or discourage entrepreneurial entry into perceived avenues for profitable activity. The entrepreneurial spirit, the potential for discovery, is always waiting to be released. Human ingenuity is irrepressible and perennial; and its release requires an environment free from special privileges or blockages against new entrants. For the successful allocative functioning of the market, and for the stimulation of dynamic growth, the entrepreneur must not be taken for granted.

Notes

1. J.A. Schumpeter, *Theorie der wirtschaftlichen Entwicklung* (Leipzig: 1912), English translation, *Theory of Economic Development*, (Cambridge, Mass.: Harvard University Press, 1934). See also Schumpeter, *Capitalism, Socialism and Democracy* (New York: Harper and Row, 1942).

2. Harvey Leibenstein, *General X-Efficiency Theory and Economic Development* (New York: Oxford University Press, 1978), p. 9.

3. See the statement by Joan Robinson, *Economic Journal* (March 1963), p. 125: "The strong case for the price mechanism lies in the allocation of scarce resources between competing uses. . . . But no one has ever been able to make out a case (on grounds of economic efficiency) for

laissez-faire in the sphere of investment." See also, I.M. Kirzner, "On the Premises of Growth Economics," *New Individualist Review* (Summer 1963).

4. See also, I.M. Kirzner, "Entrepreneurship and the Future of Capitalism," in *Entrepreneurship and the Outlook for America*, J. Backman, ed. (New York: Free Press, 1983).

5. L.H. Robbins, *Nature and Significance of Economic Science*, 2nd ed. (London: Macmillan Co., 1935).

6. G.L.S. Shackle, *Epistemics and Economics* (Cambridge: Cambridge University Press, 1972).

7. I.M. Kirzner, "Hayek, Knowledge, and Market Processes," in *Perception, Opportunity, and Profit* (Chicago: University of Chicago Press, 1979).

8. I.M. Kirzner, "Uncertainty, Discovery and Human Action: A Study of the Entrepreneurial Profile in the Misesian System," in *Method, Process, and Austrian Economics: Essays in Honor of Ludwig von Mises*, I.M. Kirzner, ed. (Lexington, Mass.: D.C. Heath, 1982), p. 157.

9. This and the succeeding sections of this chapter draw on my approach to understanding the role of the entrepreneur as developed in earlier works, especially: *Competition and Entrepreneurship* (Chicago: University of Chicago Press, 1973), and *Perception, Opportunity and Profit* (Chicago: University of Chicago Press, 1979).

10. See Kirzner, *Competition and Entrepreneurship*, p. 97 ff. See also, D.T. Armentano, *Antitrust and Monopoly: Anatomy of a Policy Failure* (New York: Wiley, 1982), chapters 1 and 2.

11. F.A. Hayek, *The Road to Serfdom* (Chicago: University of Chicago Press, 1944).

12. Kirzner, *Entrepreneurship and the Future of Capitalism*, p. 161.

13. A. Seldon, "Preface," in Kirzner et al., *The Prime Mover of Progress: The Entrepreneur in Capitalism and Socialism* (London: The Institute of Economic Affairs, 1980), pp. xi–xii.

14. R.F. Hebert and A.N. Link, *The Entrepreneur, Mainstream Views and Radical Critiques* (New York: Praeger, 1982), p. 11.

15. B. Gilad, "On Encouraging Entrepreneurship: An Interdisciplinary Approach," *Journal of Behavioral Economics* (Summer 1982).

16. See for example K. de Schweinitz, "Free Enterprise in a Growth World," *Southern Economic Journal* (October 1962).

17. See also N. Balabkins and A. Aizsilnieks, *Entrepreneur in a Small Country* (Hicksville, New York: Exposition Press, 1975) chapter 10; A.V. Bruno and T.T. Tyebjee, "The Environment for Entrepreneurship," in C.A. Kent, D.L. Sexton, and K.H. Vesper, *Encyclopedia of Entrepreneurship* (Englewood Cliffs, N.J.: Prentice-Hall, 1982).

18. A. Seldon, "Preface," p. xvi.

4

The Fiscal Environment for Entrepreneurship

Michael J. Boskin

Few topics are as poorly understood yet as hotly debated as the environment for entrepreneurship. Indeed, even a definition of entrepreneurship can cover a wide range and the list of candidates called entrepreneurs be generously or narrowly defined. Throughout history, entrepreneurs have been seen either as the source of enormous disruption in traditional societies or as the fountainhead of new economic prosperity. To some they epitomize pure self-interest; to others their acts are a necessary and perhaps even a socially motivated precondition for social progress.

To those of you familiar with my writings, it will not come as a surprise that I believe that entrepreneurship is a major contributor to long-run economic growth. Except for national security, long-run economic growth is the single most important vehicle for promoting the well-being of our citizens and the vitality, and even viability, of our society. Fostering a climate in which entrepreneurship is encouraged and economic growth is enhanced leads to benefits not only for the entrepreneurs, but for all citizens. In fact, no one has more at stake in a growing economy than those who have not yet made it on the economic ladder. Whether the growth itself will provide an environment for upward economic potential for these individuals in the marketplace, or will provide ample resources for a generous and humane population to share with those who are unable to make it on their own, this growth historically has been the primary vehicle for promoting the economic well-being of the less fortunate in our society.

But what is entrepreneurship and who are entrepreneurs? I take a very broad definition of the entrepreneurial process. I include not only those who are in the business world taking risks to invent and promote new products and processes, but also those who are disseminating them to new areas, whether regionally, nationally, or internationally, and the employees in the firms that are engaged in this process. In my view of entrepreneurship, scientists, engineers, and others doing basic research, who generate ideas that lead to new products and processes, however indirectly, are also included. In short, entrepreneurship is a process by which new ideas, products, or processes are produced, generated, and disseminated to one or more markets. But why is it important? And what drives entrepreneurs?

Entrepreneurship and Economic Growth

There are many reasons to be concerned about the level and allocation of entrepreneurial activity in society. As noted here, I included in the definition of entrepreneurship basic scientific research, product and process innovation, and the dissemination of these throughout society. Some people may value this process per se; throughout history some have opposed it as a threat to stability and continuity of tradition. Historically, entrepreneurial activity is often associated with major breakthroughs made by mankind such as the modern computer industry, but the myriad of less-noted but collectively important changes in techniques of production, product lines, and methods of dissemination—the transportation and information revolutions—have been major vehicles for promoting general increases in the standard of living in the United States. It is not surprising then that the recent abysmal growth performance of the United States economy focuses attention on the environment that tends to promote growth and on entrepreneurship in particular.

Though it is certainly clear that on occasion individual entrepreneurs have done what they did quite irrespective of the potential risks and returns in undertaking their activities, it is my opinion that the *primary* motivation of individuals—and individuals working in organizations such as firms and governments—has been the returns (usually pecuniary, but sometimes nonpecuniary) and risks involved. My interpretation of the available evidence is that a substantial fraction of productivity growth rests ultimately in such incentives. There are many ways in which an economy can improve its standard of living, and entrepreneurial activity leading to new products, improved production processes that lower costs and thereby free resources for other uses, is certainly only one. Technological change in this broad sense appears to be responsible for between one-third and one-half of our economic growth. The remainder appears to be the result of investment in the knowledge and skills of the labor force, increasing the capital/labor ratio (so-called *capital deepening*), and various other ways to improve the allocation of resources in society.

If technological change, innovation, and their dissemination are so important to the growth process, which in turn is so important to the long-run evolution of societies, and these in turn are heavily influenced by the climate for entrepreneurship, then where are we now, where are we heading, and where are we likely to head in the future?

The Current Climate for Entrepreneurship

By most standards, entrepreneurship and innovation have declined precipitously. If we look at the number of patents taken out, the ratio of research and development (R&D) spending to gross national product (GNP), and a variety of so-called scientific indicators, they have all been falling substantially. Some basic recent trends for these indicators are reported in tables 4–1 and 4–2. With the decline in R&D and patents, particularly those issued to U.S. citizens and corporations, the technological base of our future growth is threatened. We are no longer training as many scientists and engineers as a proportion of our population. Though these levels are somewhat lower for the major countries with which we compete internationally, their rates have been growing.

There are many explanations for this phenomenon, some economic, some sociological, some demographic. However, the substantial increases in the risks and the reductions in the potential returns to entrepreneurial activity that have occurred in the process of the enormous expansion of our welfare state, the concomitant high and rising tax rates, the displacement of private economic activity by government economic activity, and the substantial inflation of the last fifteen years have seriously eroded the environment for entrepreneurship.[1] During this time, Danzinger and Plotnick indicate some additional progress was made in reducing poverty in part as a result of this rapid growth of social spending. In 1965, persons below the poverty line accounted for 12.1 percent of United States population. In 1968, the incidence had dropped to 10.1 percent; in 1970, 9.4 percent; in 1972, 6.2 percent; in 1974 the figure fluctuated up to 7.8 percent; but by 1976 the rate was down again to 6.5 percent.[2] An environment of inflation, high and rising taxes, and uncertain interest rates, is quite inhibitive to the entrepreneurial process. Let us take a few examples.

It is now well documented that not only can inflation reduce the real after-tax return to investment, but it also substantially increases the risks involved. The variance of inflation increases more than proportionally with the level. Inflation renders contractual arrangements made in nominal terms much more complicated. Consider the case of a long-term bond. Its interest rate not only reflects the real return, but an inflation premium. Therefore, each year part of the real principal is being paid back and the investor has the extra interest premium (and the investor has the option to

Table 4–1
U.S. Resources Devoted to Research and Development

Year	R&D Expenditures as Percentage of GNP
1965	2.9
1969	2.7
1973	2.3
1978	2.2

Source: *Statistical Abstract of the United States, 1981* (Washington, D.C.: Government Printing Office).

Table 4–2
Patents Issued
(in thousands)

Year	Individuals	U.S. Corporations	Foreign Corporations	Foreign Residents
1973	16.9	38.6	16.5	22.6
1974	18.0	37.8	18.7	25.6
1975	17.2	34.6	18.3	25.4
1976	14.0	34.4	19.9	26.0
1977	14.0	31.5	18.2	23.9
1978	14.3	31.3	19.3	25.1

Source: *Statistical Abstract of the United States, 1981* (Washington, D.C.: Government Printing Office).

reinvest to maintain real principal). But inflation, even when fully expected and translated into higher interest rates, ends up making a long-term bond into a much more complicated financial instrument: a series of tied shorter-term bonds. In the inflationary episodes of the 1970s, with our unindexed taxed system, inflation seriously increased the tax rate on income from capital. This in turn substantially reduced its return, and as far as I can tell, substantially reduced the incentive to save and invest at a time when we should have been equipping our rapidly growing labor force not only with more but with newer and better capital.

The work of Summers reveals the decline in the share of our resources devoted to real net productive investment and personal saving. During the period 1965–1969, the share of net productive investment in the GNP, after subtracting direct pollution control expenditures from investment, was 4.1 percent. In 1970–1974, it was 3.1 percent. By 1975–1979, it stood at 2.2 percent.[3] Not only have we been generating new technology at a slower pace, but also we have been remiss in putting aside the resources to finance the deployment of more and better capital to make our labor force more productive. The current level of unemployment is a direct result of this failure. But as the President's economic report shows, even though unemployment may be up as a percentage of the labor force so is total employment as a percentage of the total population.[4] These seemingly contradictory results can be explained by the growth of the labor force as a percentage of the population. The data are given in table 4–3.

I do not think we have definitive answers as to the exact causes of inflation, recession, and economic performance in general. But I believe that there is general unanimity among economists that our inflation began in the late 1960s with the attempt to finance the Vietnam War and the War on Poverty without raising taxes, and that a necessary precondition for accelerating inflation is accelerated monetary growth.

Table 4-3
U.S. Employment and Unemployment Rates

Year	Employment as Percentage of Population	Unemployment as Percentage of Civilian Labor Force
1960	54.9	5.5
1965	55.0	4.5
1970	56.1	4.9
1975	55.3	8.5
1980	58.5	7.1

Source: U.S., *Economic Report of the President, 1982* (Washington, D.C.: Government Printing Office), Table B-31, p. 269.

I therefore believe that a primary prerequisite to restore a climate conducive to substantial entrepreneurial activity is a much more modest rate of monetary expansion, combined with low and slightly fluctuating rates of inflation instead of high and wildly fluctuating rates of inflation and interest rates. It is one thing to ask our entrepreneurs to take substantial risks; it is quite something else for government policy to exacerbate those risks substantially. It is no wonder that our rate of innovation and technological change has deteriorated.

Our tax system is another culprit. We have been substantially increasing, until recently, taxes on income from capital. Unlike most countries, we tax many forms of savings twice: once when they are earned as part of income, and once when they earn an interest return. Although recent moves to Individual Retirement Accounts (IRA) and other changes in the tax law have moved us part way to a consumption tax, I, and I believe most other younger leading economists, have long been in favor of moving from our current system of taxation to one that integrates corporate and personal taxes into a single tax at the household level which exempts all forms of reinvestment in the economy. I believe in taxing people on what they take out of the economy—their consumption—rather than what they put in—their income. There have been a variety of technical studies that detail how this can be accomplished in the context of our current tax system with a gradual transition period.[5] Although the Accelerated Cost Recovery System (ACRS) of the current tax law moved part way in this direction—even more than all the way for certain types of assets—we should replace our current system of corporate and personal income tax with a tax on consumption at the household level, with income from businesses attributed back to the owners of those businesses so that all income is only taxed once, and reinvestment taxed not at all.

Such an integrated personal consumption tax would be neutral with respect to the choice between consumption and saving, among various types of investment, and between corporate and noncorporate business activity. The gains from eliminating the distortions currently besetting our tax laws would be substantial.

The worsening disincentives to save and invest caused by the insidious interaction of inflation and our unindexed tax system were substantially reduced with ACRS. By simplifying the complex depreciation and useful-life rules, and providing more rapid capital cost recovery for most assets, ACRS was designed to offset the erosion of depreciation allowances based on historic cost and the taxation of nominal net interest. However, ACRS still left us with a differentiated structure of effective tax rates in different types of assets. The 1982 Tax Equity and Fiscal Responsibilty Act eliminated the 1984 and 1985 features of ACRS under the Economic Recovery Tax Act (ERTA) and thereby sharply reduced the prospective rate of capital cost recovery. The continual debate over depreciation rules makes long-run investment planning quite difficult. In my opinion the case for first-year write-off of *all* investment (commonly called expensing) is overwhelming on both economic and administrative grounds.

In the tax system I favor, all corporate income would be attributed to shareholders and taxed only at the personal level. Further, all saving and investment would be deductible in the year made. Thus, retained earnings of corporations (corporate saving) would be expensed, and all personal saving would be tax deductible in much the same manner as currently occurs for Individual Retirement Accounts. However, I would resist all restrictions on amounts, withdrawals, and so forth, which tend to plague our tax-exempt forms of saving.

But we are well on our way to reducing inflation. Indeed the major achievement thus far for the Reagan administration has been the cutting of inflation by more than half. Unfortunately, while it was probably predictable in advance, the supply-side incentives in the Reagan program are of much longer time horizon than a single, even severe, recession. Thus, substantial incentives are in place for an innovation and investment boom as we come out of the recession in the mid and late 1980s. We have come a long way toward redressing the disincentives that existed and were expanded in the 1970s with high, rising and fluctuating inflation, and high and rising taxes on income from capital. Unfortunately, we are in the midst of a severe worldwide recession.

It is only possible to understand the nature and severity of the current recession by realizing its worldwide dimensions. Countries following very different policies than ours, such as France, have an even worse economic performance than the United States. Against the backdrop of the frightening long-term productivity growth slowdown I mentioned earlier and the severe structural changes in our economy resulting from our changing comparative advantage in the world, we must effect an orderly adjustment of our so-called smokestack industries to their most efficient uses, and an orderly transition of excess labor and capital to more efficient uses as determined by the marketplace.

Among the important structural changes in our economy is the large increase in the proportion of young workers and women in the labor force; an explosion of early retirement; the increased life expectancy of the elderly; the continuing shift of the population to the South and West; the change of employment to services from manufacturing; the growth of world trade, particularly following major tariff reductions; the end of the era of fixed exchange rates; the huge increase in energy prices and concomitant transfer of resources from industrialized countries to OPEC; the rapid growth of government, especially transfer payments (now larger than federal spending on purchases of goods and services); and the growth of a quasi government of organizations and agencies. The result is too much attention focused on short-run performance from too many quarters. This leaves us with the impossible notion that the economy, spurred by tax cuts, could launch into such a frenzy of activity so rapidly as to avoid the problems that we have now.

But I am optimistic for the future and it is on this note that I would like to conclude.

The Future for Entrepreneurship, Innovation, and Economic Growth

I am extremely optimistic about the future of the U.S. economy although I write from what I hope is the trough of an extremely severe recession that I expect to abate only slowly. But for the first time a large fraction of our citizens and politicians are beginning to realize how bad the mess is that we are in, how deeply rooted our productivity slowdown was, and how important restoring incentives to produce income and wealth really is. This realization is reflected in the tax-law changes we have passed, the wrenching effort to slow the growth of government spending, particularly on social programs, and the lack of any credible alternative policy to the one currently in place.

Many people, myself included, have problems with some of the specifics of the recent monetary and fiscal policies. In particular the very tight monetary policy clashed with the very loose fiscal policy in a predictable manner, driving up real interest rates and choking off investment and interest-sensitive consumption. Further, with a defense buildup deemed necessary and Social Security off-limits, virtually all of the pressure to slow spending growth has occurred in about 40 percent of the budget. Additional savings will not be easy to achieve without a closer look at defense and Social Security.

Though many of the reforms in social-program eligibility standards are quite reasonable, even necessary, it is unfortunate that they have had to be implemented with such weak labor market conditions. Our political process, however, seems unable to make such changes during times of rapid economic progress; it focuses, rather, on how and to whom to distribute some of the fruits of that progress, without regard to what we will be able to afford and who really needs support in untoward times.

However, it is important to note that these tend to be attacks or complaints about some specific feature of some specific part of the program. Since silence is the most eloquent testimony, it is interesting to note the lack of a coherent, cohesive, and politically viable alternative set of policies. People and politicians do not like our current economic distress, but no group of politicians has moved forward to espouse any major alternative that promises success. Returning to wage and price controls to deal with inflation has more or less been ruled out by a public that realizes how socially damaging controls were. At a time of severe unemployment, the Democrats in the House proposed a public-works bill of $2 billion; this is, pardon the expression, peanuts compared to that launched by President Carter when he assumed office when unemployment was much lower than it is today. Is this not a tacit admission that the promotion rate to permanent private-sector jobs was so low from these programs that they proved to provide too little bang for the buck?

I am certain that our progress in the future will be uneven for several reasons. First, it is impossible to know what it is possible to know. Therefore, several different avenues of scientific inquiry may prove to be of little use. Second, it will take a considerable period of time for people to believe that we are serious about continuing to reduce inflation and to restructure our economy toward one that has a higher investment rate and a higher rate of innovation and technological activity, lower taxes, and less government intrusion by regulation. Many people, including many potential investors and entrepreneurs, are concerned that we may cycle back to our policies of the 1970s of growing government, increasing taxes, increasing regulation, and decreasing private incentives. We need to continue the general structure of the policies adopted in the last two years, although clearly a variety of mid-course corrections are desirable and some have begun to be implemented.

Finally, let me note that traditionally periods of slowdown and hardship, whether the late 1950s and early 1960s or the Great Depression, have been followed by an era of substantial improvement. This occurs for a number of reasons: the backlog of unutilized investment opportunities, and the potential availability of talented labor and valuable capital freed up as industries that have overreached themselves draw back. We are likely to move into such an era in the mid and late 1980s, but only if we do not throw out the basic structure of policies designed to redress the balance toward investment away from borrowing to finance current consumption, toward stabilizing the share of government in the economy and not increasing it, toward focusing our tax system on neutrality at the margin between invest-

Table 4–4
New Business Formations and Failures

Year	New Business Incorporations (in thousands)	Failure Rate (per 10,000 enterprises)
1965	203.9	53.3
1970	264.2	43.8
1975	326.3	42.6
1980	533.5	42.1

Source: U.S., *Economic Report of the President, 1982* (Washington, D.C.: Government Printing Office), Table B–93, p. 338.

ment and consumption, toward regulations that balance economic gains with environmental and other social goals.

We have the economic capability of reversing the deterioration of the climate for entrepreneurship, innovation, and economic growth; whether we will reinforce the political will and capability of doing so that surfaced in 1980 remains to be seen. The costs of not surmounting the obstacles extends well beyond the economic well-being of future generations of Americans. Table 4–4 indicates the continuing optimism of entrepreneurs. Despite the current economic difficulties, new-business formations are up dramatically and the business failure rate remains below one-half of one percent. If we stick to the general notion of trying to restore incentives to produce income and wealth we should be able to restore the spirit of vitality, creativity, productivity, and resourcefulness with which we so often described our nation and its economy, possibilities, and accomplishments in the past. If not, our long-run economic success will be sacrificed because we cannot bear the short-term pain.

The correlation of free political institutions, free markets, and rapid economic progress of which the United States is the leading example to the Third World societies tottering between dictatorship and democracy is still our major weapon against the possible loss of our leadership in the world economy and of world economic and social stability. The deterioration of our leadership would be an unfortunate consequence of failing to provide an environment within which entrepreneurship, innovation, and economic growth can flourish.

Notes

1. Michael Boskin, "Taxation, Saving and the Rate of Interest," *Journal of Political Economy* (April 1978); and Michael Boskin, M. Gertler, and C. Taylor, *The Impact of Inflation on U.S. Productivity and International Competitiveness* (Washington, D.C.: National Planning Association, 1980).

2. Shelton Danzinger and Robert Plotnick, "Has the War on Poverty Been Won?" Mimeo, Institute for Research on Poverty, Madison, Wisc., March 1980.

3. Lawrence H. Summers, "Taxation and Capital Investment: A q-Theory Approach," *Brookings Papers on Economic Activity* 1:1981.

4. President's Council of Economic Advisors, *Economic Report of the President 1982* (Washington, D.C.: Government Printing Office, 1982).

5. U.S. Treasury, Office of Tax Research, *Blueprints for Basic Tax Reform* (Washington, D.C.: Government Printing Office, 1982).

5 Taxation and the Entrepreneurial Environment

Calvin A. Kent

With the election of President Reagan, it appeared that the 1980s would be the decade of supply-side economics. This philosophy was based upon the highly plausible idea that if people and businesses were allowed to keep more of what they earned, there would be greater incentives for them to save and invest in the economy as well as to work harder and create new jobs.[1] Early in his administration the President communicated to Congress his plan for economic recovery.[2] After a masterful legislative campaign, the Economic Recovery Tax Act (ERTA) was passed during the summer of 1981.

The euphoria did not last long. Faced with ballooning rather than diminishing deficits, public opinion that felt business had benefited too much at the expense of the little guy, and the reluctance of Congress to significantly cut government spending, less than a year later the Tax Equity and Fiscal Responsibility Act (TEFRA) was enacted. TEFRA reduced by almost half the benefits business received in 1981. Over two-thirds of the additional revenue raised under TEFRA will come from the reduction of ERTA tax benefits, new tax increases, and accelerated business-tax payments.[3] These two acts, along with the Subchapter S Revision Act of 1982, the Miscellaneous Revenue Act of 1982, and the Social Security Program Revision Act of 1983, constitute the most significant change in the tax environment for entrepreneurship since corporate income taxation began over seventy years ago.

Has the combined effect of these laws significantly benefited business in general and the entrepreneurial sector in particular? In reviewing the reduction in the corporate income-tax rates and the accelerated cost recovery system (ACRS) for depreciation of personal and real property, the Urban Institute concluded that taxes on corporate earnings from investment in new plant and equipment would be reduced by 85 percent.[4] Using statistics supplied by Data Resources, Inc., including not only the 1981 and 1982 tax acts but the impact of the revised Social Security payroll tax as well as other miscellaneous fees, the Federal Reserve Bank of Philadelphia made a more comprehensive analysis.[5] The Federal Reserve study agreed with the Urban Institute that effective tax rates on additional corporate profits coming from new investment would be cut from 33 percent in 1980 to 4.7 percent in 1984. They concluded that, "although corporations will pay less profits tax

69

as a result of the 1981 and 1982 tax acts, other taxes levied on businesses will rise more than enough to offset the tax savings."[6] Indirect business taxes such as excise taxes are projected to rise by 32 percent in real terms for 1980 to 1984. Employer contributions for social insurance (such as Social Security and unemployment-compensation taxes) are projected to rise by 21 percent (after adjusting for inflation) during the same period. The result is a slight increase rather than a diminuation in the tax burden on the business sector.

Unfortunately for business as a whole, recent tax changes may constitute a no-sum game with businesses' position being neither significantly improved nor reduced. The entrepreneurial sector of the economy may not have fared so well. What has transpired is a redistribution of tax burden among firms of different size and capitalization. In discussing the tax changes, Topping stated the following: "Recent tax legislation with its emphasis on what is right for good old big business really didn't do anything for entrepreneurs."[7] Though the statement may be extreme, it does point out the major flaw in current strategy. Most entrepreneurships are labor-intensive with relatively low capitalization and virtually no profits during their startup phases. With these characteristics, many venture-oriented firms will be unable to avail themselves of the positive features of the recent tax acts while being affected by the negative provisions.

In designing a tax program that affects entrepreneurs, there are two goals that might be used as standards of a good tax system. The first is tax neutrality. Under this standard taxes would be revised to remove any discriminating provisions that place new ventures at a disadvantage when competing either for funds or markets with larger established entities. The second is tax subsidation. This principle sees the tax system as designed to give a competitive tax advantage to entrepreneurs that other firms do not enjoy. This goal is appropriate if it is accepted that the entrepreneurial sector of the economy will create more jobs, devise more innovations, and contribute more to economic growth than will larger businesses. The current tax treatment of new ventures fails to comply with either standard.

New ventures pass through two district phases during the initial portion of their life cycle. Stoll and Walter have identified these as the "Loss Generating" and "Emerging Profit" phases.[8] During each phase tax policy is a crucial variable in the survival of the firm. During the loss-generation phase new firms are experiencing the high costs of becoming established. Their markets are not yet developed, and cash flow is low if not negative. During the emerging-profit phase the firm has a positive cash flow but is often in need of outside financing for consolidation and expansion of operations.

For firms in the loss-generation phase the critical need is to attract capital. As likely as not this will come from the entrepreneur, friends, or relations. Short-term financing, secured by the creditworthiness of the entrepreneur, may come from banks or perhaps a Small Business Investment Company (SBIC). The ability to attract funds from outside investors and to retain the cash flow generated is essential. Tax provisions that fail to encourage venture capitalists or deplete cash retained can be fatal to business continuation. Tax credits are of little use during the phase as there are no positive tax liabilities against which these credits can be taken.

As firms enter the emerging-profit phase their need to attract capital and retain cash does not diminish. The firm may incorporate, perhaps as a Subchapter S corporation, or even go public to raise needed financial capital. Venture-capital firms may be looked to as sources for funding. Those who put their money in the venture-capital market do so usually seeking income in the form of capital gains, which are taxed less heavily than regular income. During expansion the firm relies heavily on debt, which may make it a more risky investment than a firm with more equity. Tax credits are important to the extent that there is federal tax liability or the credits can be used directly by investors against personal tax liabilities.

The competitive disadvantage of new firms arises from the ability of the large corporation with a group of diversified but incorporated divisions to manipulate its corporate tax liability. Using consolidated returns large firms can use losses in some divisions to offset taxable profits in others. Unused tax credits from divisions with no tax liability can be transferred to offset profits arising elsewhere in the corporate structure. The internal cash flow of the large corporation is an excellent source of venture finance that is not available to most new, independent businesses. The most desirable tax system would recognize these disadvantages and seek to remedy them to put new ventures on equal competitive footing.

The major question to be addressed is to what degree the recent tax changes have brought the system into conformity with the goals discussed here. Have previous discriminations been reduced or eliminated? Has the entrepreneur now any tax advantages available to allow more growth and expansion?

Corporate Tax Rates

The foremost recommendation of the White House Commission on Small Business was to "legislate a more graduated corporate income tax, reducing taxes at the low end of the rate schedule, by pushing the top of the tax rate step ladder from $100,000 to at least $500,000 of earnings."[9] Congressional response to this recommendation was puny. Under the provisions of ERTA, tax rates on the first $25,000 of income were reduced from 17 percent to 15 percent and on income in the $25,000 to $50,000 bracket reduced from 20 to

18 percent. The maximum corporate tax rate of 46 percent still applies to any income in excess of $100,000. The Small Business Administration in analyzing these changes commented, "while this provision will have a direct and immediate beneficial impact on small businesses, the impact will be relatively minor." The report notes that the maximum tax savings available to any firm is $1,000.[10]

Further reductions in corporate tax rates are not the most efficacious policy alternative to promote new ventures. Stoll and Walter contend:

> Reduction in the corporate tax rates suffer from comparison to tax credits in two respects. One, their thrust is general rather than specific. Their efficiency as a tax incentive is thereby diminished. Two, general tax reductions lessen the value of incentives already in the system.[11]

If the goal of tax policy is to specifically assist entrepreneurs, there appear to be more effective ways of accomplishing this objective than across-the-board corporate tax-rate reductions.

Subchapter S

One of the more encouraging aspects of recent tax reform as it impacts entrepreneurship has been the significant revision of the Subchapter S provision of the Internal Revenue Code. The Subchapter S provisions are designed for small, closely held businesses seeking to incorporate for legal reasons while remaining partnerships for tax purposes. Though it is widely assumed by the general public that owners of stock in Subchapter S corporations are taxed in exactly the same manner as are partners, this impression is not entirely accurate.

To quality as a Subchapter S corporation five criteria must be met. First, the firm must have no more than a specified number of shareholders. Second, it may issue only one class of stock. Third, it must be a domestic corporation. Fourth, it may not be a member of an affiliated group. Fifth, it must have only individuals, estates, and certain trusts as shareholders. Both ERTA and TEFRA substantially liberalized these criteria.

ERTA increased the number of shareholders from fifteen to twenty-five. TEFRA further increased this to thirty-five. These changes are far short of the recommendation of the White House Commission on Small Business, which contended that "by expanding the limit to 100 shareholders these vehicles could attract a great deal of capital for a wide variety of new enterprises."[12]

Changes in the law also make corporations eligible for Subchapter S if their passive investment income (rents, dividends, interest, royalties, and annuities) exceeds the old limit of 20 percent of income. The new provisions increase the allowable percentage to 25 and provide that any excess income will be taxed at regular corporate tax rates. The firm will not lose its Sub-chapter S status unless passive income exceeds the 25-percent limitation for three years in a row.

The new laws also simplify the IRS Code to allow shareholders to treat certain items in a manner identical to how they would be treated under part-nerships. Under the prior law, capital gains and net operating losses in ex-cess of the shareholders' basis (total amount invested in stock plus loans to the corporation) were treated unfavorably since they could not be used by the shareholders on their individual returns. As Pollard explains, "Now, long-term capital gain, short-term capital gain, long-term capital losses, short-term capital losses, all pass through intact. Also operating losses in excess of the shareholders stock plus loan basis is no longer lost forever but can be carried forward."[13] Since most new firms experience operating losses during their startup phase, this provision is especially attractive to potential investors. The capital-gains provision also should create an increased will-ingness of high-tax-bracket investors to participate in new ventures using Subchapter S.

In addition to these changes, several of the old tax traps that plagued Subchapter S corporations in the past have been eliminated. In particular, those provisions which would have automatically terminated a Subchapter S corporation and imposed corporate tax liability even for inadvertent technical violations of Subchapter S status were eliminated or their conse-quences reduced. In the past, these Subchapter S terminations have involved extremely costly consequences to many Subchapter S shareholders. The IRS has been given increased flexibility in dealing with unintended violations.

The improvements in Subchapter S are laudable but will principally benefit those startup companies which anticipate early losses that they can pass through to shareholders in the form of personal tax reductions. These will also benefit highly profitable companies with very low capital spending needs and high dividend distributions. But these rules will have limited im-pact on companies seeking to retain earnings for growth, many of whom "will still do just as well to continue as proprietorships or partnerships."[14]

Capital Gains Taxation

Ever since the first income tax was enacted in 1913 there has been a con-tinued controversy over the question of how capital gains should be taxed. Capital gains, which are the difference between purchase price and selling price of an asset, were originally taxed as ordinary income. Since that time taxation of capital gains has gone through seven major and a host of minor revisions. Most of these have given income received as long-term capital gains preferential treatment, resulting in a lower tax liability.

Those who contend that capital gains should be taxed as ordinary income do so on the grounds that these gains are additions to the recipient's purchasing power and therefore properly subject to taxation.[15] Those who support favorable treatment of capital gains do so on three grounds.[16] First, when combined with the progressive income tax, income received from the sale of an asset could force a taxpayer, sometimes dramatically, into a higher income tax bracket, creating a much higher tax liability than would otherwise have been the situation. Without preferential treatment of capital gains, these lumps of income cause taxpayers to feel locked into investments and unwilling to move their investment money to areas of greater efficiency.

The second reason is the impact of inflation. Much of the capital gain experienced when assets are sold does not reflect an increase in asset value, but a decrease in the value of money. In their study Martin Feldstein and Joel Slemrod revealed that in 1973 sellers of capital stock paid taxes on nominal gains of $4.5 billion, which when adjusted for inflation became capital losses of almost $1 billion.[17] Preferential treatment of capital gains is viewed as a partial corrective for the effects of inflation on the value of investments.

Since capital gains are the successful entrepreneur's principal source of gain, a third and more compelling reason is that by giving preferential tax treatment to capital gains, capital formation in the small-business sector is encouraged. Though it is recognized that such favorable treatment is of principal benefit to high-income individuals and therefore offensive to some notions of vertical tax equity, supporters contend that without this tax incentive the supply of venture capital would significantly diminish.

In the seventy years of income taxation that this nation has experienced, the preferential treatment of capital gains has varied with the political philosophy of the times and the administration in power. In recent history both the 1969 and 1976 tax-reform bills significantly increased the rate of taxation on capital gains for both corporations and individuals. Not only were rates increased but the holding period for capital gains was also increased from six months to one year. In addition, capital gains were to be included in the basis used for calculating the Alternate Minimum Tax (AMT). The result was a demonstrable decrease in the flow of venture capital.

Responding to the growing national concern about decreases in United States investment and productivity, Congress in 1978 lowered the effective capital gains rate from 49 percent to 28 percent. This was accomplished by increasing the amount of capital gains that could be excluded from the tax base to 60 percent of the total long-term gain. A recent study by the U.S. General Accounting Office has indicated that this reduction contributed to an expansion of the venture-capital pool from $2.5 billion in 1977 to almost $6 billion in 1981.[18]

The first two reasons cited for giving preferential treatment to capital gains do not appear to be valid. The problem of income bunching that results when assets are sold can be dealt with through the process of income averaging. The problem of inflation is both imperfectly and inadequately dealt with by the current method of capital-gains preferences. The current practice of excluding 60 percent of capital gains from the tax base is valid only if 60 percent of the appreciation in the asset's value is caused by inflation. If inflation during the period over which the asset is held is less than 60 percent, then the provision overcorrects and bestows an unjustified tax benefit on the recipient. On the other hand, if inflation during the period is greater than 60 percent, the taxpayer receives only a partial correction for the effect of inflation. The inflationary impact on capital gains could be handled through a system of indexation that would more accurately reflect the diminuation in the purchasing power of the dollar over the holding period of the asset than the current exclusion does.[19]

This being the case, the justification for preferential treatment of capital gains must rest with its favorable impact on entrepreneurs and those who would supply them with venture capital. The case here is not as strong as it first appears. The ERTA, by reducing the top tax rate on unearned income from 70 percent to 50 percent, reduced the maximum effective tax rate on capital gains from 28 percent to 20 percent (40 percent capital-gains inclusion times a maximum 50-percent rate). The Small Business Administration (SBA), while indicating the reduction will be an incentive for investors, also notes that of the capital gains to be realized, "over 70 percent will probably be in non-equity activities, primarily real estate, if past and current investment trends are a guide."[20] The principal benefit then of this provision does not appear to be the encouragement of capital flows to entrepreneurs, but speculation in real estate, livestock, art objects, and other nonproductive assets.

A much more sensible approach would be to permit the rollover of capital gains to go tax free. Under this suggestion capital gains accrued from investment in new ventures would not be taxed if those capital gains were plowed back either into the venture or into a new qualified alternative small business. Currently this approach is used to encourage home ownership. Capital gains on homes are not taxable if the gain is used to purchase a new dwelling. Extension of this principle to new ventures would target the tax preferences in a manner to encourage capital formation and entrepreneurship. The current preference system for capital gains, while an incentive for investment in new business, is an inefficient and less-effective alternative than would be such a rollover provision.

The Accelerated Cost Recovery System (ACRS)

The centerpiece of the 1981 ERTA was the establishment of the Accelerated Cost Recovery System (ACRS). A speedup and simplification of depreciation schedules had been strongly endorsed by the White House Commission on Small Business on two grounds. First, existing depreciation schedules and rules were so complicated that many, if not most, small firms and new ventures were unable to avail themselves of the accelerated depreciation provisions of previous acts. Second was the recognition of what inflation had done to nullify the impact of the old depreciation schedules. As the White House commission reported, "the idea that depreciation provided sufficient funds to replace obsolescent plant and equipment had been made ludicrous by inflation."[21]

The result of ERTA was that eligible personal property and certain real property would be expensed over a three-year, five-year, ten-year, or fifteen-year recovery period depending on the type of property. Three-year depreciation is assigned to most vehicles, and R&D equipment. Five-year depreciation applies to most other equipment. Ten-year expensing was to be used for virtually all other personal property. Real property is usually assigned a fifteen-year recovery period and the taxpayer can elect for either a thirty-five or forty-five year extended period. TEFRA repealed the ACRS schedules that were to go into effect in 1985 and 1986. This repeal means equipment will remain on a schedule that is close to 150 percent rather than double the amount under the previous declining-balance method of depreciation.

As an alternative, under the ERTA a taxpayer could elect to immediately expense up to $5,000 of personal property in 1982 and 1983, $7,500 in 1984 and 1985, and $10,000 in 1986 and thereafter. This expensing provision would be without regard to the life of the asset. If this immediate expensing was elected, the investment tax credit for the immediately expensed portion of the asset's value could not be taken. The Small Business Administration feels "this provision would give small businesses, especially those which make limited amounts of investment in equipment, a special incentive to make investments in depreciable property to obtain the tax benefits of immediate expensing and avoid depreciation imputations altogether."[22]

Although these depreciation alternatives will have some benefit for entrepreneurs, it has to be recognized as a general rule that new ventures are more labor- than capital-intensive and have shorter-lived assets than do larger businesses. As a result, the Treasury Department estimates that only about 20 percent of the savings of the ACRS will go to small businesses during the fiscal years 1981 to 1986.[23] From the entrepreneurial standpoint, the key benefit will be the simplified bookkeeping burdens, rather than the tax savings. This is particularly true for small businesses that have no taxable income against which depreciation can be applied. The SBA has noted that "these depreciation changes continued to expand the bias of our tax system towards capital intensive businesses and away from labor intensive ones."[24] This is not surprising since accelerated depreciation was enacted specifically to stimulate investment, not to help entrepreneurs.

Investment Tax Credit

The use of Investment Tax Credits (ITC) to stimulate the purchase of new equipment has been an off-again, on-again feature of U.S. tax policy. As originally enacted, the ITC was designed to serve two functions: first, to stimulate the capital-goods industry in the United States by encouraging the purchase of new equipment; and second, to improve the productivity of the U.S. economy and increase its competitiveness in world markets by encouraging the upgrading and modernization of facilities and equipment.[25]

Under the law prior to the ERTA, most capital investments in new equipment were entitled to the investment tax credit equal to 10 percent of the purchase price if the expected life of the asset was seven or more years. If the life of the asset was less than seven years, only a portion of the investment tax credit could be applied. Under the ERTA there was a significant change in the amount of ITC given. For assets with a life of less than three years there was no change, with a zero credit being given. For property in the three- to five-year class, the investment tax credit increased from 3.33 percent to 6 percent. For assets with a life of five to seven years, the credit increased from 6.66 percent to the full 10 percent which was awarded to any asset of seven or more years duration.

The 1982 act (TEFRA) made only one change in the ITC. The amount of a firm's total tax liability that could be offset using the investment tax credit was reduced from 90 percent to 85 percent. This reduced the attractiveness of the credit, particularly for firms with narrow profit margins.

Small businesses will undoubtedly gain some benefits from these liberalized provisions, but these benefits may not be as great as their advocates claim. To be useful the entrepreneur must have a positive tax liability in order to obtain the benefits of the ITC. In addition, the small business must also be able to have sufficient cash flow or credit available to purchase the equipment in the first place. Since most new ventures during their startup are in their loss-generation phase and crimped for either cash or credit, the value of this exemption to them can be questioned. The benefit of this exemption will be principally for firms with positive tax liabilities and cash flows that are generally larger, that is, more established firms.

Perhaps more significant from the standpoint of the venture initiator is the increase in the amount of used property eligible for the investment tax credit, which is increased in stages from the current $100,000 to $150,000 by 1985. As the Small Business Administration comments, "small businessmen, unlike large ones, cannot always afford to purchase new equipment and rely heavily on significant amounts of used equipment."[26] The limitation of $150,000 on the value of eligible use of equipment does discriminate against the small businesses, particularly in a period of rapid inflation. Although the changes reduce the discrimination, they do not eliminate it.

R&D Incentives

The perilous and precipitous decline in the portion of this nation's gross national product (GNP) spent on the research and development of new innovation and technology was documented in chapter 2 by Michael Boskin. In an attempt to remedy this problem the ERTA contains a 25- percent income tax credit for new R&D expenditures.

This revision appears more generous than it actually is. For one thing the tax credit is nonrefundable so firms with no taxable income will not be able to benefit although they may carry the benefits forward for fifteen years or apply it against three years' prior tax liabilities. Credit is also available only for research conducted within the United States. Only 65 percent of the R&D expenditures done on an outside contract basis or with universities and exempt research organizations is allowed to be included. The credit can only be claimed when the expenditures are incurred in the actual carrying on of a trade or a business. For those reasons firms engaged principally in contract research or just starting a business will find it difficult to qualify.[27]

The greatest defect in the R&D credit is that it is applicable only to additional R&D expenditures made by a firm. A firm that spends a constant amount on research and development each year, no matter how significant the amount may be, receives no benefit at all under ERTA. The credit is figured on the expenditures in excess of the average of the previous three years. The basis for this calculation will be a firm's three previous years' average expenditures for R&D. For firms with no previous R&D experience, 50 percent of the current year's expenditures are considered as its basis, thus effectively reducing the R&D credit to 12.5 percent.

This provision will provide substantial tax savings for large companies that expand their R&D budgets. It should also prove helpful to establish profit-making entrepreneurships that are out of their loss-generation phase. Existing ventures in many instances will be encouraged to start an R&D program. As an incentive for high-tech entrepreneurs its impact will be uneven and partial, giving significant benefits to some and little help to others.

Safe Harbor Leasing

As indicated earlier, one of the major problems of new firms during their startup phase is their inability to use tax credits since they have no taxable income against which these tax credits can be applied. As was recognized by Congress, many of the tax credits designed to spur investment would be of little use to new ventures during their loss-generation phase. One promising alternative for dealing with that problem was the so-called safe harbor lease.

The safe harbor lease provisions received scant attention when Congress debated the Economic Recovery Tax Act (ERTA) of 1981. Under such a lease a new venture that had no federal tax liability went through a paper transaction, transferring its tax credits to a firm with a positive federal tax liability. Title to the new machinery and equipment that the original firm purchased would be transferred to the company needing a tax write-off, which in turn would lease back the equipment to the original firm. Through this method firms otherwise unable to completely use the accelerated cost recovery allowances and expanded investment tax credits would be able to benefit. Safe harbor leases would allow parties to ship the tax benefits to the lessor as well as affording the lessee lower rental payments.[28] Before the 1981 tax act, the IRS had viewed such leasing arrangements as financing devices and had not allowed the deductions to lessor firms.

The logic behind safe harbor leases so far as entrepreneurial ventures are concerned appears correct. These provisions remained as the only way to make sure the capital-spending investment incentives would apply to all businesses. It was estimated that the Accelerated Cost Recovery System and the 25-percent R&D tax credit would reduce the cost of capital by 20 to 30 percent.[29] Without safe harbor provisions, new firms with losses could be placed at a severe cost disadvantage when compared with established, profitable enterprises. These credits would be meaningless if the firm had no positive tax liability against which these credits could be applied. The enactment of safe harbor legislation meant all firms would face the same capital cost regardless of their tax status. This would facilitate efficient allocation of investment capital within financial markets.

Testimony before Congress indicated that the majority of firms unable to use the new tax incentives were smaller businesses found in the entrepreneurial, high-technology sector of the economy.[30] It was further recognized that as these new ventures accumulated unused tax credits they became increasingly attractive candidates for mergers. Without some way to cash in on these credits many entrepreneurships faced the unpleasant option of either a severe competitive disadvantage or the possibility of being absorbed by hostile takeover.

When the ERTA was put into effect, firms had no more than ninety days to close their leases made before August 18, 1981. This limited the leasing arrangements almost exclusively to transactions among large corporations with sufficient legal and accounting skills to make the arrangements on short notice. The problem was further compounded by the complexity of the rules established by the IRS, which established high administrative fees and virtually eliminated small business from participation. Further, the IRS's temporary regulations severely limited closely held corporations from acting as lessors under the safe harbor provisions, further reducing the attractiveness of the applicability of this device to entrepreneurs.

The Joint Committee on Taxation found after the first round of safe harbor leasing that over three-fourths of the transactions and 93 percent of the benefits were ascribed to the larger corporations.[31] This concentration of benefits led to public outrage when it was revealed that several large corporations were able to completely eliminate their tax liabilities through these leasing arrangements.[32] The result was to severely restrict safe harbor leasing during 1982, and to virtually eliminate it after 1983 under the Tax Equity and Fiscal Responsibility Act (TEFRA).

Unfortunately, the demise of safe harbor leasing does not bring about the demise of the problem it was designed to cure. Its repeal in no way creates a more favorable tax environment to new-venture initiation. The use of tax credits by small firms will continue to be highly restricted until some method is devised to allow new ventures to use them for something other than bait in merger negotiations.

LIFO Inventory Accounting

One of the more promising aspects of recent tax legislation has been the reform of last-in, first-out (LIFO) inventory accounting standards to make them more usable by new ventures. The use of LIFO accounting rules is particularly important for businesses during periods of inflation. The failure of accounting rules to adequately reflect decreases in asset value due to inflation has exacted a heavy toll on the level of investment in the nation. Council of Economic Advisors chairman Martin Feldstein has estimated this failure has been the principal cause for the decrease in investment in nonresidential capital during the period of 1953 to 1978.[33]

LIFO accounting, when used to replace first-in, first-out (FIFO) rules, allows inventory sold to be valued at more nearly its current replacement cost then its historical value. Testimony before Congress indicated that small firms have generally not used LIFO accounting because of its complexity.[34] Among the simplifications in ERTA is to allow taxpayers using LIFO to make certain adjustments to their income such as market write-downs over a three-year period rather than in the single year following their change to LIFO accounting.

One of the most popular techniques for calculating LIFO is the *dollar value* method. Prior to the 1981 tax, businesses that had several product lines had to establish separate inventory pools for each type of product line. Under ERTA, small businesses using the dollar value method may use only one inventory pool. This privilege is extended only to businesses with less than $2 million in gross sales averaged over the previous three years. The ERTA further requires the Secretary of the Treasury to prepare a report specifying ways in which inventory accounting can be further simplified and adjusted for inflation.

These changes should improve the competitive position of new ventures relative to established firms. The report of the Small Business Administration comments that "inventory costs [to new businesses] are even more important than depreciation deductions and are [their] principal investment activity . . . inventory accounting simplification primarily benefits small businesses."[35] The extent to which these simplifications will be enough to encourage entrepreneurs to change accounting methods will await further investigations when data become available. While improved, the LIFO rules are still sufficiently complex to be of limited usefulness to many new ventures.

Estate and Gift Tax Provisions

Despite the significant reductions in the impact of the estate and gift taxes that were enacted in 1976, testimony before Congress indicated that "the estate and gift taxes could result in the imposition of larger estate and gift taxes on estates containing highly successful, closely held, and family businesses than their owners could afford without disposing of the businesses."[36] Delegates to the White House Commission on Small Business listed as their fourth priority a revision of the estate taxes to ease the tax burden on family-owned businesses and to encourage the continuity of family ownership.[37]

Responding to this pressure in the 1981 act Congress increased unified credit for estate and gift taxes from $47,000 to $175,625, which in effect exempts all estate or gift transfers aggregating $600,000 or less. In addition, the maximum unified estate and gift tax rate was reduced from 70 percent to 50 percent to correspond with the reduction in the maximum personal income-tax rate of the same magnitude. This reduction is to be phased in over a four-year period. In addition, the law was changed to permit virtually unlimited transfers between spouses during their lifetimes and to surviving spouses at death.

It has been contended that prior to the provisions of 1976 and 1981, estate and gift tax provisions forced the sale of many family businesses, thus increasing industrial concentration. In addition, it was felt that many firms were forced to burden themselves either with insurance or high liquidity to meet potential estate taxes, to the point where these measures threatened their financial viability and capacity to raise funds in the marketplace. In viewing these changes, the Small Business Administration comments that they will "have a substantial beneficial impact on the small business and should be regarded as one of the key elements of the act from a small business standpoint."[38]

Despite the accolades given to these reforms of estate and gift taxation, questions remain. Critics will be quick to point out that such provisions encourage the concentration of wealth and make it less difficult to pass large estates on to others at death. A more telling criticism concerns the generality of these provisions. Favorable estate and gift tax treatment is afforded to all such transfers rather than being targeted toward entrepreneurial activity. From a political standpoint this may be the only acceptable alternative, but in terms of improving the tax environment for entrepreneurship these changes suffer from a lack of specificity.

Social Security Taxes

Late in the 1970s, it was recognized that the Social Security system was by any actuarial standard in effect bankrupt.[39] There was no way the system would be able to pay the planned and promised benefits to recipients and retirees of future years. Though there was a minor crisis in the years 1982 and 1983, the real crunch would have taken place in the year 2008. The changing age structure and retirement patterns of the U.S. population would mean 3.2 workers would be supporting every Social Security recipient during the first decade of the twenty-first century compared to 16.5 workers in 1950. In order to maintain the level of real benefits it would be necessary for Social Security taxes to rise to 25 percent of taxable payroll by the year 2010. Congress responded to this crisis in 1983 by passing legislation significantly raising Social Security taxes and realigning certain benefit provisions. But even these reforms will only meet two-thirds of the projected deficit.[40]

According to the report of the Small Business Task Force on Social Security issued early in 1983, these proposed increases in Social Security taxes would place a disproportionate burden upon the small, entrepreneurial firms in the nation's economy.[41] It was the feeling of the task force that these increases would both reduce small-business investment as well as the number of new jobs that would be created within new ventures. At the same time it was recognized by the task force that employees of small firms are less likely to have private pension plans where they work and would be more dependent upon Social Security as a source of retirement income. Small, entrepreneurial firms viewed themselves as being caught in a squeeze. The integrity of the Social Security system was viewed as essential for their employees yet the adverse economic results on investment and employment opportunities made it difficult for them to support legislation significantly raising payroll taxes.

The disproportionate burden of Social Security taxes on small firms results from three distinguishing structural characteristics. First, small-business firms employ almost 60 percent of the workers covered by the Social Security program. In addition there are 12 million sole proprietors paying self-employment Social Security taxes. For that reason, any increases in the Social Security tax bill will come principally from the small-business, entrepreneurial sector.

Second, small businesses also tend to pay lower wages than do large businesses. On the whole, small firms pay only 66 percent of what firms with more than fifty employees do. As a result, fewer small-firm employees have incomes high enough to exceed the $32,400 ceiling for Social Security payroll taxes. This means the entrepreneurial sector of the economy pays more Social Security taxes per dollar of wages than do larger firms.

An even more important third structural characteristic is the inability of small firms to shift taxes forward. Taxes may shift forward to the consumer in the form of higher prices or backward to workers in the form of lower wages, reduced hours of work, or smaller wage increases. The market structure faced by most new ventures reduces their opportunity to shift taxes. Most new ventures face strong competition or are struggling to open a new market. In either case forward shifting of payroll taxes is unlikely. It has been estimated that one-third of the payroll tax is shifted backward to labor.[42] Since smaller firms pay lower wages while competing with larger firms for workers, the possibility of backward shifting is viewed by the task force as being significantly less for firms during their startup phase.

The task force also contends that because of the labor-intensive nature of most new ventures, payroll taxes present a disproportionate burden for them. Small firms employ more labor for every dollar of receipts. As a consequence, the burden of the payroll tax as a percentage of total sales is much higher than in more established, larger firms. Smaller firms have payroll costs equal to 14.4 percent of total sales while larger firms experience only a 12.3 percent payroll tax cost when compared to sales. The conclusion reached by the task force is that

> Any increase in payroll tax rates would have a more severe impact on the cost and profits of small firms as compared to large firms. These added costs of small businesses could serve as a disincentive to hire new employees. When an employer has to decide whether to create new jobs, high taxes would likely tip the balance for the decision not to do so.[43]

Conclusions and Evaluation

During the late 1970s the Small Business Administration proposed certain standards for tax reforms to assist new ventures.[44] The following standards were suggested.

Tax Reform Standards

The Retention of Capital. The tax system was criticized for discriminating against new ventures by preventing the retention of adequate capital for current operating needs and for expansion. Noting that small firms lacked the ready access to long-term sources of capital that larger firms did, they suggested certain revisions to achieve this objective.

Recent tax legislation has improved the potential of capital retention by entrepreneurs. The diminuation of both individual and corporate tax rates will improve the cash flow of firms, but the increase in payroll taxes and excises will have an offsetting effect that may leave entrepreneurs in no better position than they were at the time of the SBA report.

The centerpiece of recent tax reform, the accelerated cost recovery system (ACRS), which permits faster write-off of investment in new plant and equipment, will be of some benefit to small or new ventures. The principal beneficiaries of these alterations will be in larger, more capital-intensive firms. The disparity in tax treatment between new and struggling firms and established profitable businesses has not been diminished by the accelerated cost recovery system. Tax credit for research and development expenditures will again have some benefit for some new ventures, but its application only to additional R&D spending will be of little use to new firms or those firms who maintain a constant but high level of investment in R&D. Both of these involve tax credits that can only improve the cash flow of a firm if it is generating taxable profits.

Incentives for Long-Term Capital Formation. Evidence was presented in the SBA report indicating that the current tax system does not provide incentives to attract adequate private investment into the entrepreneurial segment of the economy. Recent tax changes have addressed this problem. More favorable treatment of capital gains is viewed as the principal incentive. Though there are more efficient ways, such as the rollover of capital gains as opposed to the current policy of reducing effective tax rates, the entrepreneurial tax environment has been improved through recent legislation. The 1981 act (ERTA) contained many provisions designed to increase the level of personal savings. These were passed with the expectation of an increased pool of funds that would be available to investors including entrepreneurs. Preliminary studies done by the U.S. Treasury reveal these expectations to be half right.[45] The supply of savings has increased dramatically but most of this new saving has eluded entrepreneurs. For example, Individual Retirement Accounts (IRAs) and Keogh plans have garnered over $89 billion. Virtually all of these funds have gone to traditional sources such as banks, thrift institutions, and life insurance companies, which are not likely to be suppliers of risk capital.

Complexity of the Tax System. The complexity of the federal tax system, both personal and corporate, was viewed as discriminating against new ventures. Entrepreneurs often did not have the expertise or the resources to obtain the expertise necessary to comply with the bewildering labyrinth of federal income and payroll taxes, to say nothing of the compounding of the problem by state and local levies. Two significant improvements have been made in this area. The simplification of the LIFO accounting rules will make this tool more widely available to small businesses and should reduce their susceptibility to inflationary increases in their profits and taxes. The revised Subchapter S rules not only reduce the complexity of the system, but also should be a vehicle to attract additional investors to new firms during their startup phases.

Maintenance of Business Independence. At the time the SBA report was written it was felt that the current tax structure discouraged small-business independence by forcing the sale of small enterprises to pay for estate and transfer taxes. The tax advantages for merging small firms have been reduced, but with the repeal of safe harbor leasing the only method that a new venture may have to make use of its tax credits is to merge. In fact the unintended result of the ACRS and R&D tax credits may be to make new ventures more attractive candidates for mergers than before recent legislation was enacted. On the other hand, the liberalization of death taxation has reduced the likelihood of forced sale of closely held family businesses to pay for death duties.

From the previous analysis it is possible to conclude that recent tax legislation has improved the tax environment for entrepreneurship only slightly. Small businesses are still at a tax disadvantage compared with existing large businesses, in their ability to both raise and retain the capital needed for startup and expansion. The tax system does not provide the positive incentives entrepreneurs need. What follows is an agenda for further improvements in the entrepreneurial tax climate.

Improvements to the Entrepreneurial Tax Climate

Rollover of Capital Gains. Allowing investors to roll over capital gains made from investments in new business ventures if reinvested in additional business startups would have a major impact in both increasing the amount of funds and retaining funds invested in new businesses.[46]

Transfer of Unused Tax Credits. Currently, large corporations experience a decided competitive advantage compared with new businesses because of their ability to more effectively use tax credits and loss write-offs. Tax credits and losses incurred in unprofitable divisions can be used by larger corporations to offset profits and reduce taxes earned elsewhere within the corporate structure. Small businesses do not have this flexibility.[47] This discrepancy could be compensated for by allowing investors in new ventures to transfer unused tax credits from investments in one new venture to profits earned from investments in other enterprises. Small firms also could be allowed to establish loss reserves that would increase the amount of retained earnings and reduce their tax liabilities.

Small Business Participating Debentures (SBPD). One of the more intriguing suggestions resulting from the White House Commission on Small Business was to create Small Business Participating Debentures (SBPD).[48] These would combine characteristics of debt with equity to open the capital markets to new ventures. The SBPDs would be essentially debt instruments, but the interest payments would be related to the company's profits. During the early years the interest rates would be low, but would increase as the company's profitability rose. The interest paid by the firm issuing the SBPD would be deductible, but investors would treat the payments as capital gains rather than ordinary income and would be taxed accordingly. The firm would achieve a tax advantage in that payments would be tax deductible interest rather than taxable profits paid out as dividends. Investors would receive a bonus in terms of favorable capital-gains treatment and the ability to get their money back without having to find a buyer for their stock. There appears to be considerable enthusiasm for this alternative in Congress, but no action has yet been taken.[49]

As a whole, these three suggestions would target tax relief to new ventures that are creating new jobs and spurring innovation. They would redress the imbalance that now exists between new and established business and increase the capacity of new ventures to compete in capital markets. These are the necessary next steps in an improved tax environment for entrepreneurship.

Notes

1. Bruce W. Kimsey, *Reaganomics* (St. Paul: West Publishing Co., 1983), pp. 13–29.

2. Office of the President, "The Economic Plan," (Washington, D.C.: February 18, 1981).

3. U.S., Small Business Administration, *The State of Small Business: A Report to the President, 1983,* (Washington, D.C.: Government Printing Office, 1983), p. 339.

4. Charles R. Holton and James W. Robertson, *Corporate Tax Policy and Economic Growth: An Analysis of the 1981 and 1982 Tax Acts* (Washington, D.C.: Urban Institute, 1982).

5. Steven A. Mayer, "Tax Cuts: Reality or Illusion?" *Business Review,* Federal Reserve Bank of Philadelphia, July 1983, pp. 3–9.

6. Ibid., p. 3.

7. Quoted in Kevin Farrell, "Entrepreneurial Economics," *Venture* (January 1983), p. 34.

8. Hans Stoll and James Walter, *Tax Incentives for Small Business* (Chicago: Heller Small Business Institute, 1980).

9. White House Commission on Small Business, *America's Small Business Economy: Agenda for Action* (Washington, D.C.: Government Printing Office, 1980), p. 27.

10. U.S., Small Business Administration, *The State of Small Business: A Report to the President, 1982*, (Washington, D.C.: Government Printing Office, 1982), p. 315.

11. Stoll and Walter, *Tax Incentives,* p. 45.

12. White House Commission on Small Business, *America's Small Business Economy*, p. 28

13. William B. Pollard, "Subchapter S Election: Attractive Taxation Alternative," *The Collegiate Forum* (Spring 1983), p. 14.

14. Robert W. Merry, "Why Subchapter S is More Alluring Than Ever," *Inc.* (January 1983), p. 94.

15. Richard A. Musgrave and Peggy B. Musgrave, *Public Finance in Theory and Practice* (New York: McGraw-Hill, 1976), pp. 244–248.

16. James W. Wetzler, "Recent Developments in U.S. Capital Gains Taxation," in Michael J. McIntyre, et al., *Readings in Federal Taxation,* second ed. (Mineola, New York: Foundation Press, 1973), pp. 421–427.

17. Martin Feldstein and Joel Slemrod, "Inflation and the Excell Taxation of Capital Gains on Corporate Stock." *National Tax Journal* (June 1978), pp. 107–18.

18. Quoted in Farrell, "Entrepreneurial Economics," p. 34.

19. Roger E. Brinner, "Inflation and the Definition of Taxable Personal Income," in Henry J. Aaron, ed., *Inflation and the Income Tax* (Washington, D.C.: Brookings Institution, 1976), pp. 121–41.

20. Small Business Administration, *The State of Small Business, 1982,* p. 306.

21. White House Commission on Small Business, *America's Small Business Economy,* p. 28.

22. Small Business Administration, *The State of Small Business, 1982* p. 310.

23. Ibid., p. 311.

24. Ibid., p. 311.

25. U.S. Congress, Joint Committee on Taxation, *General Explanation of the Economic Recovery Tax Act of 1981,* 97th Congress, December 29, 1981, p. 75.

26. Small Business Administration, *The State of Small Business, 1982,* p. 313.

27. Ibid., p. 314.

28. David E. Franasiak, *The New Tax Law: What's in For You and Your Business* (Washington, D.C.: U.S. Chamber of Commerce, 1981).

29. U.S. Congress, House Committee on Oversight, *Safe Harbor Leasing Provisions of Economic Recovery Act of 1981,* 97th Congress 1st Session, 1981, p. 84.

30. Ibid., p. 54.

31. U.S. Congress, Joint Committee on Taxation, *An Analysis of Safe Harbor Leasing,* 97th Congress, 2nd Session, 1982, p. 26.

32. Stanford L. Jacobs, "Leasing Breaks Limited for Small Firms," *Wall Street Journal,* February 8, 1981, p. 20; John R. Eswyler, "New Tax Rules on Leasing for GE Unit," *Wall Street Journal,* October 16, 1981, p. 29.

33. Martin Feldstein, "Inflation Tax Rules and Investment: Some Econometric Evidence," Working Paper No. 577, National Bureau of Economic Research, 1981.

34. *General Explanation of the Economic Recovery Tax Act 1981,* p. 149.

35. Small Business Administration, *The State of Small Business ,1982,* pp. 316–17.

36. *General Explanation of the Economic Recovery Tax Act of 1981,* p. 229.

37. White House Commission on Small Business, *America's Small Business Economy*, p. 64.

38. Small Business Administration, *The State of Small Business, 1982,* p. 21.

39. U.S., Office of Management and the Budget, "Social Security and Supplemental Security Income: Basic Program Charts," Washington, D.C., April 1981.

40. Robert W. Merry, "Major Overhaul of Social Security is Voted By Ways and Means Panel," *Wall Street Journal,* March 3, 1983, p. 2.

41. U.S., Small Business Administration, "Social Security: A Tax on Labor," Report of the Small Business Task Force on Social Security, Washington, D.C., January 1983.

42. Daniel Hammermesh, "New Estimates of the Incidence of the Payroll Tax," *Southern Economic Journal* (April 1979).

43. Small Business Administration, "Social Security: A Tax on Labor," p. 16.

44. U.S., Small Business Administration, Office of Advocacy, "The Impact of Taxation on Small Business, A Proposal for Reform," Part III of *The Study of Small Business* (Washington, D.C.: Government Printing Office, 1977).

45. "IRA's a Hit—But Costly for Uncle Sam," *U.S. News and World Report,* August 29, 1983, p. 66.

46. Carl H. Vesper, *Entrepreneurship and National Policy* (Chicago: Heller Institute for Small Business, 1983).

47. Stoll and Walter, *Tax Incentives for Small Business,* pp. 43–44.

48. White House Commission on Small Business, *America's Small Business Economy*, p. 28.

49. Kevin Farrell, "Entrepreneurial Economics," p. 35.

6 Regulation and the Entrepreneurial Environment

Kenneth W. Chilton

The decade of the 1970s might well be called the decade of environmentalism. Concern for our nation's future ecological balance reached a peak in the early part of that decade, spawning a flurry of legislative activity to protect the environment from the so-called ravages of industry. In the process, however, government regulation began to threaten the health of the United States's small-business sector—significantly degrading the entrepreneurial environment.

Of course, regulation during the past decade extended far beyond environmental concerns. Worker safety and health, consumer safety, equal employment opportunities, and a host of other social concerns brought a regulatory response from all levels of government, but most dramatically from the federal government. The side effects of this regulatory overdose on innovation, productivity, and employment were, for all intents and purposes, ignored in the frenzy to prescribe legislative solutions for those perceived social ills. The fact that the American entrepreneur survived during this period bears witness to the truth of Will Rogers's remark that "We are a nation that runs in spite of, and not on account of our government."

Fortunately, the future public-policy environment looks a good deal brighter for small business. Due in no small measure to the increased efforts of small firms and their trade-association representatives to communicate their message, federal decision makers have become aware of the economic (and political) significance of small business. The cause of the entrepreneur has gained such political momentum that David Gumpert, associate editor of the *Harvard Business Review,* recently observed, "the government is currently giving small business the kind of attention, if not money, once reserved for eradicating poverty and exploring outer space."[1]

All of this new-found concern for small business suggests an important question: What should entrepreneurs expect from their government? Rather than merely reacting to what government is doing *to* them, business executives need to formulate a philosophy of what government should or should not do *for* them as well.

The first section of this chapter documents some of the ways in which regulation degraded the entrepreneurial environment during the 1970s. The second section describes some of the recent efforts to reform regulation and other areas of government/small-business interaction. The final section examines the direction that public policy should take in order to enhance entrepreneurship in the United States.

As the reader may have already observed, I have chosen to equate the two terms *small-business* and *entrepreneurship.* Certainly, one can argue for narrower or broader definitions. As Edwin Harwood concludes in his paper, "The Sociology of Entrepreneurship," an entrepreneur is one who "takes initiative, assumes considerable autonomy in the organization and management of the resources, shares in the asset risk, shares in an uncertain monetary profit, and innovates in more than a marginal way. . . ."[2] In my opinion, this description sufficiently describes a small-business person to warrant the free substitution of these designations.

Trampled in the Rush to Regulate

There are two compelling reasons to study the effects of 1970s regulation on small firms. First, a massive regulatory carryover into the 1980s will continue to affect the prospects for successful entrepreneurship in the current decade. Second, as George Santayana warned, "Those who do not remember the past are condemned to relive it."

As table 6-1 shows, the decade of the 1970s was the most interventionist ten-year period in our nation's history. One hundred thirty major, new legislative controls over business firms were passed in that decade. The New Deal decade of the 1930s, known as a regulatory era, enacted in comparison only forty-two major statutes. The regulatory phenomenon grew so rapidly and became such a pervasive influence that decisions made by agency officials in Washington often became more important to the profitability of a firm than its own internal decisions.

Table 6–1
A Decade-by-Decade Comparison of Major Regulatory Legislation

Decade	Number of Major Regulatory Statutes
Pre-1900	10
1900–1909	6
1910–1919	18
1920–1929	15
1930–1939	42
1940–1949	17
1950–1959	26
1960–1969	53
1970–1979	132

Source: Center for the Study of American Business, Washington University, unpublished data.

Government-Induced Economies of Scale

Far from being immune to the rapid expansion of federal controls, small firms in the 1970s often experienced disproportionately adverse effects from the expanded powers of government. Major capital expenditures required to meet environmental and workplace safety standards had serious consequences for the small manufacturing firm, resulting in higher unit costs than those experienced by larger firms. In the terminology of the economist, these programs produced artificial or government-induced *economies of scale.*

One of the best-documented cases of this type of adverse impact is furnished by firms in the foundry industry. Seventy-five percent of the nation's 4,200 foundries employ fewer than fifty persons. In the period 1968 to 1975 there were 350 verified foundry closings. A survey of these firms revealed that more than 34 percent of the respondents (158 firms) cited Environmental Protection Agency (EPA) regulations as being partly or totally to blame for their closures.[3]

Similarly, in 1979 the Center for the Study of American Business surveyed active small concerns (fewer than five hundred employees) in the forging industry and the chemical-specialty industry. The results of that survey also indicated that environmental and workplace safety rules constituted major burdens and were creating new economies of scale in these industries. Nearly 70 percent of the small chemical-specialty firms indicated that EPA requirements presented the most severe regulatory burdens, and 27 percent of this group believed EPA regulation could cause them to close or change ownership.[4] Of the forging firms responding to the survey, 60 percent ranked the Occupational Safety and Health Administration (OSHA) as the regulatory agency presenting the most difficulty, with 25 percent of this group indicating that OSHA regulation could cause their firms to close or change ownership.[5]

Likewise, a study done by Charles River Associates in 1977 for the Lead Industries Association indicated that OSHA air/lead regulations proposed at that time could force the closing of about 113 single-plant battery firms. The entire battery industry totals only 143 firms.[6] Clearly, the large capital expenditures were more burdensome to small firms in these industries than to their large-firm competitors.

Regulatory Impacts on Labor Costs

Small firms are not only more sensitive to large capital expenditures, but they are also more sensitive to changes in labor costs. Many Department of Labor regulations had an important and, most often, adverse effect on labor-intensive small companies.

To many small firms in the 1970s, OSHA became a four-letter word. They felt harassed and overinspected by this agency. Bureau of Labor Statistics (BLS) figures indicate that small business may indeed have been overinspected. Even as late as 1979, 30 percent of OSHA inspections were in firms with ten or fewer employees (representing only 17 percent of the work force) and nearly 50 percent were of firms with less than twenty-five workers (accounting for 30 percent of all workers).[7] The combination of nitpicking rules—when is a hole a hole and a ladder a ladder and how high should fire extinguishers be hung—and nitpicking (often capricious) fines did not engender respect for the agency or its mission.

In addition, because of the greater use of unskilled and young workers, small enterprises have been and continue to be more adversely affected by increases in the minimum wage. Over 20 percent of the nation's small businesses hire full-time teenage help, and more than a third employ part-time teenage help (not including summer employees).[8] Thus, the costs to small firms rise significantly when the minimum wage is increased, as it was frequently in the 1970s.

A variety of labor restrictions also antagonize entrepreneurs whose businesses are labor-intensive. Small construction firms feel shut out from many federal projects because of the so-called prevailing-wage rates required by the Davis-Bacon Act. For many local construction companies, Davis-Bacon wage rates are far above normal labor rates, thus making these government contracts unattractive to them. Restaurant owners can be harassed by the Labor Department inspectors enforcing Fair Labor Standards. In addition, teenage employment restrictions are in many instances illogical and unnecessary, for instance, prohibiting teenagers from being sales clerks in shoe repair shops and from working in coin-operated laundries.[9]

Paperwork

James Madison expressed the entrepreneur's source of frustration with excessive rules for recordkeeping when he wrote in the *Federalist* No. 62 nearly two hundred years ago,

> It will be of little avail to the people that the laws are made by men of their own choice, if the laws be so voluminous that they cannot be read, or so incoherent that they cannot be understood; if they be repealed or revised before they are promulgated, or undergo such incessant changes that no man who knows what the law is today can guess what it will be tomorrow.

The small firm, unlike its large-firm counterpart, does not have a professional staff that can respond to heavy paperwork and reporting requirements. Often the owner/entrepreneur is the only individual with sufficient knowledge to comply with an agency's requirements for information. According to a 1979 Small Business Administration survey, the average small business spent about $1,270 (1979 dollars) to comply with federal, state, and local government reporting requirements—a total annual cost of $12.7 billion.[10] Reporting costs, like the other more severe burdens of federal regulation, are not proportional to the size of the firm.

Access to Capital

Access to capital is a perpetual problem for the entrepreneur. Small firms are much more dependent on short-term debt than are large firms. Thus, they are not only sensitive to the government regulations that affect their need for increased debt but also are quite sensitive to the price charged for short-term debt.

SBA Loan Programs. In most instances where the federal government has taken action to address the financing problems of smaller firms, such as Small Business Administration (SBA) aid programs, the results have been negligible, if not negative. James W. Singer, a business writer, sums up his view of the Small Business Administration loan programs. "Even within the small business community, the direct loan program has not been very popular. It has created expectations that cannot possibly be realized with limited funds and has aroused bitter feelings."[11]

One of those unrealizable expectations appears to be the SBA's expectation that these loans will be repaid. In September 1981, the *St. Louis Globe-Democrat* reviewed more than fourteen thousand small-business loans. Their findings sent shock waves through the agency and through Congress. More than 40 percent of direct loans end in defaults, and only 18 cents of each dollar loaned is collected on these defaults. More than $571 million was lost in the program from 1970 to 1978. The report estimated that program losses from 1970 to 1980 could reach $900 million if 1979 and 1980 default rates are consistent with those of previous years.[12]

The direct loan program is small potatoes however, compared with the guaranteed loan program. For example, in 1981 the SBA made 5,437 direct loans totaling $333 million while guaranteeing 23,213 loans totaling more than three *billion* dollars.[13] One would hope that the guaranteed loan experience will be better than the direct loan experience. Unfortunately, the SBA guarantee of 90 percent of the loan encourages risk taking by lending institutions that will surely result in loss rates on these loans far greater than on normal commercial loans. The sad truth is that the SBA has no idea of the eventual loss rate in this program and no established means to evaluate its effectiveness.

Equity Capital. Access to equity capital is important primarily as a source of funds for expansion. Though most small firms begin with capital from relatives, associates, and the local bank, there comes a time in the innovation process when the entrepreneur needs to share the risk taking with a larger pool of investors in order to continue to grow.

From a macroeconomic view, the biggest factor influencing such investment is, of course, the tax code. Though some may consider the tax laws to be a form of regulation—and I do not quarrel with that view—I have chosen not to do so here. There are important regulatory considerations, however, that do directly affect equity and venture-capital markets for small business that we should consider: Securities and Exchange Commission regulations, the Employee Retirement Income Security Act, and SBA investment programs.

The Effects of SEC Regulation. The Securities and Exchange Commission (SEC) was once considered to be quite insensitive to small- business problems. A 1977 *Report of the SBA Task Force on Venture and Equity Capital for Small Business* placed partial blame on several SEC rules for the poor state of venture and equity markets for small firms. The limitation of $500,000 on Regulation A offerings was cited as unrealistic because of the difficulty in underwriting such a small issue. The report also stated, "The limitations that the SEC has developed on the secondary sale of securities are probably more damaging to small business financing in the public securities markets than the high cost of registration . . ."[14] One of the most fascinating developments in the regulatory environment facing small business is the turnaround in policies at the SEC—a subject that I shall return to.

This is not to imply, however, that SEC regulations no longer have disproportionate impacts on entrepreneurs. Recently, scholars in the field of finance have been pointing out that accounting rules put forward by the Financial Accounting Standards Board (FASB) and adopted by the SEC have a differential impact on small firms. One study found that the 1975 ruling banning the capitalization of research and development expenditures and requiring them to be reported as current expenses mainly affected small companies, bringing about a reduction in their R&D expenditures.[15]

Similarly, financial-reporting costs are often disproportionate with respect to firm size. For example, the costs per sales dollar for filing 10K forms for a firm with less than $100 million in assets are nearly 60 times the cost to a firm with over $1 billion in assets.[16] Likewise, the 1970 SEC requirement for segmental sales and profit disclosures was relatively more costly for small concerns. One study of this issue concluded with a recommendation for exempting small firms from such disclosures. The authors conclude that "economic considerations suggest that the optimum level of voluntary financial disclosures for small firms is lower than it is for large firms. Thus, imposing the same level of disclosure requirements on all firms does, indeed, impose relatively greater costs on small firms . . ."[17]

The Employee Retirement Income Security Act (ERISA). The availability of venture capital for small firms was also adversely affected by the 1974 Employee Retirement Income Security Act (ERISA). Pension-fund managers were extremely reluctant to invest in small firms because of the so-called prudent-man rule and its severe penalties for imprudence. Fund managers, therefore, concentrated on the seasoned issues of established larger companies. In 1979, the Labor Department issued a guideline suggesting that "pension-fund managers could invest in a certain number of new ventures and still live up to their fiduciary responsibilities."[18]

Small Business Investment Companies. In addition to the Small Business Administration loan programs mentioned previously, this agency also strives "to improve the national economy through programs that stimulate the flow (where inadequate) of private equity capital . . . to small business concerns" through the authority conferred by the Small Business Investment Act.[19] As a result of this act, the SBA has established a program to make venture capital available through Small Business Investment Companies (SBICs).

SBICs are private companies approved by the SBA to receive government loans (at rates that are slightly above treasury bill rates) to leverage funds supplied by private investors to venture-capital pools. Once an SBIC has a half-million dollars in private capital, it can borrow up to four times that amount from the SBA. In 1981, $700 million in private capitalization and $800 million in government funds were committed to some 350 SBICs. While this $1.5 billion is 30 percent of the total capital ($5.0 billion) committed to the venture-capital industry in 1981, it is a small fraction (approximately 1 percent) of the total funds raised in the private business sector.[20]

The SBICs have not been without their problems, however. Of all the SBICs ever licensed, 23 percent have ended in liquidations because of difficulties ranging from theft and bankruptcy to regulatory violations. Total losses in the program from 1958 to June 1982 are not expected to exceed $80 million.

One investment company that recently succumbed, Commerce Capital Corporation—the sixth largest SBIC at the time—invested in a gold mine in El Salvador and a Turkish-bath chain. At one point its owners forced Capital Commerce's affiliates to purchase obsolete computer equipment for $466,500 that was sold by the trustee of the bankrupt firm for $900. Most tragic of all is the fact that the SBA could not bring federal charges against Capital's owners because the SBA knew what was going on and did not act to stop it.[21]

Regulatory Effects on Innovation Entry
and Product Viability

Barriers to Entry. Interstate Commerce Commission (ICC) regulation of the trucking industry is the most obvious case of federally erected barriers to small-firm entry into an industry. Prior to the recent deregulatory emphasis at the ICC, in case after case the commission denied even temporary authority to new companies, although existing, authorized truckers were unable or unwilling to meet the needs of shippers. State and local regulations likewise restrict entry into a host of service-oriented businesses from taxi companies to barber shops to optometrists to massage parlors.

One of the most ludicrous examples of ICC intervention in transportation came about when a midwestern trucking firm applied for permission to transport yak fat from Omaha to Chicago for 45 cents per hundred pounds. In this case, the railroads protested to the commission, citing the new rates as predatory. The ICC suspended rates on yak fat and formed committees to study the matter before they discovered that yak fat had never been produced or even sold in the United States.[22]

Product Viability In some instances, regulatory whims have virtually destroyed the market for viable products offered by small firms. For example, the first product regulation issued by the Consumer Product Safety Commission (CPSC) set standards for swimming-pool slides. As a result of this ruling the number of pool-slide manufacturers went from seven to one. That single manufacturer is the same party which petitioned the CPSC to adopt the rule in the first place. It was also the only manufacturer whose production molds conformed to the design features required by the CPSC requirements.[23]

The wide variety of regulation takes its toll on small firms in many ways. For one manufacturer of a reversible child-resistant cap for medicine vials, CPSC packaging regulations first created and then virtually destroyed the market for its product. Housing and Urban Development rules designed to promote energy efficiency preclude the use of adobe in the Southwest and threaten the use of concrete-block construction in the Midwest. The long list of governmental interference with the viabilty of small-firm products receives little attention because each individual interference affects only a small segment of the business system.

Effects on Innovation. Small business has been a major contributor of innovations in this country. For instance, an Office of Management and Budget (OMB) study found that for the period 1953 to 1973, firms with less than 1,000 workers accounted for half of all major U.S. innovations, and produced four times as many innovations per employee in research and development as did larger firms.[24] Furthermore, the National Science Foundation found that small firms produced twenty-four times the number of major innovations per R&D dollar than large firms (those with more than ten thousand workers) and four times that of medium-sized firms.[25]

In spite of this apparent historical advantage in R&D efficiency, the role of small firms in innovation is dwindling. According to the American Association for the Advancement of Science, a breakdown of the data for the 1953–1973 period examined in the OMB study reveals that firms with fewer than one thousand employees did indeed produce the greatest number of major innovations from 1953 to 1967. But the greatest number of major innovations produced from 1968 to 1973 were products of firms with more than ten thousand employees. To be sure, many factors are at work here, including economic conditions, changing economies of scale, international competition, and union wage rates. But the inhospitable public-policy environment faced by small firms in the late 1960s and early 1970s should not be overlooked as a major contributor to the declining role of small business in innovation.

Each new regulation from each agency seems to pose a special problem for entrepreneurial innovation somewhere in the economy; for example, the proposed regulations on radiology equipment promulgated by an office within the Food and Drug Administration (FDA) known as the Bureau of Medical Devices and Diagnostic Products. Dr. William Tuddenham has described the likely impact of these regulations as follows. "These controls effectively impede the development of experimental devices and equipment, even of a trivial sort, and by virtue of the 'Regulations Establishing Good Manufacturing Practices' they essentially 'freeze out' the small manufacturer of specialty products."[26]

Nor are the regulatory roadblocks always known by the innovator. For example, the creative geniuses at Apple Computer came close to tripping over the following stumbling block prior to the introduction of the Apple computer. Neither Stephen Wozniak, the mathematical and engineering genius, or Steven Jobs, the marketing wizard, at Apple were aware that their early prototype was illegal because it violated the radiation standards established by the Federal Communication Commission (FCC) for a Class I television device. Fortunately for Apple, they consulted with an electrical engineer at a major firm before advancing too far with the new product. Thus, the company that is considered one of the biggest success stories in the home computer field, were it not for a stroke of good fortune, might have been derailed by regulations its founders were not even cognizant of.[27]

The fact that these examples are not isolated cases is borne out by a comprehensive National Science Foundation survey conducted in 1981 of more than twelve hundred small high-technology firms. Nearly two-thirds of the surveyed firms listed nonprocurement regulations as a major concern.

The most affected industry appears to be the chemical manufacturers, with 84 percent of them citing regulations as a major problem.[28] These findings seem to confirm the results of the Center for the Study of American Business survey of chemical-specialty firms summarized earlier.

Conclusion

The motivation behind the rush to regulate in the 1970s was laudable. No one can argue with the goals of a cleaner environment, safer workplaces, fewer product hazards, or expanded opportunities for minority employment. But far too many of the regulatory thrusts of that decade failed to adequately consider the costs and harmful side effects of these efforts to cure social ills. Small business became, in short, an unintentional victim of a regulatory overdose.

The Changing Policy Environment

Fortunately, U.S. public policy has begun to turn in favor of entrepreneurs as the decade of the 1980s begins to unfold. For example, in order to accommodate the increased interest in small business in the Senate, the Senate Select Commission on Small Business was expanded in 1979 from nine members to seventeen. Furthermore, the White House Conference on Small Business, held in January 1980, constituted at least a symbolic turning point in public policy toward small business.

Much of the rediscovery of the virtues of entrepreneurship has come about as the result of publicizing the economic contribution made by small business. Trade associations and the SBA continued to disseminate the figures on the contribution of small business to the gross national product, employment, and total number of firms during the 1970s. But it was the emphasis on small business as an important source of economic growth that made it most attractive.[29]

The entrepreneur has historically made a major contribution to innovation in the United States—or, as Joseph Schumpeter put it, to the process of "creative destruction . . . that sets and keeps the capitalist engine in motion."[30] Furthermore, a 1979 report by David L. Birch of MIT indicated that small businesses are the primary source of new jobs. Birch reported that establishments with less than twenty-one employees created 66 percent of all net new jobs (new employment less jobs lost) in the private sector between 1969 and 1976. Firms with fewer than five hundred employees accounted for 87 percent of all net new jobs during this period. According to Dr. Birch, "it appears that it is the smaller corporations, despite their high failure rates, that are aggressively seeking out most new opportunities."[31] No public official faced with declining productivity and rising unemployment could ignore the policy implications of these data. A more recent report covering the period 1978–1980 by Catherine Armington and Marjorie Odle, senior research analysts at the Brookings Institution, indicates that Dr. Birch's figures may have been somewhat misleading. Armington and Odle point out that many major firms have multiple locations or establishments that would be counted as small businesses by Dr. Birch. However, when a small business is defined as a firm with fewer than one hundred employees, then small businesses employ 33 percent of the labor force and generate just 37 percent of the net new jobs.[32] Armington and Odle indicate that small firms are a stablizing force in declining regions, increasing employment when large firms decline. This new information has yet to gain widespread attention. Its effect may be to place policy emphasis on small firms in these declining situations, in the form of enterprise zones and job tax-credits for small firms in inner cities or rural pockets of poverty.

Regulatory Reform and the Entrepreneurial Environment

Though many inequities remain, there has been improvement in a number of key regulatory areas. Some of this improvement is the result of reform legislation recently passed—the Regulatory Flexibility Act, the Equal Access to Justice Act, and the Paperwork Reduction Act, in particular. In other instances, regulatory burdens on small businesses have been lightened by individual agency actions. Some benefits have also come about with the Reagan administration's emphasis on regulatory relief.

The extent of these improvements is not really ascertainable, since there is no good baseline measurement of the original burden to small business nor of the current level of burden. One qualitative measure of the regulatory burden, at least as it relates to other business worries, is available from a series of surveys conducted by the National Federation of Independent Business. Table 6–2 shows how government regulation and red tape have been ranked in the list of small-business worries from 1974 to 1983. This table also shows the percentage of small firms that listed regulation as the single most important small-business problem.

As the figures in table 6–2 indicate, the dissatisfaction with government controls reached a peak in 1976: it was the third most important problem overall and the single most important problem to 14 percent of those surveyed. This is only a rough indicator, however, since deep concern for other issues such as inflation or interest rates means that fewer votes can be cast for regulation as the single most important problem.

Table 6–2
NFIB Survey of the Importance of Government Regulation and Red Tape as a Small-Business Issue, 1974–1983

Year	Survey Ranking	Percentage of Firms Indicating Regulation Single Most Important Small Business Problem
1974	5	8
1975	3	12
1976	3	14
1977	3	12
1978	3	10
1979	3	9
1980	4	8
1981	5	5
1982	6	4
1983	5	8

Source: National Federation of Independent Business *Quarterly Economic Report for Small Business* (July reports) (San Mateo, Calif.).

Legislative Changes

Reg-Flex. One important regulatory reform passed by Congress was the Regulatory Flexibility Act of 1980. Reg-Flex, as the act is called, requires that federal agencies tailor regulatory requirements to the size of the firm where possible. Agencies are now required to analyze and publish reports on the economic impact of new regulations on small firms and possible alternatives to existing regulations. A mechanism to review all existing rules within ten years was included in the law.

The rationale for Reg-Flex was succinctly put by John Kenneth Galbraith.

All regulatory policy should have categories. And, without retreat on regulatory objectives, there should always be consideration of cost and reporting requirements for the small firm. By treating large and small alike, one treats them very differently.[33]

One of the interesting arguments favoring regulatory flexibility is the realization that too-onerous regulation is self-defeating. An option always available to overregulated parties is noncompliance. Just as confiscatory taxing invites underground economic activity, so too overly complex and costly regulation causes otherwise law-abiding citizens to ignore government rules.[34] In most instances, it is not only more equitable to reduce the regulatory burden on small firms, it is also more cost-effective, since greater compliance produces more benefits with less policing costs.

Not all agencies are subject to Reg-Flex: the Internal Revenue Service and the Department of Defense claim not to be. The watchdog for compliance,

SBA Chief Counsel for Advocacy Frank Swain, recently gave low marks to the Food and Drug Administration and improving ratings to the Department of Interior and the Federal Communications Commission. His best grades were reserved for the departments of Labor and Transportation, the Federal Trade Commission, and the Securities and Exchange Commission (SEC). In particular, Swain praised the SEC for its "major efforts in regulatory reform on behalf of the small business community."[35] Though Reg-Flex is no panacea, it is an important improvement over the situation that existed in the 1970s, when regulatory mandates ran roughshod over all other economic considerations in rule-making deliberations.

Equal Access to Justice. The Equal Access to Justice Act, passed in 1980, seeks to help balance the mismatch in court battles between big government and small business. Small firms (having less than $5 million net worth and less than five hundred employees) may now recover costs incurred in specific types of legal actions involving the federal government. The act has five key provisions.

1. It does not matter whether the taxpayer or the government initiates the case.
2. It is not necesary to prove that the agency acted in bad faith.
3. The burden of proof is on the agency to show that its actions were substantially justified.
4. An award can be made whether or not the small firm prevailed on all issues.
5. There is no upper limit on awards (the top hourly rate for lawyer fees is currently $75, however).[36]

The Equal Access to Justice Act did not take affect until October 1981, so there is little experience with it thus far. In the first six months, the only party actually paid as a result of the act was the Florida Farm Workers Council, which received $13,000 from the Department of Labor. Many winners that should be eligible for compensation have had their awards delayed because of interagency disputes over where the money should come from and appeals of their cases to higher courts.[37] Of course, these cases cover many areas other than regulatory disputes, but the Equal Access Act does provide the small firm with more incentive to battle regulatory inequities.

Other Legislative Changes Benefiting Entrepreneurs. Several other acts passed in 1980 also give special consideration to small business. First, the Paperwork Reduction Act is aimed at reducing the costs of paperwork imposed by regulation by setting the goal of a 15-percent reduction in paperwork in the 1982 fiscal year and a 10-percent reduction in 1983. In addition, the act attempts to standardize methods of federal information collection, retrieval, and sharing. Any reduction in federal-government paperwork is good news for small business, since filling out government forms most often falls on the shoulders of the busy entrepreneur. Second, the new Patent Law Amendments Act has a provision whereby nonprofit organizations and small firms can retain both the ownership and claims to inventions developed with federal aid.

There is also some faint hope that the ninety-seventh Congress may pass a comprehensive regulatory reform measure along the lines of Senate bill 1080. The most important feature of this bill, in my opinion, would be its requirement for cost-effectiveness analysis and justification for whatever alternative is eventually adopted. The so-called Bumpers Amendment (proposed by Senator Dale Bumpers, D-Arkansas) would eliminate the presumption of validity for agency interpretations of regulatory law in court battles. The most controversial provision of S. 1080 is the legislative veto empowering Congress to overrule agency regulations that it considers not in keeping with original congressional intent. The Supreme Court has ruled the legislative veto unconstitutional on grounds that one branch of government may not unilaterally change a law. At any rate, the benefits of this comprehensive reform are likely to be drived more from its requirements for consideration of costs rather than from any high-visibility, legislative veto actions on Capitol Hill.

Executive Branch Initiatives

The Reagan administration set the tone for regulatory reform from its first day in office. First, the President appointed people to head key regulatory agencies who are very different from the typical public-interest-group graduates who were often tapped for these posts in the past. Second, President Reagan's executive order requiring all executive-branch agencies to submit cost-benefit or cost-effectiveness analyses for all major regulatory proposals to the Office of Management and Budget (OMB) is an important step in the right direction. To the extent that the agencies have cooperated with Executive Order 12291, much of the benefit of S. 1080 has already been realized.

Lastly, the regulatory task force headed by Vice President Bush is charged with the responsibility of recommending procedural and legislative changes to existing rules in order to accomplish the social objectives of regulation in a less onerous fashion than at present. The performance of this task force has been disappointing to date. In spite of the reported savings of $9 to 11 billion in one-time regulatory costs and $6 billion in annual expenditures in the first year and a half, the task force has done little to bring about lasting changes through proposals for legislative reform.

The overall regulatory pace has already slowed to a considerable extent in this decade. OMB reported that 5,648 regulations were published in 1981 compared with 7,192 in 1980—a reduction of more than 20 percent—and proposed rules dropped by one-third—3,317 in 1981 versus, 4,979 in 1980. The reduced pace, however, may be more attributable to factors other than Executive Order 12291. Only 3 percent of the 2,803 executive-branch rule proposals were rejected by the OMB watchdog group.[38]

Another factor that promises to affect the future pace of rule writing is budgetary cutbacks within the agencies. Real federal spending for regulatory programs is scheduled to decline by nearly a sixth during the period 1981 to 1983, but this does not necessarily mean that federal burdens placed on small firms will decrease a like amount. Regulatory relief for small business has, thus far, been very spotty. There has been some relief from unnecessary OSHA inspections and recordkeeping and also SEC reporting, but there are continuing (and in some cases increasing) burdens in the environmental realm.

OSHA and Other Labor Regulations

Small firms can expect less harassment and more help from the Occupational Safety and Health Administration due at least in part to reduced staffing at the agency. Personnel cuts from 3,000 in 1981 to 2,350 by 1983 coincide with plans to cut inspections by 11 percent over that time.[39] The decision to exempt firms with fewer than ten employees from safety inspections and to concentrate efforts on firms with poor safety records gives small firms about all of the regulatory relief that can be expected at this time.

Many proposals for new labor legislation could prove harmful to the health of small business, however. In order to crack down on so-called sweat shops, Representative George Miller (D-California) has proposed H.R. 6103. The problem with this bill is that it calls for a hefty civil fine ($10,000) whether an employer willfully or unintentionally is in noncompliance with the Fair Labor Standards Act. Since criminal sanctions already exist for willful recordkeeping violations, the new law would primarily affect those who unwittingly violate the labor laws.

Similarly, the bill proposed by Senator Alan K. Simpson to control illegal aliens, the Immigration Reform and Control Act of 1982, would place the burden of policing illegal aliens on businesses. As a *Wall Street Journal* editorial pointed out, small companies would be placed at a disadvantage since they usually rely on one overburdened manager to make hiring and firing decisions. Without the threat of an OSHA-style inspection force to investigate without warning, most small businessmen would find it expedient to ignore the rules.[40]

Changes at the EPA

Budget and staffing reductions at the Environmental Protection Agency seem to be promoting a regulatory new federalism—an effort to transfer regulatory enforcement to the states. How this nascent development will ultimately affect small business is uncertain; there are no guarantees that state bureaucracies will be any more sensitive to small-business problems than their federal counterparts.

Unfortunately, the House and Senate committees responsible for environmental regulation seem to be opting for old-style regulation. They have shunned meaningful reform of the Clean Air and Water acts and may make business more difficult for some 150,000 service stations, cleaners, and painting contractors who would be affected by tighter hazardous-waste restrictions being proposed by the House Energy and Commerce Committee. Indeed, regulatory reform in the environmental area seems to have lost most of its momentum, thanks to the stalling tactics of the congressional oversight committees involved.

SEC Reforms

The Securities and Exchange Commission (SEC) has shown a very enlightened view of the need to facilitate small-firm financing while protecting the investing public. Since April 1982, a new set of rules known as Regulation D allows small firms to raise as much as $500,000 from the sale of securities without registering those securities with the SEC. There is a two-year holding period required before reselling these securities, and they are still subject to the so-called blue-sky laws of states. Regulation D also permits unregistered sales of up to $5 million to a total of thirty-five investors (actually without limit for accredited or sophisticated investors).[41] The SEC appears willing to let the investment community determine what information is necessary to protect their clients in these situations. A reliance on the market is refreshing to see.

The new attitude at the SEC actually began to develop as long ago as 1978. With the passage of the Small Business Investment Incentive Act, innovative approaches for removing barriers to small-firm equity financing began to appear at the SEC. Prior to Regulation D changes, the commission had increased the maximum amount for Regulation A offerings from $500,000 to $1.5 million and introduced a simplified registration form for public offerings of up to $5 million.

ICC Deregulation

With the passage of the Motor Carrier Act of 1980, barriers to entry in the trucking industry began to tumble. Though the Reagan administration appointee heading the Interstate Commerce Commission has been accused (not without foundation) of dragging his feet on deregulation, significant changes have taken place in this industry. The commission has been more generous in granting applications for authority to haul cargo—from a 69.8 percent approval rate for applications in 1976 to 97.5 percent in the first half of 1982. Likewise, data on the number of regulated trucking firms reflect the increased entry of smaller firms. The total number of regulated firms has risen from approxiamtely 17,100 in 1979 to nearly 22,300 in 1981. Furthermore, the growth in the largest class of carriers increased by 39 percent.[42] The recession has, of course, affected these figures adversely but the increased competitiveness is evident.

Not everyone views competition favorably, however. The American Trucking Association estimates that the value of the operating rights for carriers with annual revenues over $1 million has declined from a value ranging between $5.1 and $6.8 billion to virtually zero.[43] Shippers and ultimately consumers are the beneficiaries of the increased competition reflected by this $6 billion shift in wealth.

One of the more memorable remarks concerning the problems caused by trucking deregulation came from the president of one of the large carriers, who accused deregulation of causing chaos in the trucking industry. Even during previous recessions, he complained, "we never used to have to cut our prices just to keep our customers."[44]

Conclusion

Federal actions in the decade of the 1970s might be characterized as the dark ages of public policy affecting small firms. The decade of the 1980s has begun on a much more promising note. Though this promise may not produce a full-scale renaissance of entrepreneurship, it may well produce a modest age of enlightenment. Entrepreneurs still face many problems in the 1980s, but the current enlightened views of policymakers toward small business is encouraging.

**What Should Small Business Expect
from Government?**

The previous sections of this chapter have shown how government regulation has affected the environment for entrepreneurship: how the disproportionate effects of regulation on small business were ignored in the 1970s and how the executive and legislative branches of the federal government have set about to make amends in the 1980s. But what about the future? How far should small-business advocates go in their attempts to change the policy environment to one more favorable for entrepreneurship?

What Government Should *Not* Do

In my opinion, efforts by supporters of small business to obtain special government set-asides in procurement programs, to insist that the plethora of small-business credit programs are sacrosanct, or to emphasize small business in every public-policy issue will ultimately prove self-defeating. Such self-serving activity could well produce a public-opinion backlash that could be quite harmful.

Set-Asides

Much of the impetus for government small-business set-asides in its procurement activities stems from an apparent inequity in current purchasing patterns. Small firms generate approximately 38 percent of the nation's gross national product but receive only 23 percent of the $110 billion that the federal government annually spends on goods and services. A variety of laws have been passed to address this situation. One of the most far-reaching attempts to direct more procurement funds toward small firms is embodied in Public Law 95-507, passed in 1978. A key provision of this law is that small businesses receive all federal contracts of $10,000 or less (about 10 percent, or $11 billion, of total federal purchases involve contracts under $10,000). The law also requires all contract bids over $500,000 to contain a plan to subcontract some parts of the work to small business.[45] While the law attempts to regulate the behavior of the demand or buyer side of the federal procurement market, it does little to affect the supply (seller) side of the market.

The lower participation by small firms in federal contracting stems from many factors beyond those addressed in P.L. 95-507. For one thing, the federal contracting process is something of a mystery to many small businesses. This is not surprising, since there are 485 offices issuing procurement regulations, 877 different sets of regulations, and a total of 64,600 pages of regulations in effect, 21,900 pages of which are revised each year.[46] As if this maze of red tape were not disincentive enough, the federal government has frequently been one of the slowest-paying customers. The Prompt Payments Act of 1982 was designed to speed up federal disbursements, but many forces within the government are attempting to slow down the implementation of this law. In short, there are many good reasons why small firms themselves might not wish to compete for federal procurement monies.

The Small Business Innovation Development Act

The most recent addition to these special programs for small firms is the Small Business Innovation Development Act (SBID). In the September

1982 issue of *Inc.*, the magazine's editor hailed the recent Small Business Innovation Development Act as "the most important piece of small business legislation yet enacted in our lifetime." For anyone familiar with the act, which is an expansion of a rather successful National Science Foundation (NSF) program, this would seem a bit of an overstatement. The law will result in only $30 to $50 million in research and development (R&D) awards to small firms in 1982. Even the estimated $400 million annual value of the program when it reaches full implementation does not seem that great in light of federal procurement of $110 billion annually. The *Inc.* editorial continued, "Small business's hard-won victory represents a landmark in its revolution into a significant political force."[47] This remains to be seen.

On January 27, 1982, I was asked to testify before the House Committee on Science and Technology on the SBID bill. I testified that

> Unfortunately, I must disagree with one of the features of the current bill—the set-aside provisions. Such a segmentation of the "supply side" of research contractors is likely to have a detrimental effect on the normal market for federal research—that is, it interferes with the normal efficiency of the marketplace. Our Center for the Study of American Business has been unswerving in its pursuit of regulatory reforms that make use of markets. Further, we have been critical of most command-and-control approaches to changing private behavior. It would be at best inconsistent of me to now promote a potentially inefficient allocation of taxpayer dollars by supporting command-and-control regulation of public decision makers. . . . Frankly, I do not find the case for a small business set-aside compelling enough to warrant establishing this precedent in research funding.[48]

My objections were based as much on the symbolism of this legislation as was *Inc.* magazine's editorial support in favor of it. In my opinion, if many more such battles are waged to foster special programs for small business, we may come to view this "landmark" as the beginning of a public-opinion backlash.

A Proper Role for the SBA

Unfortunately, the role of the Small Business Administration (SBA) in developing a proper entrepreneur/government relationship has been poorly defined in the past. One of the SBA's biggest problems has been the loan-officer role forced upon it by Congress. SBA personnel are not financial professionals, and the nearly 40-percent default rate in the direct loan program demonstrates what happens when an agency is forced to do a job that it is not equipped to do.

To the extent that SBA should have a role in loan guarantee programs, they should co-participate with a financial institution experienced in making business loans. The bank or other private financial party should have a major stake in such loans, and SBA should guarantee 50 percent to 60 percent of the loan rather than the current 90 percent. This would assure a rigorous analysis and auditing of the loan portfolios by professionals. Certainly the agency should be encouraged to deemphasize its loan activities.

As mentioned previously, many of the special favors offered small firms through small-business set-asides or procurement goals prove to be ineffective at best. For example, the Section 8(a) of Public Law 95-507 Procurement Program has been worse than ineffective—it has been self-defeating. Designed to nurture small, minority-owned firms, it has largely made such firms almost totally dependent upon the federal nursemaid to stay in business. More than 30 percent ($1.7 billion) of the federal contracts awarded through this program from 1969 to 1980 went to only fifty firms. Sixty percent of these fifty firms have been on the 8(a) program for more than seven years.[49] Because of the obvious political hazards of cutting off a minority, small-business program, the only changes made as a result of the revelation of this horrendous performance has been to limit (effective November 23, 1981) the amount of time a firm may stay on the list of approved 8(a) firms to five years, with a possible two-year extension.

A more positive role for the Small Business Administration would not be hard to imagine. The SBA could be a valuable repository of management assistance and liaison between small business and sources of private capital and between small business and the federal government. For instance, the Procurement Automated Service System (PASS), created by the SBA, could if given more serious attention and publicity, provide a valuable service to small firms by matching government procurement needs to small-firm capabilities. Judging by his recent published statements, the new SBA head James Sanders seems to agree on the need for a new emphasis on management assistance.[50]

Keeping Free Enterprise Free

One of the greatest enemies of small business, or free enterprise for that matter, is the temptation to say one thing and to do another. Will Rogers addressed the issue of our inconsistent attitudes about government spending in a way that is most appropriate to our discussion of what government should do for small business.

> We say the government is nutty, and throwing away our money. But anytime any is thrown our way, we have never dodged it. Well, if the government is throwing money away, the only thing I see is for the ones they are throwing it to, have 'em refuse to take it. But you haven't heard of that, have you? So don't be so critical of the present plans as long as you are living on the loot from them.

Indeed, two very contrary-minded contemporary thinkers recently agreed with this viewpoint in a recent interview entitled "Is America Still the Land of Opportunity?" Michael Novak and Robert Lekachman both gave very similar responses to a question in the intrusiveness of government. Lekachman pointed out the ambivalent feelings of Americans in their attitudes toward government. Business groups, like everyone else, tend to rely on government intervention in times of economic hardship. "And yet," he said, "we like to think of government as bumbling, incompetent, corrupt, and bureaucratic."

Novak agreed when he commented on the government's obligation to promote the general welfare: "When people are in trouble, they try to promote the general welfare in *their* cases. But they also lose some respect for the government which does it."[51] If we wish to preserve the environment for entrepreneurship, small business must rise above this natural inclination to promote its own general welfare.

Conclusion

Much of the public-opinion clout that small business enjoys is actually based upon the public's perception of it as the last bastion of free enterprise and as the underdog in a world dominated by big institutions—big government and big business. Public-interest groups may derive their power from their apparent *lack* of power. To a large extent this is also true for small business. As well-meaning representatives of small business push for more and more special programs—set-asides, loan programs, and the like—public opinion and ultimately political clout are likely to erode.

Tom Richman points out that the many voices claiming to speak for small business and asking for government favors are creating a less-than-helpful situation. Important issues tend to be obscured by the very number of other causes said to be in the best interest of small business. Such widespread efforts could come to be viewed as crying wolf and masking the significant public-policy issues impacting entrepreneurship.[52]

The most important point, however, is that small business truly is the last bastion of free enterprise. As government favors are sought, this vital segment of our economy is likely to become less entrepreneurial and offer less opportunity as it grows in dependence on federal largesse. Would it not be tragic if the hardy entrepreneurs that survived the regulatory environment of the 1970s condemned themselves to the status of endangered species by too much feeding at the public trough?

There is a verse of scripture (Micah 6:8) that says, "what doth the Lord require of thee, but to do justly, and to love mercy, and to walk humbly with thy God?" Paraphasing this verse to apply to the question at hand, "what should small business require of government, but to do justly, and to love mercy, and to walk humbly with the private enterprise system." Regulatory Flexibility, Equal Access to Justice, and other such changes that promote justice and equity in the economic environment are in keeping with these principles. They also reflect a healthy, humble attitude, as government attempts to allow enterpreneurs more freedom to do what they do best: to produce goods and services and a rising standard of living.

Set-asides and special loan programs benefiting only a chosen few (or few thousand) only encourage further public-sector intervention in the marketplace, ultimately promoting an unhealthy haughtiness on the part of government. In the final analysis, the best way for government to have a positive influence on the entrepreneurial environment is to do as little as possible *to* small business rather than to do as much as possible *for* small business.

Notes

1. David E. Gumpert, "Future of Small Business May be Brighter Than Portrayed," *Harvard Business Review* (July-August 1979), p. 172.

2. Edwin Harwood, "The Sociology of Entrepreneurship," in Calvin A. Kent, Donald L. Sexton, and Karl H. Vesper, *Encyclopedia of Entrepreneurship* (Englewood Cliffs, N.J.: Prentice-Hall, 1982), p. 98.

3. R. Walk, "Analyses of Shipment Trends in Foundry Closings in the U.S.," *Modern Castings Market Insight,* Publication No. 739 (March 31, 1975), Exhibit IV, p. 1.

4. Kenneth W. Chilton and Murray L. Weidenbaum, *Small Business Performance in the Regulated Economy* (St. Louis: Center for the Study of American Business, Washington University, February 1980), p. 15.

5. Ibid., p. 19.

6. *Economic Impact of Proposed OSHA Lead Standards* (Cambridge, Mass.: Charles River Associates, March 1977), p. 15.

7. U.S. Small Business Administration, *The State of Small Business, A Report to the President, 1982* (Washington, D.C.: Government Printing Office, 1982), p. 162.

8. *Future of Small Business in America, Part 1,* Hearings before the Committee on Small Business, House of Representatives, 95th Congress, Washington, D.C., March 21, 22, April 18, 1978, p. 37.

9. James F. Ragan, Jr., *Minimum Wages and the Youth Labor Market* (St. Louis: Center for the Study of American Business, Washington University, August 1977), p. 7.

10. U.S. Small Business Administration, *Government Paperwork and Small Business: Problems and Solutions,* December 1979, pp. ii, 16.

11. James W. Singer, "The Enemy Is Us," *National Journal* (January 31, 1981).

12. Thomas L. Amberg and Michael R. Montgomery, "U.S. Committees to Hold Hearings on SBA Practices," *St. Louis Globe-Democrat,* September 16, 1981, p. 1; and Murray L. Weidenbaum, "Loan Subsidies: This Kind of Help Small Business Doesn't Need," *Inc.,* March 1981.

13. Small Business Administration, *The State of Small Business, 1982,* p. 140.

14. U.S. Small Business Administration, *Report of the SBA Task Force on Venture and Equity Capital for Small Business* (Washington, D.C.: Government Printing Office, 1977), p. 17.

15. Bertrand Horwitz and Richard Kolodny, "The FASB, the SEC, and R&D," *The Bell Journal of Economics* (Spring 1981), p. 249.

16. Gerald L. Salamon and Dan S. Dhaliwal, "Company Size and Financial Disclosure Requirements with Evidence from the Segmented Reporting Issue," *Journal of Business, Finance and Accounting* 7:4 (1980), p. 558.

17. Ibid., p. 546.

18. David Pauly with Pamela Abraham, "Venture Capital Comes Back," *Newsweek,* June 4, 1979, p. 67.

19. Small Business Administration, *The State of Small Business, 1982,* p. 141.

20. Ibid., pp. 144–146.

21. Brooks Jackson, "Small Business Loans Aid 'Minority' Whites, the Rich, a Porn Firm," The Wall Street Journal, June 8, 1982, p. 18.

22. "Yak Fat Story Illustrates Process: Agency's Role in Rail-Truck Fight Hit," *Washington Post,* January 28, 1975.

23. "Update: Taking a Dive at the CPSC," *Regulation* (July/August 1981), p. 7.

24. U.S. Office of Federal Procurement Policy, Office of Management and Budget, *Small Firms and Federal R&D* (Washington, D.C.: 1977).

25. National Science Foundation, *Science Indicators 1976* (Washington, D.C.: 1977).

26. William Tuddenham, "Quality Assurance in Diagnostic Radiology: An Irreverent View of a Sacred Cow," *Radiology* 131 (June 1979), p. 586.

27. Paul Ciotti, "Revenge of the Nerds," *PD* (St. Louis Post Dispatch), September 12, 1982, p. 9.

29. National Science Foundation, *Problems of Small, High-Technology Firms,* (NSF 81–305), (Washington, D.C.: 1981), p. 5.

29. Tom Richman, "Will the Real Small Businessman Stand Up?" *Inc.* (July 1982), p. 26.

30. Joseph Schumpeter, *Capitalism, Socialism and Democracy* (New York: Harper and Row, 1962).

31. David L. Birch, *The Job Generation Process* MIT Program on Neighborhood and Regional Change, (Cambridge: Massachusetts Institute of Technology, 1979), p. 8.

32. Catherine Armington and Marjorie Odle, "Sources of Job Growth: A New Look at the Small Business Role," *Economic Development Commentary* 6:3 (Fall 1982), p. 4.

33. John Kenneth Galbraith, "The Government vs. Small Business," *Washington Monthly* (September 1978), pp. 42–44.

34. Paul Sommers and Roland J. Cole, "Costs of Compliance in Small and Medium-Sized Businesses," *American Journal of Small Business* 6:1 (July-September 1981), pp. 25–33.

35. "Regflex Report Card: Some Agencies Flunk," *Inc.* (April 1982), pp. 20–21.

36. Michael Thoryn, "A Fairer Shake for Small Business," *Nation's Business* (February 1982), p. 40.

37. Robert E. Taylor, "New Law May Make It Easier To Fight Federal Government," *The Wall Street Journal,* May 24, 1982, p. 21.

38. "Administration Publishing Fewer Agency Rules," *National Journal,* May 1, 1982, p. 781.

39. Ronald J. Penoyer, *Directory of Federal Regulatory Agencies: 1982 Update,* (St. Louis: Center for the Study of American Business, Washington University, June 1982), p. 19.

40. "Employers as Cops," *The Wall Street Journal,* August 12, 1982, p. 14.

41. Andrew C. Saxlehner, "Equity Made Easy," *Inc.* (July 1982), p. 105.

42. Robert E. Mabley and Walter D. Strack, "Deregulation—A Green Light for Trucking Efficiency," *Regulation* (July-August 1982), p. 42.

43. Ibid., p. 39.

44. *Washington Post,* July 6, 1982.

45. Small Business Administration, *The State of Small Business, 1982,* pp. 164–166.

46. Ibid., p. 165.

47. Milton D. Stewart, "Small Business—and the Nation—Win a Very Big One," *Inc.* (September 1982), p. 152.

48. Kenneth W. Chilton, "Incentives for Innovation: Federal Research and Small Firms," testimony before the House Committee on Science and Technology, (Washington, D.C., January 27, 1982).

49. Comptroller General of the United States, *The SBA 8(a) Procurement Program: A Promise Unfulfilled,* Report to the Congress, (Washington, D.C.: General Accounting Office, April 8, 1981), p. 6.

50. Sanford L. Jacobs, "SBA Chief Brings New Style, But Few Policy Shifts Likely," *The Wall Street Journal,* April 26, 1982, p. 23.

51. "Is America Still the Land of Opportunity?" *Public Opinion* (June-July 1982), p. 10.

52. Richman, "Will the Real Small Businessman Stand up?", p. 28.

7 Patents and the Entrepreneurial Environment

William E. Schuyler, Jr.

Origin of the United States Patent System

Prior to 1787, when the Constitutional Convention was convened in Philadelphia, patents had been granted by Massachusetts, Maryland, South Carolina, New York, Connecticut, Delaware, New Hampshire, and New Jersey. Since some inventors had applied in more than one state for patents on their inventions, it was apparent to members of the Constitutional Convention that a centralized patent system would be required to avoid conflicting claims in the several states. Proposals to include in the Constitution authority to "grant patents for useful inventions" were accepted unanimously and incorporated in article I, section 8 of the eighth clause which reads, "The Congress shall have the Power—To promote Progress of Science and the useful Arts by securing For limited Times for Authors and Inventors the exclusive Right to their respective Writings and Discoveries."

This so-called *intellectual property* clause is the only one of the enumerated powers of Congress that includes expression of the purpose for which the power is authorized. Probably the reason for this is the novelty of an expressed monopoly power in a basic government document. It is significant that the delegates to the convention, who were divided and arguing strenuously over many provisions of the Constitution, were unanimous in their approval of the power of Congress to secure to authors and inventors a monopoly (exclusive right) in the products of their intellects.

Exercising the power authorized by the intellectual property clause, in 1790 Congress enacted patent and copyright statutes. At that time, there was no comparable provision in British law. In fact, the United States's patent statute was the first in the world to recognize the inherent right of an inventor to retain an invention and to profit from it. From this beginning, we have evolved a sophisticated patent law that carefully balances the right of the inventor and the interest of the public.

What is a Patent?

By its terms, a United States patent grants to the inventor the right, for a limited period of seventeen years, to exclude others from making, using, or selling his or her invention; it is nothing more. Issuance of a patent does not confer the right to make, use, or sell the patented invention; the patentee must still respect the right of any dominating patent and abide by any applicable governmental regulations.

In the United States, an applicant for a patent must make a complete disclosure of the invention. That disclosure of the invention is published when the patent is issued, and moves into the public domain when the patent expires in seventeen years. Thus, the patent may be viewed as a contract between the inventor and the public represented by the government. By the terms of the contract, the inventor makes a public disclosure of his or her invention in exchange for a seventeen-year monopoly; that is, the exclusive right to make, use, and sell the invention for a period of seventeen years.

By statute, a patent has all the attributes of personal property: it may be sold, assigned, licensed in whole or in part, pledged as collateral, or dedicated to the public. There is no obligation on the patentees to do anything with respect to a patented invention. They may use the patent to maintain a monopoly in the manufacture, use, or sale of the invention, they may sell or license it in whole or in part; or they may do nothing and permit the invention to remain dormant.

How the Public Benefits from the Patent System

The U.S. patent system is frequently referred to as an incentive system because it provides incentives to invent and innovate. It provides incentives for venture capital to be invested in the development of inventions; incentives to inform others about an invention by applying for a patent and making a full disclosure of the invention; and incentives to imitate by designing around a patented invention in order to compete with it or improve on it.

Incentive to Invent

Although most of the money spent for research and development is spent by the government and large corporations, most of the significant inventions of the last two centuries have been made by individual inventors working alone or in small companies. For example, even though large manufacturing companies expended considerable money and effort to produce color photography, the breakthrough invention was made by two violinists without the support of a research laboratory.

It is often the pioneer invention of an individual that is the beginning of a new industry. Chester Carlson, a patent attorney, was searching for a more efficient method of copying documents when he drew upon his knowledge of electrostatic precipitation of smoke particles to conceive the method of controlling the electrostatic adhesion of particles to paper according to different light intensities applied to different areas of the paper. Even though Carlson's xerographic experiments were successful, many years elapsed before commercial copying machines were available. Similarly, Edwin Land invented and successfully experimented with cameras and film to develop photographic prints immediately after exposing the film. But much time, effort, and money was expended before the first Polaroid® camera was marketed.

Incentive to Inform

Both Carlson and Land applied for patents to protect their inventions. In so doing, they made full and complete disclosures of their inventions as well as the best ways then known to them for making and using the inventions. When the patents were issued, this information was published and added to the store of public knowledge. Seventeen years later when the patents expired, all of the disclosed information was in the public domain.

So far we have seen how the patent system provided the incentive to Carlson and Land to work on their inventions, and to inform the public about their work by applying for and obtaining patents. These two examples also demonstrate how other incentives of the patent system work.

Incentive to Invest

In an effort to obtain financial support necessary to develop his copying machine, Chester Carlson approached every major corporation he could find, but they all turned him down. Finally, he persuaded Batelle Memorial Laboratories in Ohio to undertake the development of the invention in exchange for an interest in the invention and the patents. Batelle spent several million dollars trying to produce a commercial machine, but was unsuccessful, became discouraged, and decided to abandon the project. Carlson again solicited support and finally made a deal with the small Haloid Corporation of Rochester, New York.

Business of the Haloid Corporation had been depressed, but the management and directors of that company decided to take a momentous gamble and invest most of its available resources in the development of Carlson's copying machine. Many years after Carlson's invention, Haloid marketed the first commercial copying machine utilizing the xerographic method. That was the beginning of Xerox Corporation.

Land approached the development of his instant camera and film by interesting investors in the Polaroid Corporation. That considerable investment financed the enormous expenditures necessary to bring the camera and film to the marketplace at a price consumers could afford.

In the case of both the Carlson and Land inventions, the cost of developing was financed by venture capital made available only because both inventors applied for and obtained patents. Potential return to the investors based upon exploitation of their patented inventions could only be of sufficient magnitude to warrant the risk involved if the patent system provided the protection of a monopoly for a limited period of time.

Incentive to Imitate and Design Around

Once Xerox® copiers and Polaroid® cameras were successfully marketed, competitors began investigating ways of manufacturing and marketing competing products. This effort involved an analysis of the patent positions, negotiation of licenses, and commencement of engineering projects to produce competing products while avoiding the Carlson and Land patents.

These competitive efforts ultimately resulted in improved products made available to the public by Xerox and Polaroid as well as by their competitors. Once the basic patents expired, the disclosures of the basic patents were in the public domain and competitors were free to utilize the information and incorporate the inventions in competitive products.

Entrepreneurial Success without Patents

Although this chapter is about patents and their advantages and disadvantages in creating a healthy entrepreneurial environment, and possible measures for improving that environment, it may be helpful at the outset to digress and provide some perspective on the remainder of the discussion by pointing out that patents are not a sine qua non of success in business. On the contrary, many extremely prosperous firms do not pursue patent protection, particularly in the service industries and in retail merchandising. Patents alone are not the answer to encouraging innovation and investment—patents are merely an important element in overall governmental policy in support of technological development and a strong economy.

One broad area in which patents are almost unheard of is banking and insurance. As one court explained almost a century ago in invalidating a patent that attempted to cover a method for insuring against business losses,

The guarantying [sic] of men's financial ability to pay is not an invention of the complainant. Nearly all forms of guarantying or insuring have been in existence for many years, notably fidelity, casualty, fire, lightning, and other forms of insurance, all of which are based upon averages obtained from practical experience. It required no inventive genius to form and plan the insurance on this basis. One is not entitled to a patent for a plan or method of business which only requires good judgement and foresight.[1]

Yet the banking and insurance industries thrive, even without a foundation of patents upon which to base their successes. For example, the nation's largest commercial bank, Bank of America N. T. & S. A., is the principal asset of BankAmerica Corp., which has assets of over $120 billion, including $70 billion in outstanding loans. The holding company has 1,100 branches in the bank's state of incorporation and conducts business in 94 foreign countries, yet owns no patents. Another giant of the financial field is Aetna Life & Casualty Co., the largest investor-owned insurance enterprise in the United States. Its assets are valued at almost $40 billion, and total insurance in force exceeds $170 billion. Patents are not significant in its business.

Retail merchandising is a second facet of the economy in which patents are generally unsuitable as a vehicle for attracting investment or protecting one's markets. Companies such as Safeway Stores, Inc., and Associated Dry Goods Corp. must, by any standard, be described as successful. Safeway collects annual revenues of over $16 billion from almost 2,500 stores worldwide. Associated Dry Goods (operator of Lord & Taylor and fourteen other department-store divisions), while somewhat smaller, is still an imposing business entity with its $2.7 billion in annual revenues.

If growth rate rather than sheer size is used as a gauge of a firm's success, one of the more successful has been an ice cream plant in Woodbridge, New Jersey—the sole source of Haagen-Dazs™ ice cream. Though production in the ice cream industry as a whole was creeping upward at an annual rate of only 0.4 percent, that of Haagen-Dazs™ was bounding upward at 25 percent. Containing half again as much butterfat as ordinary ice cream, selling at almost twice the price, and in quantities no larger than a pint, Haagen-Dazs™'s amazing growth is the result not of patents (which are unavailable for food recipes),[2] but of the product's "reputation for quality and a 20-year lead time in building up the Haagen-Dazs™ name."[3]

By its nature, the patent system is better able to protect those who deal in products than those whose business it is to provide services. The latter, for the most part, exist outside the patent system, principally by virtue of the definition of patentable subject matter in 35 U.S.C.S. 101 (1981), which allows patents to be granted only for "any new and useful process, machine, manufacture, or composition of matter." Of the four patentable categories, only process (or method) may be applicable to a service firm. Furthermore, judicial construction has even narrowed this category so that a method of doing business, such as, for example, a system of bookkeeping, is unpatentable regardless of its novelty or usefulness.[4]

An example of a successful service firm is the world's largest hotelier, Holiday Inns, Inc., which operates or licenses 1,751 hotels, with a total of 308,113 rooms, in the United States and foreign countries. Hotel operations provide almost half of its $1.75 billion in revenues. Another large service organization is Hospital Corp. of America, which owns or manages 349 hospitals with a total of 49,866 beds and has annual revenues over $2 billion.

Computer Software: Patent
Protection Questionable

Of all possible inventions produced or discovered by man, one highly successful class is giving the legal system more trouble than most. This orphan of the intellectual property clause is the sui generis category known as computer software. Though it forms the foundations for two industries—software sales and data processing services—its protectibility at present is perilously uncertain. Most software does not rise to the level of invention, so patent protection even if available would apply to only a small segment of the industry.

The generally held view that software is unpatentable is a result of three Supreme Court decisions, *Gottschalk* v. *Benson, Parker* v. *Flook*, and *Diamond* v. *Diehr*[5], yet the lower-court opinions that proport to follow these three authorities sometimes reach apparently conflicting results.

The patent sought in *Benson* was for a method of programming a general-purpose digital computer to convert binary coded decimal (BCD) numbers to pure binary. Aside from the requirement for a computer, the method could be carried out by hand. Though specifically declining to find "any program servicing a computer" unpatentable, Justice Douglas, writing for a unanimous six-member Court, nevertheless declined to issue a patent to this program for reasons stated in the now-famous "nutshell" holding.

> What we come down to in a nutshell is the following: It is conceded that one may not patent an idea. But in practical effect that would be the result if the formula for converting binary code to pure binary were patented in this case. The mathematical formula involved here has no substantial practical application except in connection with a digital computer, which means that if the judgment below is affirmed, the patent would wholly pre-empt the mathematical formula and in practical effect would be a patent on the algorithm itself.[6]

The next issue in computer-software patentability involved an application for a patent on a method for updating alarm limits. The only novel feature of the invention was the formula by which the new alarm limits were calculated; but Flook, relying on *Benson*, had added two steps to the process and had limited the entire method to the context of catalytic chemical conversion of hydrocarbons. Six members of the court, led by Justice Stevens, denied Flook a patent "not because [the process] contains a mathematical algorithm as one component, but because once that algorithm is assumed to be within the prior art, the application, considered as a whole, contains no patentable invention."[7] Neither the specified end use of the calculation nor the limitation of the claims to catalytic conversion of hydrocarbons, could save the application.

The latest Supreme Court pronouncement in the area of patenting computer software, *Diehr*, concerned a process for curing synthetic rubber using a mathematical formula (the Arrhenius equation) and a programmed digital computer. In an opinion joined by four other members of the Court, Justice Rehnquist first compared the claims in the application with the Court's previous decisions and found that "a physical and chemical process for molding precision synthetic rubber products falls within the 101 categories of possible patentable subject matter."[8] He then stated that this conclusion was not altered by Diehr's use of a mathematical formula or a computer in several steps of the process, since no attempt was being made to patent the formula but only to use it, in conjunction with all of the other steps of the process, including significant postsolution activity, to lessen the possibility of overcuring or undercuring the rubber. Justice Stevens wrote the dissenting opinion, arguing that the only inventive concept was in the use of a mathematical formula and, therefore, *Flook* required denial of a patent.

The lower courts have agreed that a mathematical formula, or algorithm, is itself unpatentable; but beyond that it is unclear whether a patent will be granted for a computer program tied to more or less hardware, or coupled with steps providing for a greater or lesser degree of postsolution activity, or not involving a formula at all. *In re Abele* provides a good example.[9] Two principal claims, numbers 5 and 6, were in issue. Claim 5, for a method of displaying data in a field, contains the following steps:

1. calculating the difference between the local value of the data at a point in the field and the average value of the data in the region surrounding the data point, for each point in the field; and
2. displaying the value of the difference as a gray scale.

Claim 6 added only that the data were x-ray attenuation data produced by a computed tomography scanner. The court found claim 5 unpatentable because it attempted to patent a mathematical algorithm, yet claim 6 was allowed.

The uncertainty surrounding patentability of software has led to a search for other methods of protection.

Copyright Protection: An Unknown Quality

Though the U.S. Copyright Office began to accept computer programs for registration as books in 1964,[10] it was not until 1980 that the Copyright Act was amended to include provisions which confirm the copyrightability of computer programs. Section 101 of the act was amended to define computer programs as "a set of statements or instructions to be used directly or indirectly in a computer in order to bring about a certain result." Section 117 was completely revised to specify that certain acts of copying in the computer context do not constitute infringement. Even before these revisions, a careful reading of the 1976 version of the Copyright Act compelled the conclusion that computer programs are copyrightable.

> In the Copyright Act of 1976, *literary works* are defined as: Works, other than audiovisual works, expressed in words, numbers, or other verbal or numerical symbols or indicia, regardless of the nature of the material objects, such as books, periodicals, manuscripts, phonorecords, film, *tapes, disks, or cards*, in which they are embodied.[11]

The following section, 102 (emphasis added), identifies copyrightable subject matter.

> (a) Copyright protection subsists, in accordance with this title, in original work of authorship fixed in any tangible medium of expression, now known or later developed, from which they can be perceived, reproduced, or otherwise communicated, either directly *or with the aid of a machine or device*. Works of authorship include the following categories: (1) literary works

The italic portions of these provisions clearly pertain to computer programs. Thus, computer programs are classed as literary works and, as such, are copyrightable subject matter. This was the conclusion reached by the district court in *Tandy Corp.* v. *Personal Micro Computers, Inc.*[12]

However, copyright may not provide the extent of protection desired by the creator of a computer program. Unlike patent law, a fundamental concept of the law of copyright is that copyright protects only the expression of an idea and not the idea itself.[13] This concept is reflected in 17 U.S.C.S. 102(b) (1981): "In no case does copyright protection for an original work of authorship extend to any idea, procedure, process, system, method of operation, concept, principle, explained, illustrated, or embodied in such a work." Thus, copyright gives authors or copyright claimants exclusive rights in the arrangement of words they have chosen to explain their ideas, but it does not give them exclusive rights in the use or practical application of the ideas imparted. In the computer context, the idea/expression dichotomy appears as the unprotected idea of the operation that the computer is to perform and the protected program that instructs the computer how to do this operation. However, as the following cases illustrate, where the protection of the expression prevents others from utilizing the idea, the protection of the expression must be restricted.

Applicable to the averaging program discussed earlier is the acknowledgment by the courts that where the idea is so narrow that it is susceptible to only a few expressions, greater similarity must be tolerated. In *Decorative Aides Corp.* v. *Staple Sewing Aides*,[14] both the plaintiff and the defendant manufactured drapery headers, a premarked strip of stiffened material that, when attached to the top of drapery fabric, indicates to the home sewer how the fabric should be folded and tacked to produce pleated drapery into which hooks can be inserted for attachment to a rod. The plaintiff claimed that the defendant's instruction sheet which illustrated the use of its header infringed the copyright in its instruction sheet. In finding for the defendant, the court explained its reasoning.

> This similarity cannot be the basis of an infringement charge here, however, for it is dictated by functional considerations; instructions for applying a drapery header can be expressed only in limited ways. . . .
>
> To forbid defendant to offer similar instruction for its similar product would result, in effect, in protecting the device itself. . . . [The] defendant's instructions were not slavish copies of plaintiff's, but were merely similar expressions of the same idea.[15]

The situation in *Affiliated Hospital Products, Inc.* v. *Merdel Game Manufacturing Company* is similar.[16] The plaintiff alleged that its copyrighted rulebook for the game of caroms was infringed by the defendant's rulebook for the same game. Again the court held for the defendant:

> [Plaintiff's] copyright only protects [Plaintiff's] arrangement of the rules and the manner of their presentation, and not their content. Here, however, the simplicity of the games makes the subject matter extremely narrow, and the distinction between substance and arrangement blurs.[17]

As in *Decorative Aides*, the court concluded that to hold otherwise would result in protecting the idea; that is, the game itself.

From these cases, it is easy to see the difficulty in attempting to protect a program for averaging twenty numbers. The program is simple and capable of practical expression in only a limited number of ways. Thus, in order to employ the idea of averaging with a computer, the same program or one very similar to it must be used. Under these cases, similarity would not be actionable. This basic notion has been applied and elaborated in the insurance field where reliance on specific languge and forms to achieve the desired coverage plan is required. Because the computer field likewise relies on specific language to achieve the desired result, these cases are relevant to the discussion of the protection accorded computer programs by copyright.

In *Continental Casualty Company* v. *Beardsley*,[18] an insurance broker had published a copyrighted pamphlet, complete with forms, which explained a particular type of insurance coverage. An insurance company that sought to use the forms or, possibly, had already used similar forms, filed suit for a declaratory judgment that the forms were not copyrightable. The court found the forms to be a proper subject of copyright, but went on to find that the use of similar forms was only incidental to the use of the underlying idea.

> In the field of insurance and commerce the use of specific language in forms and documents may be so essential to accomplish a desired result and so integrated with the use of a legal or commercial conception that the proper standard of infringement is one which will protect as fast as possible the copyrighted language and yet allow free use of the thought beneath the language. The evidence here shows that Continental insofar as it has used the language of Beardsley's forms has done so only as incidental to its use of the underlying idea.[19]

Thus, in cases where specific language is required to achieve the desired result, copyright cannot prevent its use.

Perhaps *Crume* v. *Pacific Mutual Life Insurance Company* provides the clearest illustration of judicial refusal to protect the copyrighted expression of an idea where to do so would prevent the use of the idea in practice.[20] In *Crume*, even the plaintiff acknowledged the distinction between the actual plan for the reorganization of insolvent insurance companies and the pamphlet which described the plan. The plaintiff, however, claimed infringement of his expression on the basis that the defendant, in using the plan, had employed the same word coined by the plaintiff to refer to his plan. The court held that to the extent that protection of the language prevented the use of the idea, the expression could not be protected even by a valid copyright. Of the plan, the court stated:

> Its use, to which the public is entitled, can be effected solely by the employment of world descriptive thereof. In our view, where the use can be effected only in such manner, there can be no infringement even though the plan or method be copied. We realize that such a view leaves little, if any, protection to the copyright owner; in fact, it comes near to invalidating the copyright. The situation, however, results from the fact that the practical use of the art explained by the copyright and lodged in the public domain can be attained solely by the employment of language which gives expression to that which is disclosed.
>
> To hold that an idea, plan, method or art described in a copyright is open to the public but that it can be used only by the employment of different words and phrases which mean the same thing, borders on the preposterous.

It is to exalt the accomplishment of a result by indirect means which could not be done directly. It places a premium upon evasion and makes this the test of infringement. Not withstanding some authorities which support a theory permitting such a result, we think it is wrong and disapprove it.[21]

Both *Crume* and *Beardsley* stand for the proposition that the protection by copyright for the expression of an idea will expand or contract as necessary to provide for the free use of the underlying idea itself. In the computer context, this means that similarity among programs that seek to accomplish the same function, regardless of their simplicity or complexity, may not be actionable because they are merely expressions of the same idea that require use of similar language.

Neither is similarity actionable where the idea cannot be distinguished from the expression, for this too could protect the underlying idea. In *Herbert Rosenthal Jewelry Corp.* v. *Kalpakian*,[22] the plaintiff designed and coyrighted a jeweled bee pin. The defendant also produced a jeweled bee pin that the plaintiff claimed infringed his copyright. The plaintiff admitted that the idea of a jeweled bee pin was not protected, but claimed that its expression of the idea was infringed by the defendant's similar expression. The court did not agree and stated,

> The difficulty, as we have noted, is that on this record the "idea" and its "expression" appear to be indistinguishable. There is no greater similarity between the pins of plaintiff and defendants than is inevitable from the use of jewel-encrusted bee forms in both.
>
> When the "idea" and its "expression" are thus inseparable, copying the "expression" will not be barred, since protecting the "expression" in such circumstances would confer a monopoly of the "idea" upon the copyright owner free of the conditions and limitations imposed by the patent law.[23]

In denying protection to the idea, the court found it necessary to deny protection to the expression as well.

The same result was reached in the computer field in *Synercom Technology, Inc.* v. *University Computing Co.*[24] The court grappled with the question of whether the copying by the defendant of the plaintiff's input formats were "expressed ideas" (which appears to be a somewhat confused way of saying that the idea and the expression of the idea are inseparable) and found for the defendant on the issue of copyright infringement of the formats.[25]

This illustrates a major problem of copyright protection in the computer field. Since the set of instructions embodied in a computer program often can be written in several different ways and still achieve the desired result, the value of a computer program lies not in a particular expression, but in the idea that a computer can be used to perform a particular function. However, the idea itself is not protectable by copyright.

Other aspects of computer software create novel problems for copyright protection. Electronic video games provide an example. Each game has three components; the computer program in object code, the computer program in source code, and the visual display. Since the same or similar visual displays can be achieved by different programs, the manufacturers of such games have successfully relied on registration of the copyright in the display as an audiovisual work for protection as an alternative to registration of the copyright in the underlying program.[26] Frequently, manufacturers are unwilling to register the copyright in the program itself since the portions of the program that must be deposited with the Copyright Office might be used by competitors.

Reliance on the audiovisual aspect of electronic video games cannot prevent others from copying the unprotected idea expressed in the game. For example, in *Atari, Inc.* v. *Amusement World, Inc.*, Atari claimed that the registered copyright in its popular game *Asteroids* was infringed by the defendant's game *Meteors*.[27] The court cited the *Kalpakian* case discussed earlier and determined that the similarities between the games were due solely to the use of the same idea and thus did not constitute copyright infringement. Regarding the protection secured by copyright, the court stated, "It seems clear that the defendants based their game on plaintiff's copyrighted game; to put it bluntly, defendants took plaintiff's idea. However, the copyright laws do not prohibit this. Copyright protection is available only for expression of ideas, not for ideas themselves."[28] Thus, while the Copyright Act of 1980 does provide for the registration of the copyright in computer programs, a creator of computer software is unlikely to be satisfied with the limitations on protection inherent in the copyright law.

Other Protection

Faced with the voids in the protection afforded by patent and copyright law, "one is left almost by default with trade secret law."[29] The chief drawback of trade secret law, aside from its similarity to copyright law in the necessity for actual copying, is the need to guard the confidentiality of the programs. This involves entering nondisclosure agreements with everyone who assists in the development of the software and every purchaser or user.

Special legislation protecting computer software has also been proposed. One such model statute prepared by the World Intellectual Property Organization essentially combines the most desirable features of copyright and trade secret law, and makes them specifically applicable to software.[30] The owner of the software would be able to prevent any person from, *inter alia*:

1.   disclosing it to others;
2.   allowing access by others to any object storing or reproducing it;

3. copying it by any means or in any form;
4. using it to produce "the same or a substantially similar computer program or a program description of the computer program or of a substantially similar computer program";
5. "Using the program description to produce the same or substantially similar program description or to produce a corresponding computer program"; and
6. using or storing the program in a computer.

In return for this enhanced protection, the program owner would be required to deposit a copy with the appropriate government agency as notice to the public of exactly what is being protected. This model statute, if enacted, would go a long way toward removing the uncertainty surrounding protection of computer software. Until it is enacted, however, we must rely on existing modes of protection. It is compelling testimony to the value of software in our economy that, even with the present uncertain state of the law, programs are being developed and licensed or sold at an astounding rate.

Trademarks

Although the major portion of this chapter is directed to patent policies and how they affect the entrepreneur, it is worthwhile to briefly address another form of intellectual property that is also of great importance and value to the entrepreneur: the trademark. The interrelationship between patents and trademarks generally is misunderstood by most laymen and also by many attorneys who do not deal on a regular basis with these specialized areas of the law.

The fundamental distinction between patents and trademarks is found in the purpose each serves in an industrialized capitalist society. Although each of these forms of property is an intangible intellectual type of property, each performs different functions for the entrepreneur. Usually both types will be helpful if not necessary, to protect the fruits of his or her labor.

As described earlier, provision was made in the U.S. Constitution for a system of patents to reward inventors for the creation of new and useful products. Trademarks, on the other hand, are not related to invention. Moreover, the products or services with which trademarks are used need not even be useful, although such is usually the case.

A trademark is defined as any "word, name, symbol or device or any combination thereof adopted and used by a manufacturer or merchant to identify his goods and distinguish them from those manufactured or sold by others."[31] The trademark selected as this indication of origin may be a commonly known word or symbol. However, the *first* person to use that particular word or symbol, or combination, in connection with a particular product or service so that the trademark becomes associated with that product or service, is entitled to exclude others from using the same or similar mark on the same or similar products or services. Of course, what constitutes *similar* marks or similar goods or services is a matter of much litigation, but the basic issue is whether the ordinary consumer would be likely to be confused.

Patent rights are limited in duration by federal statute. Upon the expiration of the patent, the product that is covered by the patent enters the public domain free for anyone to copy. Trademark rights, however, may be of infinite duration. For as long as a trademark continues to identify and distinguish the goods of one person from those of another, the trademark owner has a protectable property right in the mark. This right, under appropriate circumstances, may be used to extend the monopoly on a particular product that the entrepreneur enjoyed by virtue of a patent that has expired. If, during the life of the patent, widespread consumer recognition of and demand for the product was created because of its association with a trademark, such recognition and demand will continue after the patent has expired, resulting in a de facto extension of the monopoly. The trademark identifies the product with which everyone is familiar and has purchased for the seventeen-year life of the patent. Other manufacturers of identical products must spend time and money developing that sort of trademark identification. Thus, the trademark can become the entrepreneur's most valuable asset once the patent expires, as it is the only thing that distinguishes his or her product from now-identical products of other manufacturers.

One of the dangers inherent in associating a trademark with a patented product is too great an association between the product and the trademark, resulting from the product being the only one of its kind on the market for a certain period of time. This situation happened with a very famous trademark—Xerox® . When the Haloid Corporation obtained the original Carlson patents on the process of xerography, it created the arbitrary trademark Xerox® to identify its photocopy machines (also changing its corporate name). During the life of the patents, whenever anyone wanted to make photocopies using this patented process, a Xerox® copier was the only type of equipment available. Tremendous advertising and promotion, coupled with a new and unique product, accelerated the demand, and strong trademark recognition quickly developed. Upon expiration of the patents, new copier manufacturers entering the market had to fight for recognition, not because of the patent monopolies of Xerox Corporation, but because of the frame of the trademark Xerox® and the strong consumer identification it enjoyed.

However, the danger of so much trademark recognition quickly became apparent. Because Xerox® brand copying machines had been the only ones available for an extended period of time, the trademark had, for many, become synonymous with all photocopying equipment. Consumers and others had begun to misuse the trademark by using the trademark Xerox® to indicate any copying machine.

The Xerox Corporation has taken steps in recent years to police these types of misuses, even to the extent of placing full-page advertisements in major newspapers and magazines reminding readers that Xerox® is a trademark. Loss of the exclusive right to use the trademark Xerox® for photocopying machines and related supplies would be of incalculable proportions. The owners of former trademarks such as Aspirin, Thermos, Shredded Wheat, Cellophane, and the recently invalidated trademark *Monopoly*, know that all too well.[32] All of the skill and hard work involved in the creation and development of a business reputation built on a combination of patent and trademark rights (and often copyright protection as well) can be destroyed by abuse of the company's trademark. However, with proper use, advertising, and promotion of a patented product in association with a trademark, the entrepreneur may be able to maintain and extend the monopoly that the patent originally provided.

Where Do Patents Have an Impact?

Examples of patented products and processes that have been responsible for creating new markets and industries are all about us and are recorded in the archives of the Patent and Trademark Office. The Morse telegraph, the McCormick reaper, the Bell telephone, and the Edison incandescent lamp benefited from patent protection and have provided immeasurable benefits to our society. Agriculture has prospered from such inventions as patented insecticides and food-processing machines. Modern electronic technology, spurred by the patent system, has benefited mankind with lasers, transistors, and computers. Patented plastics, textiles, and pharmaceuticals have created new markets and industries.

It has been said that the patent system offers the same protection, the same opportunity, the same hope of reward to every individual. In this sense, the system is as democratic as the Constitution that begot it. Notwithstanding the truth of this statement, the patent system does appear to serve different industries and different inventions in different ways.

Technological change has been characterized as occurring in three main ways: invention, innovation, and imitation. Based on this premise, four variables have been identified upon which the incentive to invent and innovate depends: 1) the cost of invention and innovation; 2) the risk; 3) the payoffs potentially obtainable if one is technically and commercially successful; and 4) the rate at which competitive imitation occurs (which in turn depends on the strength of patent protection and other factors such as reverse engineering lags, secrecy, know-how advantages, and first-in reputation advantages).

Some inventions would be made whether or not a patent system existed. However, there are surely innovations and inventions that would not occur or would be delayed in the absence of patent protection. There are certain market conditions under which patent protection is more important to invention and innovation than others. Much depends upon the market position of the would-be innovator. Firms well established in the market need patent protection much less than enterprises contemplating entry through technical innovations into some new field without the benefit of brand reputation, existing distribution channels, and accumulated production know-how.

Small firms, and especially small new firms, are likely to find the prospect of some patent protection essential before undertaking sizable innovative ventures The patent system is perhaps most important for these small firms and for independent inventors. One study done in 1969 found the patent system in general to be "a crude and inconsistent system" that "lacks logic" and is "wasteful."[33] Nonetheless, this study found that for the small firm or independent inventor struggling to market a new idea, the patent right is critically important. It is the only resource the inventor or firm may possess and, fragile and precarious as the patent right may be, without it, small firms or inventors would have nothing by which to establish a claim to a reward for their work. It was found that the sale of ideas directly, or the raising of capital, would be very difficult for this class of inventor without the patent.

In addition to the size of the firm, innovations and inventions most dependent for protection are those that embody key features expensive to develop but quickly and cheaply copied. Also, patent protection provides a more essential incremental incentive the smaller the market is in relation to development costs and the greater the technological marketing uncertainties associated with the innovation.

The impact of patents varies not only with the market position or market structure within an industry or a particular technology. Patents also appear to have a different effect on different technologies, although findings are inconclusive and not very well documented. In the pharmaceutical industry, a Batelle-Columbus Laboratories study in 1973 found unmistakable evidence that the exclusive right of patent protection has a strong and pervasive influence on the willingness of firms to undertake research and development and to commercialize new drugs. About half of pharmaceutical research and development and associated innovation was found to be dependent on patents. Several other areas stood out as being significantly effective by the exclusive patent right. These included agricultural chemicals, plastics, and special-purpose industrial chemicals.[34]

The innovation lag, that is, the total time from invention to commercialization of new technology, also is a factor in determining whether patents will have a significant impact on a particular technology. Where the innovation lag is relatively long, patents become more important; where the innovation lag is short, patents become less important. The innovation lag certainly is not uniform but varies with industry, product, market, and resources used. In a recent study of "Innovation, Competition, and Government Policy in the Semiconductor Industry," it was found that the patent system is not serving its intended purpose because "the time required to obtain a patent is long in relation to the speed with which semiconductor technology changes."[35] Engineers and inventors in the electronics field have found that parts of their field are moving so fast and are so competitive that an invention can be obsolete in the time it takes to obtain a patent.

In the report prepared by Batelle-Columbus Laboratories, twenty-one factors of probable importance to the direction and rate of the innovation process were selected from the general literature. These factors were rated according to the degree of importance to each of the decisive events of each of several innovations studied. One of the twenty-one factors was the existence of patent protection for inventions. Patent considerations were ranked ninth among the twenty-one factors and rated moderately or highly important in 47 percent of the decisive events during the innovation process. Of interest, patent considerations were found to be more important to the innovation process than competitive pressures and general economic factors.

Patents have a significant impact not only in the domestic development and commercialization of technology, but also in the international transfer of technology. It is widely accepted that patents play an important role in the export and import of goods and in the international licensing of technology. Patents provide a means of evaluating the subject matter of the license that unpatented technology may not provide. Patents also ensure that the licensee can obtain the exclusive right to make, use, and sell the subject matter of the patent, which is not ensured by a know-how license alone. The patent license also facilitates the simultaneous transfer of unpatented know-how.

Economic analysis and statistical information regarding the impact of patents are interesting and helpful. However, the process of technological development is so complex, involving myriad legal, economic, and social factors, that perhaps it is nearly impossible to isolate and quantify the effects of a single factor such as patents. At least one visitor to the United States some time ago thought that patents were the primary factor responsible for the greatness of the United States. A story reported in the *Congressional Record* states that in 1900, a Japanese government official visited the United States and upon his return to Japan reported, "We have looked about us to see what nations are the greatest so that we can be like them. We said, what is it that makes the United States such a great nation? And we investigated and found that it was patents, and we will have patents.''[36] Today Japan's patent system is one of the most active in the world.

Problems Involved in Utilization of the Patent System

The High Cost of Obtaining a Patent

Until recently, Congress had considered the patent system as serving both the public and the inventor. Though an applicant for a patent has always been charged a fee, this fee has traditionally provided only a fraction of the cost of operating the Patent and Trademark Office, usually between 30 and 60 percent. Although many other countries have imposed taxes (politely called maintenance fees) periodically after issuance of a patent in order to continue it in force, the United States until 1981 had not added that burden to other taxes imposed upon the successful entrepreneur/inventor. Despite efforts by successive administrations to collect sufficient fees from inventors to fully support the Patent and Trademark Office, the Congress declined to do so because it was concerned that added expense would discourage inventors when the intent of the patent system is to encourage them.

Since the enactment of the first patent law near the end of the eighteenth century, Congress had specified precisely the fees to be charged each applicant for a patent. In 1982, policies continuing for almost two centuries were drastically changed. First, the Congress decreed that the inventors should bear the entire cost of the Patent and Trademark Office in examining applications and issuing patents. Second, maintenance fees were authorized for the first time. And third, the Commissioner of Patents and Trademarks was authorized to establish the fees necessary to cover the cost of operating the Patent and Trademark Office. To partially alleviate the impact of these higher fees on the individual inventor and small businesses, the legislation provides that small entities pay one-half of the fees established by the commissioner for patent applicants. This concession does not apply to maintenance fees.

As the Supreme Court has stated, "the specification and claims which constitute a patent is one of the most difficult legal instruments to draw with accuracy."[37] That instrument may be subject to extraordinary scrutiny in litigation. Hence, when an inventor contemplates applying for patent, he or she is usually well advised to consult a competent patent lawyer. Most patent lawyers have scientific or engineering backgrounds that enable them to understand and communicate the inventor's technology. Because they are well trained and experienced, they are well paid. Much of the effort of the lawyer is expended in drafting the claims of the patent that define the metes and bounds of the patented invention. Unless these claims are skillfully prepared, a competitor may find a way to avoid the patent claims and still utilize the invention.

Because most fees of patent lawyers are based on time expended on behalf of their clients, the cost of the preparation and prosecution of an application for a patent depends on the complexity of the invention and the difficulties encountered in processing the application through the Patent and Trademark Office. Even the simplest of inventions may involve legal fees of one or two thousand dollars; more complex (or more important) cases may involve tens of thousands of dollars.

Enforcement of a Patent

Even though the statute (35 U.S.C.S. 101) specifies that a patent is presumed valid, more than half of the patents that are litigated are held invalid by the courts. Hence, even though the inventor has expended a great deal of time, money, and effort to obtain a patent, he continues to run risks if he resorts to litigation in order to enforce his patent right in an effort to exclude competitors from using his patented invention.

Moreover, once a patent has been held invalid by a court from which no appeal is or can be taken, the doctrine of collateral estoppel renders the same patent unenforceable in subsequent litigation.[38]

A major reason why so many patents are found by the courts to be invalid is that the inventor is charged with knowledge of all that has been publicly known before he made his invention, and his patent must define an inventive advance beyond that which was previously publicly known. Unfortunately, neither the inventor nor the patent examiner has any feasible way of ascertaining all prior public knowledge. As a result, many patents are found to be invalid because they fail to distinguish from a prior public use or publication that was not known to the inventor or the patent examiner even though they made every reasonable effort to ascertain all relevant prior art.

Expense of Litigation

Patent litigation, along with antitrust litigation, is considered one of the most complex handled by the federal judiciary. Just as in the case of lawyers who assist inventors who apply for patents, most patent litigation is handled by highly trained (and highly paid) specialists. Both parties to a patent-infringement suit may incur legal expenses of one hundred thousand to one million dollars or more. Because the outcome of patent litigation is so uncertain, very few lawyers will represent patent owners on a contingent fee basis. Also, even the out-of-pocket expenses incurred in an average patent suit amount to tens of thousands of dollars, so only the well-financed patent owner can afford to proceed with litigation even if the lawyer's services were available on a contingent fee basis.

Recently, an entrepreneur has undertaken to underwrite, for a premium, 40 percent of the attorney's fees as well as the out-of-pocket expenses of patent litigation.[39] Where a qualified lawyer gives the underwriter an opinion that the patent will probably be held valid, the expenses of the litigation are insured in the event the patent owner loses. This may encourage more patent owners to undertake litigation to enforce their patents, and more lawyers to take cases on a contingent fee basis. It will enable small entrepreneurs to negotiate from a position of strength, because the extraordinary cost of litigation will no longer be an obstacle.

In addition to the high expense of patent litigation, a long period of time may elapse before the matter is resolved by the courts. Because of prolonged pretrial discovery undertaken by both parties, the congestion of court calendars, and exhaustion of all appeals, patent litigation may not be concluded for many years after it is initiated.

During all of this time of uncertainty, large amounts of time must be expended by the lawyers and by the management personnel of the parties. So it is not only the financial outlay that is involved, but the diversion of key officials from more productive efforts that must be considered as part of the decision making prior to instigating litigation to enforce a patent.

Major Changes in Patent Law Recently Adopted

Reexamination of Issued Patents

On July 1, 1981, H.R. 6933, previously signed into law on December 12, 1980, by President Carter, became effective as Public Law No. 96-517. A key component of this law is a procedure for the administrative reexamination of issued patents. Reexamination has been hailed as one of the most important reforms of this country's patent laws since the first Patent Act of 1790.[40]

An expressed legislative purpose of the reexamination provision is to strengthen investor confidence in the certainty of patent rights.[41] Unfortunately, a general erosion of confidence in the validity of issued patents has purportedly curtailed the availability of venture capital needed to develop inventions, especially inventions made by independent inventors. Strengthening investor confidence will substantially increase venture capital and thereby promote industrial innovation, particularly innovation by independent inventors and small businesses. Many of the most significant innovations in our country's history have been made by independent inventors.

Another expected benefit of the new reexamination system is a moderation of the steadily rising cost of patent litigation. Litigation costs often create an exorbitant financial burden for many small businesses and independent inventors.

A way to correct an often-cited malady of our patent system; that is, the routine issuance of patents of doubtful validity, is now available: the reexamination statute.[42] The reexamination statute provides a quick and relatively simple vehicle for resolving certain questions about the validity of issued patents without having to resort to the protracted nature and often prohibitive expense of patent litigation. Reexamination is available to both patent owners/inventors and adverse parties; that is, to prospective licensees or potential infringers. In fact, there is no requirement that the party requesting reexamination have standing or show any special interest in the validity of the patent.[43] Under the statute, reexamination is initiated simply by filing a request for rexamination under 35 U.S.C. 302 and paying a fee of $1,500. Such a request may be filed by any person and at any time. Provision is made for the Commissioner of Patents and Trademarks to initiate a reexamination, *sua sponte* (by his or her own initiatve).

To start this proceeding, the requestor cites any patents or printed publications that are believed "to have a bearing on the patentability of any claim of a particular patent."[44] Also, the requestor must demonstrate the pertinency of the cited references as well as describe how the references are to be applied to every claim for which reexamination is requested.[45] Within three months after the request has been filed, the commissioner determines whether the newly cited art raises "a substantial new question of patentability affecting any claim of the patent."[46]

In practice, the standard being applied with respect to "a substantial new question of patentability" appears to present a very low threshold. To date, a substantial new question has been found in over 80 percent of the requests filed. The commissioner has refused to grant reexamination requests in instances where a federal court has previously upheld the validity of the claim on the basis of the same or equivalent art.[47] According to statute 35 U.S.C.S. 301-3 (1981), a finding of no "substantial new question of patentability" is final and nonappealable. Under rules that implement the statute, however, such a finding can be reviewed by petition to the commissioner.[48] Under the current rules, 80 percent of the fee is refunded if no "substantial new question of patentability" is found.

Once a substantial new question of patentability is found, an order for reexamination is entered and prosecution before a patent examiner proceeds at an accelerated rate.[49] Although not required, the patent owner initially has two months within which to file a statement on the patentability issue.

In adversely initiated reexaminations, the requestor then has two months to reply. If the patent owner does not file a statement initially, then participation by an adverse requestor ends with the initial request. Thereafter, prosecution proceeds in the normal *ex parte* manner. The patent owner bears the same duty of disclosure during reexamination as imposed on an applicant during the original *ex parte* examination. Claims may be amended or cancelled, and new claims may be added.

As in normal *ex parte* prosecution, any final decision by the primary examiner adverse to any claim in the reexamination application is appealable by the patent owner first to the Board of Appeals, and then to the courts.[50] At present, there is no procedure available for an adverse requestor to appeal a decision favorable to the patent owner. At the close of every reexamination, the commissioner issues a certificate: 1) cancelling any claim determined to be unpatentable; 2) confirming any claim determined to be patentable; and 3) incorporating any new or amended claim determined to be patentable.

The first Reexamination Certificate was issued on December 29, 1981, to Jenn-Air Corporation for U.S. Patent 3,367,320, "Self-Ventilating Cooking Range." As of February 10, 1983, fifty-one additional certificates have issued; two certificates have issued cancelling all claims. About 58 percent of the reexamination requests that have resulted in certificates were initiated by adverse parties. Based on reexamination requests filed, over 64 percent have been initiated by adverse parties. The difference may be an indication that adversely initiated reexaminations are experiencing longer prosecutions, possibly resulting in decisions unfavorable to the patent owner in the Patent Office and thereby necessitating further appeal. Apparently, only one of the patents for which a certificate has issued, U.S. 3,703,718, for an "Infrared Intrusion Detector System," has been involved in published litigation. While denying defendant's motion for summary judgment and for a stay pending the reexamination request filed on plaintiff's patent, the district court did indicate that trial should await the reexamination result.[51] In this case, the reexamination was concluded nine months after the request was filed, less than eight months after the court's opinion. The average pendency of concluded reexaminations has been about one year.

Although the new reexamination statute does provide a relatively quick and inexpensive procedure for resolving certain questions about the validity of issued patents, it does not address all issues bearing on validity. In particular, the reexamination forum is not available for resolution of prior-art issues other than those involving patents and printed publications. Instances of prior public use and prior sale are specifically omitted. Such supplementary validity issues present factual questions that do not readily lend themselves to resolution in the *ex parte* environment of the Patent Office.

Whether reexamination will have the desired beneficial effect on the certainty of patent rights even within its own limited sphere of influence depends heavily on judicial acceptance of the Patent Office's determination of patentability. As a general proposition, courts do not usually invalidate a patent based on references specifically considered by the Patent Office during prosecution of an application. In fact, many courts find a strengthening of the presumption of validity where references cited within litigation were previously considered by the Patent Office. Notably, however, the reexamination statute is entirely void of any reference to the statutory presumption of validity.[52]

Though the congressional purpose of the statute clearly warrants application of the presumption to claims that have survived a full-scale reexamination, it is uncertain whether courts will apply the presumption to cited references leading to a denial of a request for reexamination because of a finding of no substantial new question of patentability. Commentators have also questioned whether reexamination will satisfy the original high expectations because of the limited nature of third-part participation.[53] Indeed, initial judicial reaction seems to support this position. In one case, for example, a district court judge denied a plaintiff's motion, and issued an order for the plaintiff to apply for reissue as a condition of maintaining the action.[54] Patent Office statistics indicate that as of February 19, 1983, in litigation known to involve patents for which reexamination has been requested, courts have issued stays in only about 10 percent of the cases.

The finality of the reexamination process has also been identified as a potential problem source for patent owners.[55] Unless a patent owner can successfully merge a reexamination into a subsequently filed reissue application, the only avenue available from an unsuccessful review before the board of appeals is court review. There is no machinery available in the reexamination procedure for filing continuation applications. Consequently, an initial failure to prepare a complete record before the Patent Office, including affidavit evidence, may significantly jeopardize the patent's chance of surviving reexamination.

Single Court of Appeals for Patent Cases

United States district courts have exclusive original jurisdiction of civil actions arising under the patent and copyright statutes.[56] Until October 1982, all appeals from the district courts were taken to the courts of appeal for the respective circuits.

Review on the decisions of the circuit courts of appeal is possible only by a petition to the Supreme Court for a writ of certiorari, which is infrequently granted. Since 1966, when the Court decided the trilogy of cases[57] interpreting for the first time the "obvious" section[58] of the patent statute enacted in 1952, issues of validity of patents have been decided in only two cases at the Supreme Court level.[59]

Even when the Court grants a writ of certiorari, the odds have heavily favored a result adverse to the patent owner. Many people were blaming the Patent Office for large numbers of invalid patents. This led Justice Jackson to observe in 1949, ". . . I doubt that the remedy for such Patent Office passion for granting patents is an equally strong passion in this Court for striking them down so that the only patent that is valid is one which this Court has not been able to get its hands on."[60]

Often the Supreme Court has refused certiorari even when two or more circuits were in conflict in their interpretation of the patent statute. As a result, interpretation of the patent law in some circuits has differed from the interpretation of the same law in other circuits.

In addition, the decision of some circuit courts, at least statistically, seemed to be antipatent compared with other circuits. This disparity among the several circuits led to forum shopping for the jurisdiction that seemed most favorable to a particular cause. Many times there was even a race to the courthouse when a prospective defendant tried to select the best anti-patent jurisdiction by filing a declaratory judgment action.

Over the last several decades, many proposals have been advanced to establish more uniformity in the application of the patent laws by different circuits, but most of these efforts did not even reach the stage of pending legislation. In 1978, responding primarily to demands for reduction in the load of the Supreme Court, the Department of Justice recommended the establishment of a National Court of Appeals to substitute for the Supreme Court in certain specialized areas, including patents, taxes, trademarks, and copyrights.

This proposal encountered a storm of protest from those interested in each of the fields of law involved. It was opposed by the American Bar Association. Even the patent bar was divided. But that part of the juris-diction concerned with patent cases was supported by a recommendation of the Committee for Economic Development that a single patent appeals court be established to eliminate inconsistency.[61] As ultimately enacted the Court of Claims and the Court of Customs and Patent Appeals were com-bined into the Court of Appeals for the Federal Circuit and combined juris-diction of the two courts enlarged to include appeals in patent cases.[62]

In addition to elimination of conflicts and other disparities among the several circuits, the expertise of the judges of the Court of Customs and Patent Appeals may bring a better understanding of the intricacies of patent law to the new court. It is hoped that the practice of filling at least some vacancies with patent specialists will be continued to achieve more certainty and more uniformity of the interpretation of the patent laws. Establishment of the Court of Appeals for the Federal Circuit does not mean that the Supreme Court will henceforth avoid patent cases. Since 1966 when the Court held that the Court of Customs and Patent Appeals was an Article III court to which certiorari could be granted,[63] the Supreme Court has decided four cases appealed from the Patent Office to the court of Customs and Patent Appeals, reversing two and affirming two.[64] Thus, we may expect the Supreme Court to continue to grant certiorari on a very selective basis when it considers the issues to be of sufficient importance.

Arbitration of Patent Disputes

"A major deterrent to using the patent system, especially by small businesses and independent inventors, is the inordinately high cost of patent litigation."[65] This observation was recently articulated by President Reagan as he signed a bill expanding the range of arbitrable patent disputes to include the issues of patent validity and patent infringement. The new act, which became effective on February 27, 1982,[66] authorizes voluntary, binding arbitration in these cases under the U.S. Arbitration Act.[67] It is expected to improve the patent system, stimulate innovation, and aid in relieving the burden on the federal courts brought about over the past few decades by a litigation explosion.

Arbitration has long been recognized as an attractive alternative to expensive and lengthy court litigation. The U.S. Arbitration Act, enacted in 1925 to decrease delay and expense through binding arbitration, has served as a guide in the arbitration of disputes since its inception, and most states have adopted some rendition of this federal act. Historically, mediation and arbitration were used to settle controversies, and these methods are currently utilized internationally to a large degree instead of the courts. In spite of its widespread acceptance as an economical and effective means of resolving disputes, judicial decisions since about 1930 have held arbitration inappropriate for patent disputes involving validity and infringement issues. Although courts have generally enforced arbitration awards in patent disputes in which royalties, licensing agreements, and other factual questions were at issue,[68] they have consistently refused to uphold awards where a question of validity or infringement was concerned.[69]

The U.S. Arbitration Act provides for arbitration of controversies resulting from commerce or maritime transactions.[70] In *Zip Mfg. Co.* v. *Pep Mfg. Co.,* the court rejected a request to stay litigation pending results of an arbitration proceedings.[71] The court based its decision on its determination that the controversy arose from alleged infringement of a patent and involved neither commerce nor maritime transactions as defined by the act. Other courts have applied the same narrow construction in limiting the scope of the act to maritime and commerce issues.[72]

"The great public interest in challenging invalid patents" was established as additional rationale for holding questions of validity and infringement inappropriate for arbitration in *Lear* v. *Adkins*.[73] In using the public-interest theory, the court in *Diematic Mfg. Corp.* v. *Packaging Industries, Inc.* stated that

> Questions of patent law are not mere private matters. The patent laws, in sharp contrast to the general federal policy encouraging free competition expressed in the antitrust laws, grant limited monopolies to inventors. Thus, the . . . grave public interest in questions of patent validity and infringement renders them inappropriate for determination in arbitration proceedings.[74]

The latter public-interest theory has emerged in more recent cases as controlling precedent in proscribing arbitration in validity and infringement disputes.[75]

Several prior attempts to legislate patent arbitration were unsuccessful in spite of continuing support by the patent bar, the American Arbitration Association, private industry, and the American Bar Association.

The advantages of arbitration are many. It is cheaper, faster, more informal, and more private than litigation, and parties can stipulate to discovery processes to minimize abuses of those processes.[76] But perhaps the most significant advantage of the new act is that experts in patent matters can be chosen by the parties as arbitrators. If the selected arbitrators are experienced patent litigators, they will require less time to grasp technical and legal issues, and will be able to control pretrial discovery. This should result in dramatic reductions of time and costs.

In its report accompanying H.R. 6260, the House Committee on the Judiciary emphasized the fact that arbitrators are usually better versed than judges and juries in the area of technologies involved in patent disputes.[77] The importance of this concept was acknowledged by Chief Judge Henry J. Friendly of the Second Circuit in *General Tire & Rubber Company* v. *Jefferson Chemical Co.* "This patent appeal is another illustration of the absurdity of requiring the decision of such cases to be made by judges whose knowledge of the relevant technology derives primarily or even solely from explanations by counsel. . . ."[78]

An experienced litigator is also of great import to the success of an arbitration proceeding. A knowledge of the procedural and evidentiary rules used in court litigation is rudimentary to the application of simpler ones that allow more flexibility. One major weakness of most arbitration structures is that arbitrators are not compensated adequately.[79] To assure success of the new act, arbitrators should be carefully chosen from the patent profession and compensated accordingly.

Arbitration under the new act, with its many advantages, can enhance the patent system and encourage innovation. Most importantly, it can serve to remove the prolonged uncertainties of patent litigation and lessen the disruption of parties' businesses. These are often more significant than the actual costs of patent litigation.

International Arrangements

In today's world of instant communications, supersonic travel, and global markets, an entrepreneur must contemplate protection of an invention in countries other than his or her own. This is essential to exclude competitors in other countries and to facilitate the transfer of technology. There is no substantive international patent law. Patents have no extraterritorial effect; patent protection does not extend beyond the borders of the country granting the patent.

In 1883 most of the western European countries with the United States negotiated the Paris Convention for the Protection of Industrial Property, which is the basic international arrangement concerned with patents and trademarks.[80] Now more than one hundred years old and having survived two world wars, the Paris Convention for the Protection of Industrial Property has more than eight members. The Paris Convention for the Protection of Industrial Property is based on a fundamental principle of international law known as *national treatment*, which means that any country may establish whatever national law it wishes concerning patents and trademarks, but guarantees the same rights and obligations to foreigners as it applies to its own nationals.[81]

In addition the Paris Convention for the Protection of Industrial Property provides uniform priority periods.[82] Priority periods are times within which a national of any member state may apply for a patent or trademark in another state and gain the benefit of the original filing date in the country where he or she first applied. These priority periods are twelve months for patents and six months for trademarks.

Each member of the Paris Convention for the Protection of Industrial Property undertakes certain minimum obligations. For example, patents in each member country are independent of patents obtained for the same invention in other countries[83]; a period of at least six months grace is accorded for the payment of fees to maintain patents or trademark registration[84]; registration of trademarks may not be refused or cancelled because filing or renewal has not been effected in the country of origin[85]; registered trademarks are independent of marks registered in other countries[86]; there are prohibitions against registration as marks of flags, state emblems, and so on[87]; and there are prohibitions against seizure of articles bearing a trademark registered in the country.[88]

Unlike the United States, many countries impose upon patent owners an obligation to use the patented invention. The patent owner must manufacture the patented article or utilize the patented process in the country where it is patented. Failure to work the patented invention may subject the patent owner to sanctions such as compulsory licensing of the patented invention or forfeiture of the patent. The Paris Convention for the Protection of Industrial Property places certain limitations upon the sanctions that may be applied. An application for a compulsory license may not be made until the latter of four years after the filing date or three years after the patent grant[89]; and forfeiture of the patent may not be effected until two years after grant of the first compulsory license.[90] Since 1980, a diplomatic conference has been underway for revision of the Paris Convention primarily to negotiate some concessions demanded by developing countries such as compulsory exclusive licenses; forfeiture of patents without prior compulsory license; and advance protection in all countries of geographic name indigenous to developing countries. Sessions of the diplomatic conference of a month's duration were held in 1980, 1981, and 1982. Another session is scheduled for late 1983 or early 1984.

In addition to the basic Paris Convention for the Protection of Industrial Property, there are several subsidiary treaties, the most significant of which are the Patent Cooperation Treaty and the Trademark Registration Treaty. The Patent Cooperation Treaty was negotiated in 1970; most industrial countries, including the United States,[91] have adhered to it. This treaty provides some uniformity in the formal requirements of patent applications in all countries and recognizes a single application in one country as an application in all designated countries, subject to later compliance with the requirements of each designated country.

The Trademark Registration Treaty would similarly provide greater uniformity of applications for registration of trademarks in various countries as well as a centralized filing system. As yet, the United States has not adhered to the Trademark Registration Treaty because it would require some modification of our trademark law, which bases the rights in trademarks and registration of them on actual prior use of the trademarks in interstate commerce.

Potential Future Improvements

Protecting Inventions of Lesser Importance

Because the U.S. Supreme Court applies such a high standard of invention to determine what is and what is not patentable (that is, what patent is or is not valid), there have been many proposals that the statute be amended to define a lower standard of invention. That, in fact, is what the proponents of the so-called *obvious* test tried to do by including 35 U.S.C. 103 in the Patent Act of 1952. However, the Supreme Court has repeatedly said that there is a constitutional standard of invention that must be met in order to be patentable, and that the Congress does not have the power to define a lower standard in the statute.

Those who desire to improve the standard of patentability (standard of invention) by lowering the standard are really asking how we can protect the vast area of innovation and technological development between that which is in the public domain and that which satisfies the constitutional standard of patentability. An answer to that question is found in the patent laws of Germany and Japan. Both of those countries recognize two standards or levels of innovation: one of a certain scope and term for the higher level, and a second of lesser scope and shorter term for the lower level.

This approach has already been recognized in some specialized areas. A few years ago, the U.S. Congress responded to pressure from the seed growers by supplementing the patent protection of asexually produced plants.[92] (The Plant Variety Protection Act protects sexually produced seeds and plants; that act is administered by the Department of Agriculture.)[93]

In 1977, a committee of nongovernmental experts, working in Geneva under the auspices of the World Intellectual Property Organization, evolved a Model Law for the Protection of Computer Software.[94] That model law would provide different levels of protection for algorithms, flow charts, source codes, and object codes.

Limited protection for such lower levels of innovation or invention will induce more venture capital to be invested in development of new products that are not now exploited. By offering the entrepreneur even a short-term monopoly against imitation and copying, new products can be brought to the marketplace, thereby aiding the economy and increasing employment. We must balance the social and economic gains from such encouragement to the entrepreneur against the imagined evils of a limited monopoly. If as a matter of policy we decide that limited protection of lesser innovations and inventions is desirable, we still have problems to solve in the implementation of such a system. According to the Supreme Court, inventions must satisfy the constitutional standard of invention in order to enjoy the monopoly authorized by article I, section 8 of the Constitution. Perhaps Congress may find the power under the commerce clause or exercise the treaty power to legislate protection,[95] limited in scope and term, for innovations and inventions that do not satisfy the constitutional standard. Otherwise, the only solution will be by way of amendment to the Constitution.

Better Examination

An issued patent is presumed to be valid by the courts. This presumption, however, extends only to those matters actually considered during the proceedings before the Patent and Trademark office. Thus, if new prior art surfaces after a patent is issued and if it contains subject matter similar to the invention, the patent's presumption of validity is destroyed. A court is then free to evaluate the patentability of the invention *de novo*.

The quality of the examination, therefore, can directly affect the value of a patent. The better the prior art considered by the Patent and Trademark Office, the stronger the patent's presumption of validity. If the examination of the patent considers the best art, enforcement of the patent should be more predictable, making strategic planning less risky. Furthermore, it would reduce the number of instances where close prior art comes to light after issuance of the patent when the patent owner has lost the option of maintaining the invention as a trade secret.

There are benefits to be gained in the areas of predictability and enforcement, therefore, when a patent application is subjected to a rigorous examination. Even the courts have tempered the presumption of validity, as a result of a perceived lack of quality in Patent and Trademark Office examination.[96] Thus, improved examination by the Patent and Trademark Office should result in patents of greater value to their owners and strengthen the presumption of validity of patents in our courts.

Certainly, the foundation of high-quality examination is finding the best or closest prior art and bringing it before the patent and Trademark Office. The revolution in information sciences is beginning to have an impact on prior-art searches. Computerized databases are being used and as these databases expand, the reliability of prior-art searches will increase accordingly. Probably the largest accessible database in technical fields is the full text of all United States patents issued since 1970. Those issued since 1975 are included in the LEXPAT search service recently announced by Mead Data Corporation. Though it is in the patent applicant's interest to conduct the most thorough prior-art search possible, the reality is that the burden often falls on the Patent and Trademark Office, and automation should improve the result. The planned automation of the Patent and Trademark Office and the access of examiners to computerized databases will also play an important role.

A more fundamental change in the methods employed by the Patent and Trademark Office could lead to higher-quality examinations. The Patent and Trademark Office currently conducts examinations *ex parte*. Patent applications are maintained in confidence by the Patent and Trademark Office so that third-party comments do not generally play a role in Patent and Trademark Office proceedings. Except for appeal, a single examiner is usually responsible for searching the prior art and determining the patentability of an invention. Thus, the quality of an examination can vary widely depending on the ability of the particular examiner and the examiner's grasp of the prior art.

Examination by the Patent and Trademark Office can be contrasted with examination conducted by the European Patent Office, which is responsible for issuing European patents. Established by the European Patent Convention (EPC),[97] European patents issued by the European Patent Office have the effect of national patents in the 103 member countries designated by the applicant.[98] The European Patent Office conducts possibly the most thorough examination of any patent office in the world. The differences between European Patent Office and U.S. Patent and Trademark Office examinations highlight methods that could improve Patent and Trademark Office procedures.

Each European patent application is examined at two different locations by at least four specialized examiners. A preliminary review of formal requirements comes first.[99] Each application is reviewed by the Receiving Station at The Hague, Netherlands, to ensure that the minimum requirements of content and form have been met before granting a filing date. Each application is submitted to the Search Division of the European Patent Office located at The Hague.[100] The prior-art search, conducted by a specialized search examiner, results in a search report that is published with the application. The search usually takes three to six months and systematically includes, at a minimum, the patent literature of France, the Federal Republic of Gemany, Japan, Switzerland, the Soviet Union, the United Kingdom, and the United States, as well as important periodicals and texts. The search report contains a listing of the art relevant to the pending claims, but does not comment on the ultimate patentability of the claims.[101]

The search report and the patent application are then published.[102] Generally, publication occurs as soon as possible eighteen months after the earlier of the filing date or date of priority. Publication of the application confers limited protection on the applicant that can vary among the member countries. Each country, however, is at least required to provide reasonable compensation for infringement after publication.[103]

After publication of the application and search report, the applicant can then request substantive examination to determine patentability.[104] The Examination Division, located in Munich, is composed of three technical examiners and, if necessary, one "legally qualified" examiner.[105] In certain simplified cases the number may be lowered to one examiner in an examining division. Although generally only one of these examiners handles the initial prosecution of a particular application, the entire examination division makes all final decisions on whether to allow or deny an application.

The system employed at the European Patent Office offers several advantages over that employed by the U.S. Patent and Trademark Office. First, full-time search examiners conduct the prior-art search. This results in skilled, efficient, and thorough searches. Second, more than one examiner is involved in the determination of patentability, including special legally trained examiners. The collective decisions of such a group are probably better than that of a single examiner. Adoption of these methods would improve the quality of examinations at the Patent and Trademark Office simply because more human resources would be applied to each application. Of course, such a reform would doubtlessly be more expensive.

Publication of patent applications might also be considered in the United States since it can have several benefits. A modified EPC approach workable in the United States might involve publishing a patent application after the applicant has had a chance to review the search report and request substantive examination. In return for early disclosure, the patent application could be granted limited protection. A patent applicant would, therefore, retain the opportunity to abandon the application in light of all the prior art and maintain the invention as a trade secret. Alternatively, the applicant could obtain early protection for the invention by publication. Furthermore, competitors would be able to evaluate their strategic planning in light of the potential patent rights, as well as have the benefits of the applicant's research sooner.

Extension of the Patent Term

Another proposed improvement in the U.S. patent system is designed to compensate for problems caused by government regulations, not any inherent problem in the patent system. A patent has a seventeen-year term that runs from its date of issue. There is a presumption that a monopoly of seventeen years is a fair exchange for the disclosure to the public of the invention. In certain regulated industries (particularly the food and drug industry and chemical industries such as agrichemicals), a product must be submitted to years of testing and receive federal certification before it can be commercially exploited. Some in the regulated industries claim that the average regulatory delay is in the neighborhood of seven to nine years. Federal regulatory proceedings, therefore, often substantially reduce the useful life of a patent to its owner.

Legislation designed to compensate the patent owner for these regulatory delays yet maintain vital safety regulation by the federal government has been proposed. In the ninety-seventh Congress, a bill passed the Senate that would extend the term of the patent up to seven years when its useful life was shortened by protracted regulatory proceedings.[106] The bill was aimed primarily at food, drugs, cosmetics, insecticides, pesticides, and rodenticides. The House, however, failed to pass either the House equivalent of the Senate bill[107] or a much more complicated bill[108] that would have restricted patent-term extension vis-à-vis the Senate bill. All of these bills died at the close of the ninety-seventh Congress.

One minor patent-term-extension bill was passed by the ninety-seventh Congress and enacted into law. It is called the Orphan Drug Act, and it is designated to compensate a manufacturer for its investment in the development of a drug for which there is a limited market.[109] Compensation takes the form of an extension of the patent term. The law is intended to benefit a very small group: those afflicted with a severe, rare disease where the economics would not attract drug-company investment in a cure.

Incontestable Patent

Incontestability is a familiar concept in U.S. industrial property law. It was introduced into the Lanham Trademark Act in 1947. However, the incontestability of trademarks, and that which might be proposed for patents, is perhaps better referred to as a *limited incontestability* because under existing trademark law and under any proposal that would be acceptable for the patent law, trademarks and patents could always be contexted at any time under certain grounds. The concept of incontestability for patents discussed herein is intended to refer to the removal of some bases of invalidity after a certain period of time has elapsed since the patent was issued.

A reasonable period beyond which the validity of a patent could no longer be challenged under certain grounds would appear to be from five to seven years. This is consistent with the five-year period used in the Trademark Law. Prior to the beginning of the incontestable period, all defenses against a patent could be asserted against its validity. After the incontestable period has begun, that is, five to seven years after the patent has issued, the validity of the patent could only be challenged by certain limited defenses under section 102 of patent law 35 U.S.C.S. (1981), which requires novelty, or for fraud in the procurement of the patent. Questions of infringement would not be affected by the incontestable patent.

Essentially, the proposal for an incontestable patent would eliminate the more subjective defenses of challenges to the validity of the patent, such as obviousness under section 103 of the patent law. With these more subjective challenges eliminated, an entrepreneur could, with much less risk, invest in an invention and bring it to the marketplace with a significantly greater certainty that its validity will be maintained. To an entrepreneur, the process of innovation may be viewed as a process of uncertainty reduction.

As an invention proceeds thorugh the stages of innovation, the investment increases and information is produced that allows a more accurate estimate of a project's economic and technical potential. As the investment becomes larger, the evidence must increasingly point out the profitability to justify continuation. A patent that becomes incontestable approximately five to seven years after its issuance would provide a much more certain basis on which an entrepreneur could judge the risk of proceeding with an invention.

Conclusion

The patent system in the United States provides incentives for entrepreneurs to invent, to invest in the inventions of others, to inform the public about the technology involved in inventions, and to imitate inventions of others by designing around their patents. As Abraham Lincoln said, "Patents add the fuel of interest to the fire of genius."

For almost two centuries, our patent system has served us well; it is at least partially responsible for the technological leadership our nation has enjoyed. Though Congress has imposed on inventors added costs of obtaining and maintaining patents, it has provided mechanisms that may make it less expensive and more certain to enforce their patent rights.

These legislative improvements are the result of an awakening of the patent industry (patent bar) to the need for increasing the awareness of government decision makers to the needs of entrepreneurs and industry for a strong and dependable patent system. This political activity should result in further improvements and added incentives for entrepreneurs to make and exploit inventions.

Notes

1. United States Credit System Co. v. American Indemnity Co., 51 F. 751, 754 (N.D. Ill. 1892).

2. *In re Levin*, 178 F.2d 945 (C.C.P.A. 1949).

3. Morrison, "Ice Cream Chic at Haagen-Dazs," *Fortune*, March 9, 1981, at 120.

4. Hotel Security Checking Co. v. Lorraine Co., 160 F. 467 (2d Cir. 1908).

5. 409 U.S. 63 (1972); 437 U.S. 584 (1978); 450 U.S. 175 (1981).

6. 409 U.S., at 71–72.

7. 437 U.S., at 594.

8. 450 U.S., at 184.

9. 214 U.S.P.Q. 682 (C.C.P.A. 1982).

10. Melville B. Nimmer, *Nimmer on Copyright* (New York: M. Bender, 1978), 204(c).

11. 17 U.S.C.S. 101 (emphasis added).

12. 524 F. Supp. 171 (N.D. Cal. 1981).

13. Baker v. Selden, 101 U.S. 99 (1879).

14. 497 F. Supp. 154 (S.D.N.Y. 1980), *aff'd* 657 F.2d 262 (2d Cir. 1981).

15. 497 F. Supp., at 157–58.

16. 513 F.2d 1183 (2d Cir. 1975).

17. Id. at 1188.

18. 253 F.2d 702 (2d Cir. 1958).

19. Id. at 706.

20. 140 F.2d 182 (7th Cir. 1944).

21. Id. at 184–85.

22. 446 F.2d 738 (9th Cir. 1971).

23. Id. at 742.

24. 462 F. Supp. 1003 (N.D. Tex. 1979).

25. Id. at 1014.

26. Midway Mfg. Co. v. Arctic International Inc., 547 F. Supp. 999 (N.D. Ill. 1982); Midway Mfg. Co. v. Dirkschneider, 543 F. Supp. 466 (D. Neb. 1981); Stern Electronics, Inc. v. Kaufman, 523 F. Supp. 635 (E.D.N.Y. 1981), *aff'd*, 669 F.2d 852 (2d Cir. 1982).

27. 547 F. Supp. 222 (D. Md. 1981).

28. Id. at 230.

29. Shoor, "Software Litigation Trends," *Computerworld*, December 29, 1980, p. 71.

30. World Intellectual Property Organization, *Model Provisions on the Protection of Computer Software* (Washington, D.C.: 1978).

31. Federal Trademark Act of 1946 (Lanham Act), 45, 15 U.S.C. 1127.

32. Bayer Co. v. United Drug Co., 272 F. 505 (D.C.N.Y. 1921); King-Seeley Thermos Co. v. Aladdin Industries, Inc., 321 F.2d 577 (2d Cir. 1963); Kellogg Co. v. National Biscuit Co., 305 U.S. 111 (1938); DuPont Cellophane Co. v. Waxed Products Co., 85 F.2d 75 (2d Cir. 1936), *cert. denied*, 299 U.S. 601 (1936); Anti-Monopoly, Inc. v. General Mills Fun Group, Inc., 684 F.2d 1316 (9th Cir. 1982).

33. Jewkes, Sawyers, and Stillerman, *Sources of Invention*, 2d ed. (New York: Norton, 1971), pp. 187–188.

34. Batelle-Columbus Laboratories, *Interaction of Science and Technology and the Innovative Process* (Washington, D.C.: National Science Foundation, 1973).

35. Charles River Associates, Inc., *Innovation, Competition and Government Policy in the Semiconductor Industry* (1980) (report prepared for the U.S. Department of Commerce, Washington, D.C.), pp. 13–46.

36. *Congressional Record* (January 29, 1962), p. 991.

37. Topliff v. Topliff, 145 U.S. 126 (1982).

38. Blonder-Tongue Laboratories v. University of Illinois Foundation, 402 U.S. 313 (1971).

39. Atlas Underwriters, Ltd., Washington, D.C.

40. Kaberon, "New Patent Law Becomes Effective Today," *The Chicago Law Bulletin*, July 1, 1981; Quigg, "Post-Issuance Re-Examination: An Inventive Attempt at Reform," *National Law Journal*, June 1, 1981.

41. H.R. Rep. No. 1307, 96th Cong., 2d Sess. (1980).

42. 35 U.S.C.S. 301–307.

43. United States Patent and Trademark Office, *Manual of Patent Examining Procedure*, 2212 (4th ed., rev. 8, October 1981), (Washington, D.C.: Government Printing Office, 1981).

44. 35 U.S.C.S. 301.

45. 35 U.S.C.S. 302.

46. 35 U.S.C.S. 303.

47. *In re Pearne*, 212 U.S.P.Q. 466 (Comm'r Pat. 1981); *In re Wichterle*, 213 U.S.P.Q. 868 (Comm'r Pat. 1982); *In re Hunter*, 213 U.S.P.Q. 211 (Comm'r Pat. 1982).

48. 37 C.F.R. 1.515 (1981).

49. U.S.C.S. 305.

50. 35 U.S.C.S. 134; 35 U.S.C.S. 141–145; Committee Report on the Patent Reexamination Subcommittee, *American Patent Law Association Bulletin*, March-April 1981, at 150–51.

51. Raytek, Inc. v. Solfan Systems, Inc., 211 U.S.P.Q. 405 (N.D. Cal. 1981).

52. 35 U.S.C.S. 282.

53. Adamo, "Reexamination—To What Avail? An Overview," 63 *Journal of the Patent Office Society* (1981).

54. Dresser Industries, Inc. v. Ford Motor Co., 530 F. Supp. 303 (N.D. Tex. 1981).

55. Morgan, "Hobson's Choice: Reexamination or Reissue?" 14 *Intellectual Property Law Review* (1981).

56. 28 U.S.C.S. 1338(a).

57. Graham v. John Deere Co.; Calamar, Inc. v. Cook Chemical Co.; Colgate-Palmolive Co. v. Cook Chemical Co., 383 U.S. 1,865 S.Ct. 708, 15 L.Ed. 2d 545 (1966); United States v. Adams, et al., 383 U.S. 39 S.Ct. 708, 15 L.Ed. 572 (1966).

58. 35 U.S.C.S. 103.

59. Anderson's Black Rock, Inc. v. Pavement Salvage Co., Inc., 396 U.S. 57, 90 S.Ct. 305, 24 L.Ed. 2d 258 (1969); Sakrida v. AgPro, Inc., 425 U.S. 273, 96 S.Ct. 1532, 47 L.Ed. 2d 784 (1976).

60. Jungerson v. Ostby, 335 U.S. 560, 69 S.Ct. 269, 93 L.Ed. 2d 235 (1949).

61. Research and Policy Committee of the Committee for Economic Development, *Stimulating Technological Progress* (New York, 1980).

62. Federal Courts Improvements Act, P.L. 97-164 96 Stat. 25 (1982).

63. Brenner v. Mason, 383 U.S. 519 (1966).

64. Gottschalk v. Benson, 409 U.S. 63 (1972); Parker v. Flook, 437 U.S. 584 (1978); Diamond v. Chakrabarty, 447 U.S. 303 (1980); Diamond v. Diehr, 450 U.S. 175 (1981).

65. Statement by the President, White House Press Release (August 28, 1982).

66. 35 U.S.C.S. 1.

67. 9, U.S.C.S. (1981).

68. Hanes Corp. v. Millard, 531 F.2d 585 (D.C. Cir. 1976); Levin v. Ripple Twist Mills, Inc., 416 F. Supp. 876 (E.D. Penn. 1976).

69. Diematic Mfg. Corp. v. Packaging Industries, Inc., 381 F. Supp. 1057 (S.D.N.Y.) 1974); Zip Mfg. Co. v. Packaging Industries, Inc., 44 F.2d 194 (D. Del. 1930).

70. 9 U.S.C.S. 1.

71. 44 F.2d 194 (D. Del. 1930).

72. Leesona Corp. v. Cotwool Mfg. Co., 204 F. Supp. 141 (W.D. S. Car. 1962).

73. 395 U.S. 653 (1969).

74. 381 F. Supp. 1057 (S.D.N.Y. 1974).

75. Beckman Instruments, Inc. v. Technical Developments Corp., 433 F.2d 55 (7th Cir. 1970); Foster Wheeler Corp. v. Babcock & Wilcox, Inc., 440 F. Supp. 897 (S.D.N.Y. 1977).

76. Hoellering, 188 *New York Journal* No. 115, p. 1 (Dec. 1982).

77. H.R. Rep. No. 542, 97th Cong., 2d Sess. (1982).

78. 497 F.2d 1283 (2d Cir. 1974).

79. Janicke and Borovoy, "Resolving Patent Disputes by Arbitration: An Alternative to Litigation," *Journal of the Patent Office Society* 337 (1980).

80. Stockholm Act 21 U.S.T. 1583; Treaties and International Agreements Service 6923, 7727 (1967).

81. Id., article 2(1).

82. Id., article 4.

83. Id., article 3.

84. Id., article 5 bis.

85. Id., article 6(3).

86. Id., article 6(3).

87. Id., article 6 ter.

88. Id., article 9.

89. Id., article 5A(4).

90. Id., article 5A(3).

91. Treaties and International Agreements Service 8733 (1978).

92. 35 U.S.C.S. 161–164.

93. 7 U.S.C.S. 2321–2583.

94. World Intellectual Property Organization Doc. AGCP/NGO/IV/7 (June 7, 1977).

95. Protection of utility models is covered by the Paris Convention.

96. *See, e.g.,* Graham v. John Deere Co., 383 U.S. 1, 18–19 (1966); Lemelson v. Topper Corp., 450 F.2d 845, 849 (2d Cir. 1971); Lorenz v. F.W. Woolworth Co., 305 F.2d 105 (2d Cir. 1962).

97. Convention on the Grant of European Patents and Attached Annexes and Draft Guidelines, *entered into force* October 7, 1977, J. Sinnott, 2H *World Patent Law* (1978). Hereinafter referred to as European Patent Convention.

98. Member countries include Austria, Belgium, France, Federal Republic of Germany, Italy, Liechtenstein, Luxembourg, Netherlands, Sweden, Switzerland, and the United Kingdom.

99. European Patent Convention, articles 90 and 91.

100. European Patent Convention, article 92.

101. Id., European Patent Convention, Implementing Regulations, rules 44–46 (hereinafter cited as rules).

102. European Patent Convention, article 93; rules 48–49.

103. Id., article 67.

104. Id., article 94.

105. Id., article 33(3).

106. S. 255, 97th Cong., 1st Sess. (1981).

107. H.R. 1937, 97th Cong., 1st Sess. (1981).

108. H.R. 6444, 97th Cong., 2nd Sess. (1982).

109. Pub. L. No. 97-414, 11(a), 96 Stat. 2065 (1983), (to be codified at 35 U.S.C. 155).

8

The European Environment for Entrepreneurship

Madsen Pirie

I could start this discussion by listing the obstacles and impediments to entrepreneurs in Europe, and then outline the reforms needed to improve the situation. I shall not do that. I shall not follow that procedure (1) because it is inherently dull, and (2) because it would give a wrong impression. The barriers to the entrepreneur in Europe are many and formidable, but life is a lot more fun if one treats such barriers as problems to be solved, as temporary aberrations to be removed.

Belgian Free Zones

I shall start with some of the good news. On December 29th, 1982, the Belgian government published an act to authorize the setting up of *free zones* within Belgium.[1] Industry and business inside those free zones will have seven different company taxes abolished. Out will go the tax on profits, and those on dividends and interest. Off goes the tax on landed property and the tax on the registration of share capital. The taxes on energy consumption and labor will not apply either.[2]

Bureaucracy will be reduced in the free zones because only one agency, the zone authority itself, will deal with the issue of permits, and this body is expected to reach its decisions within one month of the application. There is a certain amount of deregulation, because many Belgian laws covering employment will not apply to foreigners within the zones. Finally, the act, which the Belgians call the T-Zone Act, says that there will be no local taxes in the free zones, and that regional and local powers on such things as pollution and building codes must be delegated to the zone authority.

The bad news is that none of this applies to the rest of Belgium. Businesses outside these tiny zones will still pay a profits tax of 45 percent, a 20-percent tax on dividends and interest, a 3-percent tax on property, a 1-percent tax on the registration of share capital, a tax of just over $6 on every kilowatt of engine power, and a tax of about $4 every year for each employee! Outside of the new free zones, Belgian business will remain heavily regulated at both local and national levels, and business will still face an avalanche of paper whenever they try to do anything at all.

Yet the news is good. It is good because it represents a new outlook, a new mood, and the start of a new way of treating business activity. Business

155

is the source of wealth for society. It is the goose that lays the golden eggs. When a country wishes to inaugurate welfare programs, to initiate public projects, or to finance what it regards as worthwhile activity, it is the golden eggs, dutifully laid by the business goose, that give it the means.

The traditional way in which governments have treated that goose has been to bind its feet, clip its wings, and wring its neck; and then, perhaps, to complain that it was failing the nation. The good news about the new attitude is that governments are beginning to think that if you leave the goose alone and maybe give it a little more space, then perhaps you will get more eggs out of it. This change in attitude is evidenced by the trend toward enterprise zones, which create deregulated areas in which business can prosper. The United Kingdom and Belgium have already passed such legislation, while several other EEC (European Economic Community) countries are moving toward it.

If the Belgian free zones are successful, maybe the Belgian government will want more of them. Perhaps the whole of Belgium will demand equal freedom. Certainly the rest of Europe will not be left out. But more of that later. Belgium perfectly illustrates the entrepreneurial climate in Europe. In four words, it is *bad but getting better*.

Impediments to Entrepreneurial Activity

There are three main sources of impediment to entrepreneurial activity: government, unions, and bureaucrats. Anyone wishing to start up in Europe with a new product or process has to deal with all three. Governments impose taxes that raise business costs directly, and impose regulations costly to comply with. Unions increase the wage bill by enforcing the inefficient use of labor. Bureaucrats require compliance with an array of detailed rules, many of them baffling and even absurd to the outsider, but all of them expensive and time-consuming.

There is a fourth drag on successful enterprise, one that is harder to pin down. It is the climate of public opinion. There is no doubt that for several decades opinion in Europe has been more hostile to business activity than has opinion in the United States. Businessmen have been regarded as selfish, interested only in gain. Profit making has been sneered at as worship of money. Trading itself has been regarded as sordid. The British Broadcasting Corporation (BBC) in Britain, for example, was established as a state broadcasting service, supported by taxation so it would not face contamination by the commercial world. Until very recently orchestral music and the arts in much of Europe was supported more by state subsidy than by commercial sponsorship. Regulations controlling advertising are much tighter in Europe than in the United States.

By contrast Europeans have admired public service, and the celebrities who make a name in the professions. Polls taken just three years ago in Europe showed that more than four times as many students regarded a career as a public servant worthwhile as did a career in business. The prevalent view was that of the well-to-do middle classes. With their own paychecks from the government secure, they showed a passionate and genuine concern that the environment should be protected from unpleasant industrial activity, and that the wealth of business should be redistributed in the interest of social justice to make a fairer society.

Good News

Despite all these impediments, there is good news. Governments and unions can be influenced, and bureaucrats can be sidestepped. All of this has happened recently with considerable success in Europe. Even the negative public attitude toward entrepreneurship is changing. The general view of entrepreneurship is more favorable than it has been for decades, probably in no small part a result of the current world recession.

Over a hundred years ago, when Queen Victoria sat on the throne in England, people looked at the rising industrial chimneys and thought of jobs, wealth creation, and a rising standard of living. For much of this century, certainly in the second half of it, people in Europe have thought of industry as a blot on the landscape, a kind of curse that afflicts the environment. Now opinion has spun full circle, and local communities across Europe bid against each other to attract the once-hated factories. This is evidenced by the public money now offered to foreign businesses prepared to move in. John DeLorean, who misspent millions of pounds of British taxpayers' money to produce luxury sports cars in Belfast, is only one among hundreds of foreign business beneficiaries across Europe. Pressure groups that once campaigned against the noise and dirt of industrial development have been replaced by those which campaign for its expansion. Once more the talk is of jobs and prosperity instead of pollution and exploitation.

The once-admired career of public servant has never stood lower in popular esteem. The word *bureaucrat* is taken to be an insult, and there is wide recognition that those who are called public servants have to be carefully controlled if they are not to become our masters. The bureaucrat is now a figure of fun. He carries a rolled umbrella, a briefcase, and a copy of the London *Times*. He sits at a desk and shuffles paper all day, pausing for frequent cups of tea. He is perceived as a small-minded nitpicker whose life is governed by the rulebook, and who arrives late, leaves early, and retires on an overgenerous index-linked pension paid for by honest people. This popular image is important as well as amusing. It serves to lower the caliber of people entering the profession, and make the ambitious and talented seek a more highly esteemed outlet for their energies.

There is no longer in Europe the high regard there once was for the operations of government. Until very recently there was a prevailing view that important services could not be left to the chance operations of the market. If something was necessary, then the state should take care of its provision. There grew up an enormous panoply of state monopoly production, covering just about every conceivable range of goods and services. The statistics show a higher segment of the European economies in public-sector operations than is true of the United States. The British figure was 43.5 percent of the GNP accounted for by public spending in 1979, at the start of the Thatcher government.

The average man in Britain might wake to the strains of the national state-run radio service, brush his teeth with local-authority-supplied water, and boil his government Egg Marketing Board egg. He might eat it with a British Steel spoon, and perhaps have some cereal with state Marketing Board milk. His toast might be cooked by courtesy of the Central Electricity Generating Board, or maybe the British Gas Corporation.

He would set out for work in his British Leyland car, pausing to say hello to the municipal garbage collectors as they spilled his trash can onto the street. Dropping his children off at their state school, he would park his car at the British Rail station, post a letter through the General Post Office to his older child at a state-owned university, and catch a nationalized train to his work with the British Ports Authority.

During the day he might buy his airplane tickets from British Airways, using his British Telecom phone, and on the way home he might call on his National Health Service doctor to see if he needed a stay in a state hospital. In the evening it could be BBC Television, a visit to the municipal squash courts, or maybe a book from the local public library read in front of a blazing fire provided by the National Coal Board.

With so many areas of life dominated by public-sector supply, it is hardly surprising that entrepreneurs found themselves rather crowded out. In the first place, a public monopoly often prevented them by law from entering certain types of business. Mail delivery and telephone services are frequently run as state monopolies. By 1979 in the United Kingdom, these two were supplemented by laws that forbade private generation and sale of electricity and gas or private rail transport or coal mining, with negligible exceptions. In the second place, the cost of keeping public corporations going took a major slice of the money entrepreneurs might have used for investment capital.

It may seem strange, but the fact is that it took us many years in Europe to appreciate that these state-run services were worse than the private alternatives. Perhaps it was because many of them started out so well, and only gradually began to run downhill. We noticed with increasing irritation that they were becoming shoddy and unreliable, and that they were expensive not only in their prices, but in the losses we had to make good out of taxation. In 1982, railway losses cost the taxpayer over £ 1,000 million, with coal losses at just over half that figure. Between them they lost roughly £ 5 million *per day,* for a country roughly the size of a U.S. state.

The phrase *private affluence and public squalor* sprang to the lips of liberal politicians, who told us we were not spending enough on public-sector services. But the truth that eventually came out, even after we had spent more, was that government-run operations were no good. The effect of their cost on private alternatives may be gauged from the fact that only 7 percent, the very rich, can afford to pay for private health care or private education in the United Kingdom, after having paid for the public-sector provision. They have built-in weaknesses that eventually prove fatal.

In a competitive private economy, firms have to keep the service good and the prices low, or customers move elsewhere. In a public monopoly the consumer has no choice. There is no incentive to offer good or efficient service. The administrators and the unions find it easier to meet each other's needs, and the service becomes producer-oriented, run for the benefit of those who provide it instead of for those who receive it.

The biggest pressure is on wages because, however high wages are, a public monopoly cannot be priced out of the market. The only limit is what taxpayers can be persuaded to part with. What this means is that public services are always short of capital. Any capital they do have gets sucked toward wages, leaving them without enough to invest in new equipment and labor-saving technology. The result is out-of-date and shoddy equipment and an inefficient service. Compare Britain's National Health Service with the U.S. medical industry. Table 8–1 shows how far behind an undercapitalized service can fall. The same could be shown for any of the big utilities.

There is now widespread understanding in Europe that public-sector operations, far from guaranteeing a service, almost guarantee that it will be interrupted. With nowhere else for the public to turn, the unions have the

Table 8–1
United Kingdom's National Health Service vs. U.S. Medical Industry

Category	U.K.	U.S.
Percentage of health spending by government (1976)	89.0	43.0
Pacemakers per 100,000 of population (1976)	9.8	44.2
CAT scanners per million population (1979)	1.0	5.7
Kidney dialysis and transplant rates per million population (1976)	71.2	170.0

Source: Adam Smith Institute, London, unpublished data.

power to shut down the entire service by strike action. All of the big strikes since 1979 have been in the public sector—workers in the steel, railway, health, water, civil, and social areas—rather than in private business.

I said that government could be pushed around, unions bludgeoned, and bureaucrats sidestepped. Now I shall give examples of all of these very worthwhile activities, and show what has been achieved.

Pushing Governments Around

In democratic societies legislators listen to public opinion. The trick is to market your idea so that it catches popular imagination. At the Adam Smith Institute we found that there were 3,068 bureaucratic bodies that were outside the control of Parliament, and they were breeding like rabbits. We looked for a good name for these groups and settled on an American word, QUANGO, standing for Quasi-Autonomous Non-Governmental Organization. The word made them sound like some unpleasant little animal and invited popular contempt and derision. Just to make sure of the impact, we published the list of them on a single twelve-foot-long page.[3]

To cut a long story short, the government responded to pressure from the media and set up an inquiry. It recommended that two hundred of these organizations should be chopped.[4] We responded with our own "Death List" of 707, printed in black with a noose on the cover for dramatic effect.[5] The score to date is 660 of them disbanded—not a bad effort; over 20 percent of the total. The important thing is that they are now thought of as disreputable. People used to be proud of having jobs in such organizations; now they keep quiet about it.

Bludgeoning Unions

Second on the agenda is the bludgeoning of unions. Europe has nothing to teach the United States in this respect, after the U.S. government's handling of the strike by the air traffic controllers. Though I know of no union recently in western Europe that has been outlawed and its leader led away in chains, nonetheless, I can give several examples in which the interests of the actual workers were advanced by doing down union leadership. The policy in Europe has increasingly been for management to appeal to the work force by direct ballot, over the heads of the union bosses. The spectacular illustration is afforded by Sir Michael Edwardes of British Leyland, who broke the power of militant unions by repeated direct ballots of the membership. More often than not, a militant line by the leadership is flatly contradicted by a secret vote of the work force.

In the Adam Smith Institute we took on the union control of local-authority services. Municipal services such as clearing garbage, repairing streets, cleaning windows, and running parks and gardens, show all of the features of public monopoly. They use far more labor than their private equivalents, use their equipment inefficiently, charge more, and do not give the service people want. Why should they when they get paid no matter what happens, and the public has nowhere else to go for service?

When you try to save money on local government, as I am sure you must have found in the United States, it is usually the most popular services that are threatened. A notorious example occurred in the United States when the U.S. Customs Office was required to take a budget reduction. Immediately, the officers who search for drugs at entry ports and airports were pulled off, without a single "desk jockey" put at risk. It seems there just are no savings to be made in administration or working practices; only by closing a cripples' hospital or an old peoples' home can money be saved. The media leap in with graphic stories of the suffering to be caused, and the local legislators give up the foolish idea of trying to save money. This account is slighly unfair but basically accurate.

The Adam Smith Institute tried a new tack. We produced a survey on the use of private business to perform public services around the world.[6] The average saving in costs was about 40 percent. The survey was sent to local legislators throughout Britain as part of an information pack. Meanwhile, we fed articles and stories to the press and television about the privatization of local government, and created a storm of interest.

Each service that was put out to contractors was heavily publicized, to encourage others to do the same. The formula was simple: the private business would do the service better and at less cost than the local council's own work force. The magic 40-percent saving rate seen in the rest of the world began to appear in the United Kingdom. The savings to local governments vary from area to area, and are affected in Britain by lay-off payments that have to be made in the first year. Despite this, first-year savings usually hit the 20- to 40-percent mark. The local councils of Kensington and Chelsea cut their £340,000 expenses by £140,000, over 40 percent. Tandridge saved 20 percent, High Wycombe 24 percent, Hammersmith 25 percent. Southend, Wandsworth, and Eastbourne all hit the same range in the first year, rising nearer to the 40-percent figure for subsequent years. North Norfolk saved 32 percent, Chelsea 40 percent. More spectacular savings still are made in services other than garbage collection. Salisbury saved 60 percent of its office-cleaning bill by using contractors; Hull saved 59 percent of its bill for cleaning school windows.

The public-sector unions, meanwhile, saw a position of control that had taken half a century to build up melt in a moment. The private contractor might well offer jobs to the old labor force, but on new terms. There is a long way to go, but every week now some council somewhere privatizes some part of its services. It is like a snowball rolling downhill. There are examples everywhere; and the change is too rapid to measure. Statistics are out of date by the time they are collected. Wandsworth privatized its garbage collection, street cleaning, grass cutting, and care of its parks and gardens, and was the trailblazer for a full review of all services with a view to privatization.

So far we have seen private contractors move in to collect the garbage in a couple of dozen British cities. They clean the streets in others. They wash the windows of public buildings in some, clean the schools in others. They sell houses here, design buildings there, and provide security in many areas. They do catering, transport, and laundry. They manage golf courses, leisure centers, and deck chairs. You name it, and it is happening somewhere. It is a huge transfer of power away from unions and back to consumers, and it happened even without new legislation. The days are passing forever of the corporation municipal garbage truck that employed five men to do the work of two, and spent a significant part of each day parked outside the local bars. No longer do two men ride on a truck representing the men who used to hold the horse and feed it in the old days, and whose jobs the union had insisted on retaining.

The password now is *competition*, with penalty clauses to keep firms to their contracts, and the need for profits keeping them lean and efficient. This one victory has done more than almost anything else to open opportunities for local entrepreneurs. Enterprising businessmen are setting about getting local contracts for all kinds of activity closed to them until a couple of years ago.

Moreover, this is spreading across Europe. A recently compiled list gave over three hundred West German towns that have now privatized local services.[7] The word has spread to Denmark, where *Privatisering* is in the news.

The response of the unions has been interesting. They are spending over $2 million on a campaign against the use of contractors, but they do not really know who to fight. The opposition to their rule comes in a thousand different towns at once, and covers dozens of services. Their standard tactic has been to try and outbid contractors by offering big savings themselves. Our advice to local councils trying to save money is to mention the word *privatization* in council chambers. That saves an immediate 20 percent as the unions rush in with a counter offer of magically discovered savings. By going through with the contracting process, they will save a further 20 percent.

Many of those councils who accepted a revised bid offering savings from their unionized labor a year ago are now going through the process of bringing in local businesses after all. The promised savings did not materialize, and they have decided they would rather have a private firm under contract than a public labor force that can please itself. The first to complete this move was the local council for Milton Keynes, which opted for an in-house solution after considering contractors in 1982, and handed its garbage collection to private contractors after a year's experiment failed to yield the promised economies. The most fascinating aspect of this whole operation has been that the propagation of a simple idea has led not only to huge savings for local taxpayers combined with more responsive services; it has also led to the creation of billions of dollars' worth of entrepreneurial business across Europe.

Sidestepping Bureaucrats

What about sidestepping the bureaucrats? Here one needs to be more subtle than with governments or unions. The tradition in Europe is for a permanent civil service, without the top layer of political appointees who change with each new administration. European civil servants are supposed to be nonpolitical, serving whatever government happens to be elected.

In fact, of course, they come to regard themselves as the ruling class. Governments may come and go, but the bureaucracy remains. Bureaucrats take the long view on policy, regarding elected ministers as no more than temporary inconveniences to be dealt with. There is, thus, in Europe very much an *attitude* held by a particular department because of the traditional view of its bureaucracy.

This is bad news for entrepreneurs. Most of these departments are staffed by people who acquired their training and their experience when the theories of John Maynard Keynes were the prevailing orthodoxy, and when people took John Kenneth Galbraith seriously. Those days are gone, but the bureaucratic legacy remains, in the form of a civil service that thinks of business as something that must be finely directed and controlled by the instruments of state, instead of being encouraged to develop and expand in response to demand.[8]

Sidestepping bureaucrats is tricky. They oppose deregulation, and will persuade government ministers to think the same in the absence of other pressures. This provides the key: if enough political and public pressures can be brought to bear, the minister will tell his or her bureaucrats to implement the necessary changes.

Let me give you a case history. We at the Adam Smith Institute decided it would be a good thing to have *freeports* in Britain.[9] A freeport is an entry port that is treated as foreign territory for tariff purposes. Goods from other countries that come into it are not charged customs duties. This means that a lot of trading and processing can go on without these taxes being levied. Not surprisingly, freeports are very attractive to traders, and tend to act as magnets for all kinds of enterprises.

The idea was not exactly new. The Phoenicians used freeports nearly thirty centuries ago, and they have had a consistent and respectable history since then. Maybe *respectable* is not quite the right word; freeports are often places where anything and everything goes on. Of such is enterprise made. However, this long and distinguished history has never included Britain. Since there are now over four hundred freeports in the world, and best estimates put them as taking 20 percent of international trade within two years,[10] it seemed a good idea for the United Kingdom to have some.

It did *not,* however, seem a good idea to the bureaucrats of the Customs and Excise Department of Her Majesty's Treasury. They expressed their determination that there should be no such things. It would mean all kinds of new rules and special cases, and they might not be able to keep close tabs on what went on in these freeports. They advised the minister that these were not possible and not desirable. (This determination is usually expressed through the minister, but in this case press statements were issued casting doubt on the merits of such ports, culminating in a letter to the *Daily Telegraph* from Sir Douglas Lovelock, the head of Customs and Excise, on January 31, 1983. The letter, listing five points against freeports, raised serious questions in Parliament about who controlled government policy.)

The Adam Smith Institute advised the minister what freeports were, and planted several articles about the idea in the financial press. Two sympathetic pieces in *Accountancy Age* in December 1981 and February 1982 prompted pieces in the *Financial Times, Guardian,* and London *Times* in February 1982. From there it was picked up by the regional and Sunday press, where stories have appeared ever since. Areas that saw themselves as potential candidates for freeport status grew hungry for the jobs the ports would bring. Some of them asked us how to put their case, and then started lobbying the government.

Stage three was to get the businesses that stood to gain to clamor for the duty-free areas. The local press in every case, with only a little prodding, picked all of this up and spread around a few banner headlines in 1982. By 1983, no less than 40 potential sites had entered the picture, each with massive press coverage.

The bureaucrats were becoming quite angry with all this foolish talk. They could sense, correctly, a political wave building up against them. They began showing people a weighty report they had compiled showing what a bad idea freeports were. Could we see the report? "Oh no. It is a private memo." Questions mysteriously appeared in the House of Parliament. "Would the minister please place a copy of that report in the House of Commons library by Wednesday morning?" The response, after an initial flap, was to deny that any such report existed. This was good enough for us. If it did not exist, then they could not use it again—nor did they.

The bureaucrats decided to kill the campaign by holding an official inquiry and reporting against the ports. It was sprung in early December, to finish at the end of January, and consisted largely of Customs and Excise officials. The joint working project was announced in Parliament in response to a Parliamentary Question in December 1982. A story in the *Sunday Times* of January 23, 1983, suggested that Customs and Excise pressure had dismissed the Trade Minister, Iain Sproat, from the working party. It was discovered in addition that the representative of Chambers of Commerce was a retired customs officer. Meanwhile we waited until the last week and then assailed them from all directions. They said it would involve too much paperwork; we sent in evidence from the British firm that ran the Miami foreign-trade zone without any paper, using computer control of goods in cooperation with United States Customs. They said that British firms would have no advantage; a leading computer manufacturer wrote to the London *Times* pointing out that he paid a 17-percent duty on his components, but saw his competitors bringing in finished goods at only 6 percent. Now if he had a freeport, he could create more jobs in Britain instead of having to expand abroad.[11]

If this sounds like a complicated game of cat and mouse, that is because it is one. The aim is to use public and political pressure in one half of the scales to outweigh the power of bureaucratic inertia in the other. We suggested that the *Daily Telegraph* might run a pro-freeport editorial on the last day of the inquiry. The editorial, in the *Daily Telegraph* of January 28, 1983, referred to the Treasury's "notorious preoccupation" with immediate revenue loss. It further expressed the view that freeports "represent a creative policy, the lighting of a candle rather than the saving of candle ends." The Customs and Excise people were so outraged that their leader wrote the public letter of January 31 setting out all the arguments against the freeports.

Since bureaucrats are not supposed to make policy, a storm of criticism descended on them for coming out so openly. The point was that they had been flushed into the open because they knew they were losing. They were being sidestepped. Finally, in his budget speech of March 15, 1983, Chancellor Sir Geoffrey Howe announced that "two or three experimental freeports" were to be established in Britain.

In December 1982 the French decided to make Marseilles into a freeport, the Germans launched an investigation into possible freeport sites in early January 1983, and the Dutch have decided to proceed toward the acquisition of both freeports and free zones as soon as possible.

Once an idea is in circulation and is marketed effectively, there is no limit to how far it can spread or what effects it can have. If, as a result of that campaign, there are a few more areas in Europe in which new businesses can set up and prosper, then the exercise will have been worthwhile.

But of course our aims were wider than that. Customs and Excise opposed freeports for exactly the same reasons that made us support them: once you have them in operation, there is no telling what they will lead to. Once there is a duty-free area with a fence around it, all kinds of experiments in deregulation can be tried out. We intend to push for suspension within the freeports of health and safety regulations. We think there should be no outside controls on zoning or building standards; that the Protection of Employment Act should not operate; that laws and agreements covering minimum wage should not hold.

In other words, part of the aim of establishing a freeport is to acquire experimental laboratories in which the hindrances to entrepreneurial activity can be tested by removing them selectively. Our assumption is that the results will be so beneficial as to justify reproducing those conditions elsewhere in the country.

Sidestepping the bureaucrats calls for delicate footwork but, along with pushing governments around and bludgeoning unions, it can work wonders for the entrepreneurial climate. The last three years have witnessed several successes in Europe, and the pace is accelerating. One very important point is that there would still be changes even if we did not have several reformist administrations in power in Europe. Countries that do not have such governments are swept along by the logic of events just as surely as those who think they lead the way.

There are intellectual truths about the market economy that influence events even when M. Mitterrand is president. The fact that those truths are widely perceived across Europe today is evidence of a victory in the world of ideas. The lesson that could be drawn from this is that if you wish to influence events, "put not your trust in Princes." Instead of dissipating your energies in the attempt to elect favorable candidates, you might consider contriving circumstances that will influence the legislators who emerge as the products of time and chance. The candidate you elect may suffer a change of mind or bow to other pressures; but when you elect an idea, its influence endures. "Practical men, who believe themselves to be quite exempt from any intellectual influences, are usually the slaves of some defunct economist." That was said by John Maynard Keynes, and he ought to know.[12]

Micro-Politics

There is another lesson buried in all of this experience. It is that when you are tinkering with the political process in order to improve the climate for entrepreneurs, you can often achieve in stages that which would have been impossible to do in a jump. It is a very good thing to have good criticisms of public-sector blocks on free enterprise. It is also a good thing to have a picture of that which you would like to see taking their place. But this alone does not bring changes.

What is needed in addition is a mechanism by which the present state of play can be transformed into a better world. You have to create that small change which gradually widens until it takes over the entire area. Do not try to blow up the whole public sector of the economy in one go. What you do is to make a small hole in the public-sector dam so that some people can opt out of its provisions. As more and more do so, the gap widens. What started as a trickle becomes a torrent, then a flood. Eventually the public provision is still there, but no one uses it anymore. We call this approach *micro-politics:* like microeconomics, it is grounded in the individual decisions that people make.

Let me give a couple of quick examples. When governments try to cut their spending, road building is one of the first items to go. This, being a capital expense, is easier to chop than the jobs or wages of bureaucrats. The result is that roads deteriorate, potholes are left unfilled. Much-needed by-pass routes are delayed, and traffic costs increase. Everyone starts screaming for more public money, of which there is none.

Our answer was to devise a scheme under which private investors can fund and build public roads. They can either be repaid by tolls from the motorist, or from tolls paid by the government, depending on how much the road is used. The result is that the government gets its road, the public gets the convenience, and business gets the opportunity. Two conferences and two books later,[13] and after acres of press coverage, the British government has accepted the idea. In May 1983 the first public road was put out for tender to be financed and built by private business.

I can guess what will happen next. Governments will like the idea. It is an easy option to get roads built with somebody else's money. They will do more of it. Then they will get the idea of using the same trick for other public works. Sewers and public buildings will be next, and over the course of years we will move into a world in which public capital projects are financed by entrepreneurs on a risk and reward basis, instead of being lavishly built at direct taxpayer expense.

Another idea we are on the point of introducing should spread rapidly right across Europe, and may even find its way over to the United States. We call it the *portable enterprise zone.*[14] The idea behind it is simple. Enterprise zones try to give special concessions to lure businesses to deprived areas. One of their failings is that they are used by governments to direct businesses to places that businesses would really prefer not to go. Why not locate the principle of selective deregulation not in a particular place, but in a sector of the economy?

Our suggestion is that small business should be made a portable enterprise zone, exempt from most of the burdens of taxation and control that are imposed on their big brothers. Small businesses provide new growth, the new jobs. They need selective encouragement to help them get going.

We think of small businesses rather like teenagers. When they are big and strong they can take a full share of society's burdens; but while they are growing we should give them a little more space to stretch themselves, a little more room to develop. Just as we allow our teenagers a fairly loose rein, and let them run wild a bit as they gain strength and ability, maybe we should give a looser rein to our new businesses, not burdening them or inhibiting their growth with excessive regulations and crippling requirements. If successful, we might gradually extend the treatment to the rest of our businesses.

We look at the inhibitions on entrepreneurial activity, asking government to waive them for new firms, offering new jobs and economic growth as the bait. Our proposal is that firms employing less than one hundred persons should not be subject to the zoning and building restrictions that make the acquisition of suitable premises so costly and so difficult. Their labor should not be as protected, making up in opportunity what it lacks in security. Their tax burden should be lower. We shall ask for all firms with an annual turnover of less than $200,000, to be exempt from the 15-percent value-added tax.

Some small firms make it even now, but there could be many more. For example, a friend of mine, Clive Sinclair, makes domestic computers. He started three or four years ago with a loan of $10,000. His worth is now put at about $200 million, and he makes more small computers than anyone else. He enables consumers to buy a computer at less than $100, and is responsible for the jobs of a few thousand people. What we seek is an entrepreneurial climate in which enterprising creative people like Sinclair become a much more common phenomenon, the commonplace rule instead of the rare exception.

Nine Roads to Happiness

I shall close with what I believe to be the most important step that governments can take. It is the transfer of public resources and activities into the private sector of the economy. The Adam Smith Institute has identified nine ways of doing this, all of which are now being tried in the United Kingdom, and some of them elsewhere in Europe. We call them the nine roads to happiness. We echo the view of F.A. Hayek in his *Road to Serfdom* that, although economic freedom does not necessarily bring happiness, it helps create the conditions under which values may be expressed, and happiness sought.[15]

Profitable operations can be sold to the private sector, restoring them to the world of economic discipline. This is the first road. Amersham, a public electronic communications company, went this route.

If you cannot sell an operation, perhaps because it makes a loss like so many public activities, it may be possible to sell part of it (road number two). This happened with the British Rail hotels and the cross-channel ferry services, even though we could not sell the railways themselves.

If you cannot sell part of the whole, you can perhaps sell the whole (road three). By offering 51 percent for sale, you might attract private investment and take decisions away from government, while keeping a fair quantity of public capital in the business. In this way 51 percent of the British National Oil Corporation was sold off, and 51 percent of Telecom is being offered for sale.

Even if the public cannot or will not buy any of it, it can still be sold to the work force (road four). This happened to the National Freight Corporation, which became a worker-owned business, and turned a loss into a very healthy year profit.

Even if no one at all will buy, there is road number five, that of giving away public operations. This proved very successful as a means of transferring housing from the public to the private sector in Britain. Very few wanted to buy until the government started giving away from one-third to one-half of the market value to prospective buyers. Since then the rate of sale has climbed. It is estimated to reach about 8.5 percent by the fall of 1983, since the policy was instituted in late 1979. This represents roughly 250,000 houses sold out of a stock of 6 million.[16]

The sixth road is that of privatizing finance, if not production. This means charging for services instead of funding from taxation. Elements of this have been introduced into the British Health Service, and much is being done with city services in St. Paul, Minnesota, in the United States.[17]

More promising to our eyes is road seven, privatizing production, even though payment is still publicly funded. This is the road of contracting out to private businesses. It has started to spread in British cities, as I have explained, and is now to be introduced into hospital ancillary services, following a ministerial commitment to the idea given in Parliament in February 1983.

The eighth way is by dilution, bringing in private capital for all new projects, even though the existing public effort is left in place. This will dilute the proportion of public holding over the years, as private development becomes the norm. We may do this with our roads.

The last route is that of creating bolt-holes, or openings in the public sector through which both demand and supply can exit. If we give people the opportunity to opt out, and to make their own provision, ever-increasing numbers of them will do so. The result will be a vestigial public sector, catering for a diminishing band of those who still value its services. This is the route we make take with our state health and education services.

The nine roads add up to a program to revitalize the climate for entrepreneurship; but they promise more than that. They offer to give us a society in which people allocate their own resources, live by their own values, and face the state as its equals and its citizens, instead of its dependents and its serfs. The nine roads lead us toward a free society.

Notes

1. *The Enterprise Zone Act* (Brussels, Belgium: Government Printing Office, 1982).

2. Michael van Notten, "Boosting Enterprise: The Belgian Experience," *Journal of Economic Affairs* (July 1983) (Institute of Economic Affairs, London).

3. Phillip Holland, *Quango, Quango, Quango!* (London: Adam Smith Institute, 1979).

4. *Non-Departmental Public Bodies: A Guide for Departments* (London: Her Majesty's Stationery Office, 1980).

5. Phillip Holland, *The Quango Death List* (London: Adam Smith Institute, 1980).

6. Michael Forsyth, *Reservicing Britain* (London: Adam Smith Institute, 1981).

7. Published by the Konrad Adenauer Stiftung, Rathausallee 12, 5205–Sankt Augustin 1, West Germany.

8. Teresa Gorman, *The Portable Enterprise Zone* (London: Adam Smith Institute, 1983).

9. *A Proposal for the Establishment of Freeports in the United Kingdom* (London: Adam Smith Institute, 1981).

10. Walter H. Diamond, "Tax-Free Trade Zones of the World," *Business Week, Transatlantic Perspectives* (Washington, D.C.: German Marshall Fund, 1982).

11. Clive Sinclair, letter, London *Times,* 3 February 1983.

12. John Maynard Keynes, *"The General Theory of Employment, Interest and Money"* (New York: Harcourt Brace and World, 1936), bk. VI, p. 383.

13. Eamonn Butler and Gabriel Roth, *Private Road Ahead* (London: Adam Smith Institute, 1982); and Eamonn Butler, ed., *Roads and the Private Sector* (London: Adam Smith Institute, 1982). The conferences were in London on June 22, 1981 and June 24, 1982 by Adam Smith Institute.

14. Gorman, *The Portable Enterprise Zone.*

15. F.A. Hayek, *Road to Serfdom* (Chicago: University of Chicago Press, 1944).

16. Linda Schluster, "New Law Transforms Britain Into Nation of Homeowners," *The Wall Street Journal* September 14, 1983, p. 35.

17. Robert Poole, *Paying for City Services* (Santa Barbara, Cal.: Local Government Center, 1983).

The New Entrepreneurs

Calvin A. Kent

The explorations into the entrepreneurial environment in this book have continued to raise questions about the extent to which conscious governmental policy may be an aid or an impediment to innovation, job creation, and capital formation. The moral of these chapters is that it matters greatly what circumstances the entrepreneur faces as to whether or not these objectives will be achieved. The urge to create is so powerful and so universal that, as Pearce writes, "Entrepreneurship can never be suppressed, only misdirected."[1]

Entrepreneurship in Command Economies

The truth of Pearce's statement is no more obvious than in the misdirection of entrepreneurial effort in command economies. Examples of three countries upon which there is considerable research and comment in the popular press will serve to illustrate this point. These are the Soviet Union (USSR), the People's Republic of China, and Hungary. Each of these represents an economy operating under a different degree of central direction and planning.

USSR

Of the three the Soviet economy is by far the most rigidly planned. Levin relates that

> Commands, in the form of obligatory plan targets, are issued by the central leadership and communicated down through an administrative hierarchy, organized primarily by branch of production, to the basic producing units responsible for their fulfillment. Lines of authority are strictly delineated: Orders are issued by superiors in the hierarchy to their subordinates; information about production possibilities flows up the hierarchy. The Soviet economy is thus administered by means of a massive, comprehensive bureaucrcy.[2]

In the Soviet system the possibility of entrepreneurship arises in two places: in the planning of innovation and the introduction of technology, and in the black market. Levin details a large number of barriers to the planning of technological change that he feels retard innovation and entrepreneurial activity in the Soviet Union. One is the strict hierarchy of authority through which proposals for innovation must pass, which not only slows down the introduction of the planned innovation, but also makes it likely that someone in the bureaucratic structure will veto the idea and prevent its introduction. And since each department or industry is planned separately with little communication or cross-fertilization, ideas generated in one place are highly unlikely to invade another sphere of the economy no matter how desirable or productive they might be.

A third problem is the desire for stability. The Soviet Union stresses the achievement of growth targets. Though innovation might assist in achieving those targets, it involves upsetting existing patterns of production and destabilizing the planning process. Closely related to this is a fourth problem: risk aversion. Bureaucracies tend to penalize failure more than they reward success. For that reason taking a risk with innovation is likely to threaten a bureaucrat's prestige and power as well as benefits if the innovation fails after introduction. Fifth, the Russian system neglects to provide adequate measures of performance or rewards. The penalties for failure are very great if the production manager should introduce an unsuccessful new technology. On the other hand there is very little compensation if the new technology succeeds. In fact the introduction of innovation almost always disrupts the productive process at first and may lead to a failure to fulfill the plan. In the Soviet economy perpetual shortages constitute the sixth problem. Since the producer is always paid no matter how shoddy the good or how inefficiently it is produced, there is little incentive to innovate either to reduce cost or develop better products.

In contrasting the Soviet economy with one organized around markets, Levin comments that

> [i]n competititve market economies, the innovational process responds in a positive way to both high rewards for successful innovation and the firm's fear of being driven out of business by dynamic competitors. . . . The absence of competition, bankruptcy, and creative destruction in the Soviet economy removes the most potent force behind the defusion of new technology—the fear of death, and the drive to survive. . . . In view of the systematic barriers to innovation in the Soviet centrally planned economy, one would anticipate a very low rate of introduction and defusion of new technology . . . compared with the advanced market economies of the West. . . . [R]ecent research shows that the Soviets are clearly behind the West in this respect. However, the relative position of the Soviet Union is perhaps not as bad as one might expect.[3]

Considering the ossified condition of the Soviet planning mechanism it should surprise no one to find much of the entrepreneurial genius of the

Soviets has been directed to the black market or what is called the *second* or *left* economy. Not all of the activities in the Soviet underground economy are illegal, but since most are, entrepreneurs run not only the risk of failure but of incarceration as well. Grossman has provided an intriguing insight into the operation of this system.[4] The legal part of the Soviet private economy is in agriculture, where peasants are allowed not only to produce on privately owned plots, but also to sell any excess produced above the planned target from communal plots on the open market at whatever price it can bring. It is estimated that without this free market in agriculture that the Soviet economy would be strained to maintain adequate levels of nutrition for its people.[5] The fact that private farming includes only 3 percent of the cultivated land in the Soviet Union but provides 25 percent of the nation's farm production is sufficient testimony to the effectiveness of market incentives.

Grossman finds many examples of illegal but highly profitable entrepreneurial activity in the Soviet nonfarm economy. These range all the way from theft of inputs and equipment from socialist enterprise and their sale on the black market to the establishment of illegal factories in homes as well as in socialist enterprises. In the latter case this is called *parallel production*, in which the enterprise devotes part of its efforts to the achievement of the targeted planned outputs but diverts a portion of its time to production of goods to be sold on the black market. In fact, this private production behind the facade of a state enterprise may be the least risky way to operate on the so-called left. Simis, an expatriate Soviet lawyer, notes that

> The tenacity of the entrepreneurial instinct in the USSR has proven amazing: neither the huge obstacles in the path of private enterprise nor the threat of harsh penalties—even capital punishment—have been able to curb the vigor of these human impulses.[6]

Whatever the method employed, the illegal entrepreneurs in Russia do seem to be amply rewarded for their risks. Both Simis and Grossman see the inevitable impact of this type of entrepreneurship as being the corruption of public officials at all levels. It is well to be aware of Simis's conclusion, that "this is the awesome cost of a system dedicated to stifling the most basic impulses of personal freedom."[7]

The People's Republic of China

A step removed from the Soviet economy is that of mainland China. In recent years research has come to light that indicates that since 1979 and the reforms which followed the mayhem of the cultural revolution, the People's Republic of China in some sectors is moving toward greater reliance on free markets. Principal among these reforms have been those in agriculture, where the concept of the *iron rice bowl* has been replaced with the *responsibility system*. Under the iron rice bowl, workers were hired but never fired or demoted. Everyone was assured of not only a slice, but an equal slice of the productivity of all. Under the responsibility system the state contracts with a commune, a group of people, or an individual to produce a certain amount of agricultural products. Land and machinery are either assigned to producers or rented by them. Whatever is produced in excess of the contract is again available for private sale. This change in agricultural policy apparently is producing two desired results. Not only is the production of basic foodstuffs up, but communes are using their profits to adopt more efficient technologies and to try new methods of production that may lead to even greater levels of plan overfulfillment.[8]

Achievements have not been as impressive in the rest of Chinese industry. Johnson has noted that in theory, if not in practice, certain reforms have been enacted.[9] Among these is to allow industry to sell output beyond the amount established by the plan in the free market. The industry can use the surplus to develop and adopt new technology or as bonuses to its workers. While there are strict limits on the extent of this activity and its implementation is only fragmentary, the objective is the same as in agriculture: to stimulate more growth of output from the same resource base.

A third movement toward acceptance of the market by The People's Republic of China has been the establishment of *special zones*.[10] Currently these have been limited to the area surrounding Hong Kong but seem to be patterned after the enterprise zones discussed by Madsen Pirie in chapter 8 of this book. The early reports on these special economic zones are not encouraging as they still seem to be bogged down in bureaucratic red tape. But they do represent a further admission that a free market is more likely than a controlled one to produce economic progress.

Hungary

Perhaps the most striking example of how entrepreneurship can exist in a command economy is that of Hungary. Economic reform was introduced in 1968, was renounced in 1973, and has been reinstated since 1978. The result of these reforms is that Hungary is now the economic showcase of the Eastern Bloc, producing an agricultural surplus for export as well as a rising standard of living for its population.[11]

Rupp, an expatriate Hungarian economist, has explored these reforms and their effects.[12] At the heart of these reforms has been the establishment of the semiprivate enterprises. Rupp describes them as small industrial organizations established and run by private entrepreneurs. Formally they operate within the framework of public organizations, as agricultural cooperatives. Originally the semiprivate enterprises were established to shore up the vitality of failing agricultural cooperatives. The semiprivate enterprises were designed to produce inputs to be used by the agricultural cooperatives in the production and marketing of agricultural products. While the enterprises are privately owned they sometimes received initial financial assistance from the cooperative. Of the profits, 60 percent are turned over to the agricultural cooperative for investment in the cooperative and 40 percent can be retained within the enterprise either for expansion or as payment to owners or workers. The latter is severely restricted because of Hungary's continued insistence on policies designed to nearly equalize incomes.

These semiprivate enterprises are combined with the free market that exists in the production and distribution of many consumer goods produced by individual artisans and privately owned firms. In his analysis Rupp finds that the semiprivate firms were highly profitable as well as adaptive to changes in market conditions: "The semi-private organizational form provides incentives to realize potential sources of profitability that have not been realized in the framework of bureaucratic organizations because of disincentives."[13] Even so there is a note of pessimism to his writing: "Hungary is still a tightly controlled totalitarian society. This fact not only limits human rights and political reform, but is also a serious barrier to the rationalization of economic organization."[14]

This overview of entrepreneurship in command economies was designed to further demonstrate the point that the political environment establishes constraints on the scope, direction, and success of entrepreneurship within a nation. As these case studies have indicated, governmental policies in the command economies are creating a new class of entrepreneurs who are responding to the incentives, both positive and negative, that those systems provide. This can also apply to entrepreneurial activity in the United States.

Paper Entrepreneurship in the United States

The current political environment in the United States has had the effect of diverting a significant amount of entrepreneurial skill and energy from the development of innovation and the commercialization of new ideas and technology. Instead, the focus of the entrepreneur's attention is often on meeting standards of political conduct associated with taxation and regulation that may be of dubious value. These activities may neither increase national income, produce any new products, nor generate additional jobs. Several observers of the contemporary scene have commented on the transformation of entrepreneurship in this nation, transformation brought about by an environment created by political activity. In the past, entrepreneurs followed the models of Schumpeter and Kirzner. Entrepreneurs were the exploiters of technology, the innovators of new products and processes, the niche-finders who saw something others had failed to see and profited from its exploitation. The new entrepreneurs according to Hughes must "be adept in the exploitation of federal, state, and local regulations at a time when the predominance of power is on the side of the legislators who mold the entrepreneurial function to a large extent. The government is now the market to be exploited."[15]

Robert Reich has referred to this as *paper entrepreneurialism*. He draws our attention to the structure of our economy and its underlying organization. "The incentives it offers has discouraged long term growth in favor of short term paper profits. An even larger portion of our economic activity is focused on rearranging industrial assets rather than on increasing their size. Instead of enlarging the economic pie we are busy reassigning slices."[16] This statement points clearly to the problem this nation faces in its desire to provide for a more equal distribution of income: it has lost sight of the question of how increased income is to be generated. In our concern with equality and the quality of life we may have lost sight of the role of entrepreneurship and economic growth in enlarging the pie so that all can have a larger slice.

Among the new entrepreneurs are the accountants, lawyers, and financial analysts who are able to discern methods to increase profits by seeing loopholes in federal taxes and regulations that others have not seen; by discovering the escape hatches in agency regulations; by organizing mergers; by managing high leveraged buyouts; and by reorganizing assets to show a reduced pretax but an increased after-tax return to investors.

> The basic idea behind paper entrepreneurship is to keep money moving into the areas of highest return and profit. Unfortunately today this rarely involves investing in new factories, new technologies, new products, or expanding capacity. All of these alternatives involve risk; the payoffs on which will be severely taxed. . . . All of these activities may produce spectacular short term profits for the firm, but do nothing to raise the productivity of American business or to increase the satisfaction of the American consumer.[17]

In recent years the United States has been caught up in a debate about the adoption of a national industrial policy (NIP).[18] Although there are as many variants of this proposal as there are advocates, all share a common policy prescription that would require the government to determine the new areas into which the expansion of the economy and its resources are to be directed. Tax subsidies, financial incentives, and other assistance programs are to be directed toward moving resources into these new areas of presumed high profitability.

Much of the support for the adoption of such a strategy comes from the example of Japan. Since the 1960s when Japan adopted its national industrial policy administered by its Ministry of International Trade and Industry, its economic performance has outstripped that of the United States. Katsuro Sakoh contends that while Japanese economic success and planning have occurred simultaneously there is no causal relationship between them.

> The Japanese government has undoubtedly contributed to the economic success of Japan since World War II. The irony is that the contribution has been based not so much on what it did for the economy, but on how much it restrained itself from doing. Interference in the economy has been sporadic and slight—including efforts aimed at industrial development.[19]

More important in Japan's success, according to Arthur Denzau, appears to be a small government sector with a nearly balanced budget, low and stable interest rates, taxation at levels below those of the United States, combined with a firm commitment to quality control in the production of Japanese products. He finds that the industries most heavily aided under the Japanese industrial program have been the least successful, while those which have received the least government attention have achieved the most.[20]

The fallacy of a national industrial policy both here and abroad is the assumption that entrepreneurship can be planned; that those who draft plans are more likely than entrepreneurs to respond to the signals of the marketplace and see the unforeseen opportunities to innovate that are the foundation of the entrepreneurial event.

Governmental policy alone is not to blame for the misdirection of entrepreneurship in the United States. Part of the problem stems from the pressure being placed on managers for high short-term profits as opposed to long-term growth. Hayes and Abernathy have described the new principles which "encourage a preference for (1) analytic detachment rather than an insight that comes from hands on experience and (2) short term cost reduction rather than long term development of technological competitiveness." They feel this "new managerial gospel" has been a significant factor in retarding the growth of the U.S. economy.[21] The result has been a stress on today's profits at the expense of tomorrow's, low investment in research and development, and a reduced emphasis on the modernization of plant and equipment. Hayes and Abernathy conclude that the important elements remain, as always, "to invest, to innovate, to lead, to create value where none existed before." To achieve these goals requires leaders, not just managers and financial manipulators.[22]

In the United States a disproportionately large percentage of our students taking advanced training do not do so in science and technology, but in the fields associated with paper entrepreneuship—accounting, law, and financial analysis. Public policy could promote entrepreneurship in the United States, but is not now doing so. Entrepreneurship is not dead, but misdirected. This misdirection will continue until the environment for entrepreneurship is significantly improved.

Notes

1. Ivor Pearce, "Reforms for Entrepreneur to Serve Public Policy," in Arthur Seldon, ed., *Prime Mover of Progress: The Entrepreneur in Capitalism and Socialism* (London: Institute of Economic Affairs, 1980), p. 132.

2. Herbert S. Levin, "On the Nature and Location of Entrepreneurial Activity in Centrally Planned Economies: The Soviet Case," in Joshua Ronen, ed., *Entrepreneurship* (Lexington, Mass.: Lexington Books, 1982), p. 237.

3. Ibid., pp. 254–255; see also J. Berliner, *The Innovative Decision in Soviet Industry* (Cambridge, Mass.: MIT Press, 1976).

4. Gregory Grossman, "Notes on the Illegal Private Economy and Corruption," *Soviet Economy in a Time of Change*, U.S. Congress, Joint Economic Committee, 95th Congress, October 10, 1979, pp. 834–835.

5. David Brand, "Free Enterprise Helps to Keep Russians Fed, But Creates Problems," *Wall Street Journal*, May 2, 1983, pp. 1 and 19.

6. Konstantin Simis, "Russia's Underground Millionaires," *Fortune*, June 29, 1981, p. 38.

7. Ibid.

8. Gale Johnson, "Progress of Economic Reform in the People's Republic of China," (Washington, D.C.: American Enterprise Institute, 1982); June Keonholz, "China's Communes Get a Lot Less Communal as Incentives Boom,' *Wall Street Journal*, July 18, 1983, pp. 1 and 15.

9. Johnson, "Progress of Economic Reform," p. 32.

10. Louis Kraar, "A Little Touch of Capitalism," *Fortune*, April 28, 1983, pp. 121–128.

11. Lawrence Minard, "The Ultimate Chastity Belt," *Forbes*, July 4, 1983, pp. 76–82.

12. Kalman Rupp, *Entrepreneurs in Red* (Albany: State University of New York Press, 1983).

13. Ibid., p. 196.

14. Ibid., p. 231.

15. Jonathan R.T. Hughes, "Entrepreneurship," in Glen Porter, ed., *The Encyclopedia of American Economic History* (New York: Charles Scribners Sons, 1980), p. 226.

16. Robert B. Reich, "Pie slicers vs. Pie enlargers," *Washington Monthly* (September 1980), p. 15.

17. Calvin A. Kent, "The New Entrepreneurs," *Journal of Social, Political, and Economic Studies*, Summer 1983, p. 169.

18. Stan N. Lundine, "Now is the Time for a National Industrial Strategy," and Murray L. Weidenbaum, "Industrial Policy is not the Answer," *Challenge* (July/August 1983), pp. 16–26.

19. Katsuro Sakoh, "Industrial Policy: The Super Myth of Japan's Super Success," *Asian Studies Center Backgrounder* (July 13, 1983), p. 14.

20. Arthur T. Denzau, "Will an Industrial Policy Work for the United States?" (St. Louis, Mo.: Center for the Study of American Business, Washington University, September 1983).

21. Robert H. Hayes and William J. Abernathy, "Managing Our Way to Economic Decline," *Harvard Business Review* (July/August 1980), p. 68.

22. Ibid., p. 77.

Index

Abernathy, William J., 179
Academic values, 31–32, 37
Accelerated Cost Recovery System
    (ACRS), 13, 63, 64, 69, 75–76, 79,
    84, 85
Accountancy Age, 164
Adam Smith Institute, 160, 161, 163–
    166, 168
Advertising, 30, 156
Aetna Life & Casualty, 121
Affiliated Hospital Products, Inc. v.
    Merdel Game Manufacturing Co.,
    125
Alertness, 53, 55, 56
Alice, 33
All in the Family, 33
Alternate Minimum Tax (AMT), 74
American Arbitration Association, 142
American Association for the Advance-
    ment of Science, 99
American Bar Association, 140, 142
American Trucking Association, 107
Amersham, 169
Antioquenos, 26
Antitrust laws, 34
Apple Computers, 99
Arbitrage, 52, 53
Arbitration Act, 141–143
Armington, Catherine, 101
Arrhenius equation, 123
Aspirin, 131
Associated Dry Goods Corp., 121
Atari, Inc. v. *Amusement World, Inc.,*
    128
Austin, Texas, 29

BankAmerica, 121
Bank of America N.T. & S.A., 121
Banks, 33–34, 120–121
Bannock, Graham, 1, 7
Batelle-Columbus Laboratories, 132,
    133
Batelle Memorial Laboratories, 119
Battery industry, 93
Belgium, 155–156
Binks, Martin, 3, 10
Birch, David L., 5, 100–101
Black markets, 174, 175

Borland, 26–27
Brabant, 26
British Broadcasting Corporation, 156
British National Oil Corporation, 169
British Rail, 169
Brockhaus, Robert H., 9
Brookings Institution, 5
Bumpers, Dale, 104
Bureau of Labor Statistics, 94
Bureau of Medical Devices and Diag-
    nostic Products, 99
Bureaucrats, 16, 156, 157–158, 163–
    166, 174, 177
Business failures, 67
Business schools, 31

Cantillon, Richard, 2
Capital, 70–71; and regulation, 14,
    95–97, 106; retention of, 84; and
    taxation, 12, 63–64
Capital deepening, 60
Capital gains: rollover, 34, 75, 84; and
    taxation, 13, 34, 73–75, 84; and
    venture capital, 71, 74
Carlson, Chester, 118–119
Carroll, J.J., 26
Carter, Jimmy, 66, 136
Cellophane, 131
Center for the Study of American
    Business, 93, 100, 109
Charles River Associates, 93
Chelsea (U.K.), 161
Chemical industry, 93, 100, 132, 148
Chinese, 26; *see also* People's Repub-
    lic of China
Chrysler, 32, 35
Cities, 33, 36
Clean Air and Water Act, 106
Cole, Arthur D., 4
Collateral estoppel, 135
Command economies, 16–17, 173–177
Commerce Capital Corporation, 97
Committee for Economic Develop-
    ment, 140
Communities and entrepreneurs, 7, 22,
    33–34, 36, 38–39
Company formation, 23–28, 29–30
Computer software, 15, 122–129, 145

Congressional Record, 133
Construction industry, 94
Consumer Product Safety Commission, 98
Continental Casualty Co. v. *Beardsley,* 126
Coordination problem, 54–55
Copyright, 117, 124–128
Cork, Ireland, 26
Court of Claims, 140
Court of Customs and Patent Appeals, 140–141
Coyne, John, 3, 10
Creativity, 4, 23
Crume v. *Pacific Mutual Life Insurance Co.,* 126–127
Cultural climate and entrepreneurs, 11, 22–23, 25–26, 30–31; *see also* Public opinion

Daily Telegraph, 165
Danzinger, Shelton, 61
Data Resources, 69
Davis-Bacon Act, 94
Decision to become entrepreneur, 24–25
Decorative Aides Corp. v. *Staple Sewing Aides,* 125
DeLorean, John, 157
Demand-side economics, 10
Denmark, 162
Denzau, Arthur, 179
Depreciation, 64, 69, 76
Diamond v. *Diehr,* 122, 123
Diematic Mfg. Corp. v. *Packaging Industries Inc.,* 142
Disequilibriums, 3
Dollar value accounting, 80
Douglas, William O., 122
Drugs. *See* Pharmaceutical industry
Dun & Bradstreet, 21, 23

Eastbourne (U.K.), 161
Economic development programs, 38–39
Economic growth, 3–4, 12, 41–46, 59–60; and allocation of resources, 46, 48–50, 51, 56; and markets, 46–50, 51, 53–54
Economic Recovery Tax Act (ERTA), 13, 69, 71–72, 75, 78; and safe harbor leasing, 79; and savings, 84
Economics of Small Firms (Bannock), 1
Economies of scale, 14, 93

Education, 9, 11, 37–38
Edwardes, Michael, 160
Emerging profit phase, 70–71
Employee Retirement Income Security Act, 96, 97
Employment: and entrepreneurs, 2, 5–6, 101; entry-level, 5–6; and investment, 62; and large corporations, 5
Enterprise zones, 156, 167–168, 176
Entrepreneur, definition of, 2–4
Entrepreneurial event, 11, 23–39
Entry, freedom of, 12, 34, 54, 57, 98
Environment and entrepreneur, 28–32, 35–36
Environmental Protection Agency, 93, 106
Environmental regulation, 13–14, 91, 93, 106
Equal Access to Justice Act, 14, 101, 103, 112
Estate and gift taxes, 13, 81–82, 85
Ethnic groups, 26
Europe, 16, 155–180; bureaucrats, 16, 156, 157–158, 163–166; cultural attitude towards business, 25, 30–31; enterprise zones, 156, 162–168; freeports, 163–166; patents, 143–144, 147–148; taxation, 155, 156, 168
European Economic Community, 156
European Patent Office, 147–148
Excise taxes, 70
Executive Order 12291, 104, 105
Expensing, 64

Fair Labor Standards, 94, 105
Family and entrepreneur, 26–27, 32
Federal Communications Commission, 99, 103
Federal contracts, 108, 110
Federal Drug Administration, 36
Federal Regulatory Flexibility Act, 14
Federal Reserve Bank of Philadelphia, 69–70
Federal Trade Commission, 103
Feldstein, Martin, 74, 80
Filipinos, 26
Financial Accounting Standards Board, 96
Financial Times, 164
Finney, B.R., 26
First-in, first-out (FIFO) rules, 80
Florida Farm Workers Council, 103

Food and Drug Administration, 99, 103
Ford, Henry, 28, 31
Foundry industry, 93
France, 23, 64, 165
Freeports, 163–166
Free zones, 155, 165
Friendly, Henry J., 142

Galbraith, John Kenneth, 102, 163
General Tire & Rubber Company v. *Jefferson Chemical Co.,* 142
Germany, 145, 147, 162
Gilad, Benjamin, 56
Gorokans, 26
Gottschalk v. *Benson,* 122
Government, 10–11, 16–17, 55; economic activity, 61; in Europe, 16, 156, 158, 160; fiscal policy, 12; *see also* Regulation
Grossman, Gregory, 175
Gross national product: production investment in, 62; research and development as percent of, 7, 12, 60–61, 78; small business as percent of, 32
Guardian, 164
Gujeratis, 26
Gumpert, David, 91

Haagan-Dazs, 121
Haloid Corp., 119, 130
Hammeed, K.A., 26
Hammersmith (U.K.), 161
Harris, J.R., 26
Harwood, Edwin, 2, 4, 92
Hayek, F.A., 54–55, 168
Hayes, Robert H., 179
Hazardous waste disposal, 106
Hebert, Robert F., 2
Herbert Rosenthal Jewelry Corp. v. *Kalpakian,* 127
High technology, 21, 31, 99–100
High Wycombe (U.K.), 161
Holiday Inns, Inc., 122
Hong Kong, 176
Hospital Corp. of America, 122
Howe, Geoffrey, 165
H.R. 6103, 105
Hughes, Jonathan R.T., 178
Hull (U.K.), 161
Hungary, 16–17, 173, 176–177

Ibos, 26
Illegal aliens, 105

Imitation, competitve, 131–132
Immigration Reform and Control Act, 105
In Business, 23
Inc., 109
Incentives, 4, 53–54, 57; and patents, 118–119, 136–137
Incontestability, 149–150
Independence of character, 28
India, 26
Individual Retirement Accounts (IRA), 63, 64, 85
Inflation, 12; and investment, 64, 66; and risk, 61–62; and taxation, 74, 75, 80
Innovation, 6–7, 52–53, 133; and regulation, 98–100; and small companies, 98–99
In re Abele, 123
Insurance, 120–121
Intellectual property clause, 117
Interest, cultural bias against, 30
Interest rates, 35, 63
Internal Revenue Service, 102
International Harvester, 32, 35
Interstate Commerce Commission, 98, 107
Invention, 6, 118–119; *see also* Patents
Inventory accounting, 80–81
Investment, 62–63, 64, 66; and taxation, 34, 63–64, 66–67, 74, 84–88; *see also* Investment tax credits
Investment tax credits, 77–78, 79, 84, 85–86
Ireland, 26
Islam, 30
Italy, 25–26, 30

Jains, 26
Japan, 133–134, 145, 147, 179
Jeffersons, 33
Jenn-Air Corporation, 138
Jews, 26, 31
Jobs, Steven, 99
Johnson, Gale, 176
Joint Committee on Taxation, 80
Jones, L., 26

Kensington (U.K.), 161
Kenya, 26
Keogh plans, 84
Keynes, John Maynard, 10, 163, 166

Kilby, Peter, 2, 3, 10
Kirzner, Israel, 3
Kleenex, 15
Knight, Frank, 2
Kodak, 15
Krasner, O.J., 6

Labor costs, 14, 93–94
Land, Edwin, 119, 120
Lanham Trademark Act, 149
Last In, First Out (LIFO) inventory accounting, 13, 80–81, 85
Lead Industries Association, 93
Lear v. *Adkins,* 142
Lebanese, 26
Leibenstein, Harvey, 41–42
Lekachman, Robert, 111
Levin, Herbert S., 173–174
LEXPAT, 146
Lincoln, Abraham, 150
Link, Albert N., 2
London *Times,* 164
Lord & Taylor, 121
Loss-generation phase, 70–71, 77
Lovelock, Douglas, 164

Madison, James, 94
Markets, 46–50, 51, 53–54
Marris, P., 26
Marseilles, 165
Martin, Albro, 4
Media, 33
Medical industry, 159, 169
Megatrends (Naisbit), 1
Mennonites, 26
Mergers, 85
Mexico, 35
Midland, Texas, 29, 33
Miller, George, 105
Milton Keynes (U.K.), 163
Minorities, 8, 34, 35, 110
Miscellaneous Revenue Act of 1982, 69
Mitterand, Francois, 166
Model Law for the Protection of Computer Software, 145
Monetary policy, 62–63, 65
Monopoly, 131
Mormons, 26
Motor Carrier Act, 106

Naisbit, 1, 9
National Court of Appeals, 140

National Federation of Independent Business, 101
National Freight Corporation, 169
National industrial policy, 178–179
National Science Foundation, 6, 99–100, 109
National treatment, 143
Netherlands, 26, 165
New Deal, 92
Nigeria, 26
North Korea, 26
North Norfolk (U.K.), 161
Novak, Michael, 111

Obvious test, 145
Occupational Safety and Health Administration, 93, 94, 105
Odle, Marjorie, 101
Office of Management and the Budget, 6, 98–99, 104, 105
Omenn, D.S., 6
Orphan Drug Act, 149

Paper entrepreneurs, 177–180
Paperwork, 14, 17, 94–95
Paperwork Reduction Act, 14, 101, 103–104
Parallel production, 175
Paris Convention for the Protection of Industrial Property, 143–144
Parker v. *Flook,* 122–123
Parsis, 26
Patent Act of 1952, 145
Patent and Trademark Office, 134–135, 146–147
Patent Cooperation Treaty, 144
Patents, 14–15, 104, 177–150; appeals courts, 15, 139–141; arbitration, 141–143; computer software, 15, 122–129, 145; costs, 134–135; duration, 117–118, 130, 148–149; enforcement, 135; entrepreneurship without, 120–122; examination, 146–148; incontestable, 149–150; international, 143–144, 147–148; of less-important inventions, 144–145; litigation, 135–136, 137, 139; number of, 12, 60–61; public benefits, 118–120; reexamination, 15, 136–139
Patents Appeals Court, 15
Patents Law Amendments Act, 104
Pearce, Ivor, 173
Peers, 27
Pensions, 82, 97

People's Republic of China, 16, 173, 175–176
Personal consumption tax, 63–64
Pharmaceutical industry, 36, 132
Phoenicians, 164
Plant Variety Protection Act, 145
Plotnick, Robert, 61
Polaroid, 119
Pollard, William B., 73
Portable enterprise zones, 16
Poverty, incidence of, 61
Prager, D.J., 6
Previous job, dissatisfaction with, 9
Privatization of public service, 160–163, 168–170
Procurement Automated Service System (PASS), 110
Product viability and regulation, 98
Professional societies, 37
Profit, 12, 53, 55, 69–70
Property rights, 12, 55
Psychology of entrepreneurs, 9–10, 11
Publications, 23
Public Law 95-507, 108, 110
Public opinion and entrepreneurs, 16, 25–26, 156–157; *see also* Cultural climate and entrepreneurs
Public resources, 35
Pyongan, 26

QUANGO, 160
Quebcois, 26

Radiology equipment, 99
Reagan, Ronald, 13, 14, 64, 69, 141; and regulatory reform, 101, 104–105
Refugees, 25, 26
Regulation, 13–14, 35–36, 67, 91–112; and Europe, 156; and patents, 148
Regulatory Flexibility Act, 101, 102–103, 112
Rehnquist, William, 123
Religion, 26, 30
Report of the SBA Task Force on Venture and Equity Capital for Small Business, 96
Research and development: depreciation recovery period, 76; expenditures, 7, 12, 60–61; federal contract, 108–109; and small companies, 98–99; tax credits, 13, 78, 79, 84, 85
Resource allocation, 46, 48–50, 51, 56
Restaurant owners, 94
Retail merchandising, 121

Richman, Tom, 111
Risk, 2, 4, 9, 61–62
Road to Serfdom (Hayek), 168
Robbins, Lord, 50
Rogers, Will, 91, 111
Roubidoux, J., 26
Rupp, Kalman, 176–177

S. 1080, 104
Safe harbor leasing, 78–80, 85
Safety and health regulation, 91, 93, 94, 105
Safeway Stores, Inc., 121
St. Louis Globe-Democrat, 95
St. Paul, Minnesota, 169
Sakoh, Katsuro, 179
Sakong, Il, 26
Salisbury (U.K.), 161
Sanders, James, 110
Santayana, George, 92
Savings, 62, 63, 84
Say, J.V., 2–3
Sayigh, Y.A., 26
Schumpeter, Joseph, 3, 6, 41, 100, 178
Securities and Exchange Commission, 14, 96–97, 103, 106
Seed growers, patents for, 145
Seldon, Arthur, 55, 56
Semiconductor industry, 133
Service firms, 121–122
Set-aside funds, 34, 35, 105, 112
Shredded Wheat, 131
Simpson, Alan K., 105
Singer, James W., 95
Slemrod, Joel, 74
Small Business Administration: and entrepreneur employment, 5, 8; failure of programs, 14; loan program, 95, 109–110; and regulations, 91, 95, 101; and taxation, 72, 75, 76, 81, 83–86
Small Business Innovation Development Act, 108–109
Small Business Investment Company (SBIC), 71, 96, 97
Small Business Investment Incentive Act, 106
Small Business Participating Debentures, 86
Small Business Task Force on Social Security, 82
Small companies: and communities, 7, 22, 33–34, 36, 38–39; equity capital

disadvantages, 96–97; failure, 8; and gross national product, 32; innovation, 6–7, 21–22; and interest rates, 35; and patents, 132; publications, 23; and regulation, 35–36; wages, 83
Smith, Adam, 3
Smoeland, Sweden, 26
Social insurance, employee contributions, 70
Social Security, 65; taxes, 13, 69–70, 82–83
Somerset, A., 26
Southend (U.K.), 161
Soviet Union, 16–17, 147, 173–175
Speculative entrepreneurs, 52
Sproat, Iain, 165
Start-up phase, 73, 83
State governments, 35
State monopolies, 158–159
Steel industry, 22
Stevens, Potter, 123
Stoll, Hans, 70, 72
Subchapter S, 13, 69, 71, 72–73, 85
Summers, Lawrence H., 62
Supply-side economics, 9–10, 13, 55, 64, 69
Swain, Frank, 103
Sweden, 26
Swimming-pool slides, 98
Switzerland, 147
Synercom Technology, Inc. v. University Computing Co., 127

Tandrige (U.K.), 161
Tandy Corp. v. Personal Micro Computers, Inc., 124
Taxation, 12–13, 61, 69–86; complexity of, 85; corporate rate, 71–72; in Europe, 155, 156, 168; and inflation, 64, 66; and investment, 34, 63–64, 66–67, 74, 84–85; neutrality, 70; subsidization, 70
Tax Equity and Fiscal Responsibility Act (TEFRA), 13, 64, 69; and Accelerated Cost Recovery, 76; and safe harbor leasing, 80; and Subchapter S, 72–73
Technological advances: and economic growth, 42, 44–45, 46–48, 60; and patents, 131–132
Teenage employees, 94
Telecom, 169
The Hague, 147
Thermos, 131

Topping, 70
Trade association, 100
Trademark Registration Treaty, 144
Trademarks, 14–15, 129–131, 143–144, 149
Trade secret law, 128–129
Trucking industry, 98, 106–167
Tuddenham, William, 99
T-Zone Act, 155

Unions, 16, 156, 159–163
Unit costs, 14
United Kingdom, 1; employment, 5; enterprise zones, 156; freeports, 163–166; health service, 159, 169; innovation, 7; patents, 147; private contracting, 161–163, 168–170; public spending, 158–159; small firms, 7
U.S. Constitution, 14, 117, 129
U.S. Customs Office, 161, 165
U.S. Department of Agriculture, 145
U.S. Department of Defense, 102
U.S. Department of Housing and Urban Development, 98
U.S. Department of Labor, 93–94, 97, 103
U.S. Department of the Interior, 103
U.S. Department of Transportation, 103
U.S. General Accounting Office, 74
U.S. Supreme Court, 122–128, 132, 139–140, 141, 144–145
Urban Institute, 69

Venture capital, 71, 74, 136
Video games, 128

Wage and price controls, 66
Wages, 83
Wall Street Journal, 105
Walter, James, 70, 72
Wandsworth (U.K.), 161, 162
White House Commission on Small Business, 5, 7; on regulation, 100; tax recommendations, 71, 76, 81, 86
Wisconsin, 7
Women, 8–9, 25
World Intellectual Property Organization, 128–129, 145
Wozniak, Stephen, 99

Xerox, 15, 119, 130–131

Zip Mfg. Co. v. Pep Mfg. Co., 141

About the Contributors

Michael J. Boskin is professor of economics at Stanford University and a research associate for the National Bureau of Economic Research. He completed his undergraduate and graduate work at the University of California, Berkeley. Dr. Boskin is well known for his studies on the impact of taxation on innovation and economic growth. He is author or editor of five books and over fifty articles dealing with taxation, labor, and government finance. Dr. Boskin has been an advisor to committees in both the U.S. House and Senate as well as the U.S. Treasury.

Kenneth W. Chilton is associate director of the Center for the Study of American Business at Washington University, St. Louis. He is also a faculty member of Fontbonne College in Clayton, Missouri. He has held a variety of positions in the private sector and was owner and operator of a small business. He is coauthor of studies documenting the perverse impact of federal regulation on the small business sector. Mr. Chilton holds both engineering and management degrees from Northwestern University. Among his more significant publications is the Congressional report, "Federal Government Regulation and Small Business Performance."

Israel M. Kirzner received the B.A. from Brooklyn College and the Ph.D. from New York University, where he is now professor of economics. He is the author of five books, including *Competition and Entrepreneurship* (1973), *Perception, Opportunity, and Profit* (1979), and *Method, Process and Austrian Economics* (Lexington Books, 1982). Dr. Kirzner is the founder of the doctoral program in Austrian economics at New York University.

Madsen Pirie is president of the Adam Smith Institute in London. He is a graduate of Edinburgh and St. Andrews Universities, and was associate professor of philosophy at Hillsdale College in Michigan. Dr. Pirie's books include *Trial and Error, The Idea of Progress, The Logic of Economics,* and *Economy and Local Government* (1981). His work with the Adam Smith Institute has included studies on privatization, mass transit, and freeports. He developed many of the ideas for privatization of the public sector that are now part of the economic program of the British government. His current interest is encouraging reform of the European Economic Community.

William E. Schuyler, Jr., was commissioner of patents for the United States from 1969 to 1971 and now is a partner in the patent law firm of Schuyler, Banner, Birch, McKie, and Beckett. He is also adjunct professor of law at

Georgetown University Law Center in Washington, D.C. Mr. Schuyler was cochairman of the U.S. delegation and chairman of the main committee at the Washington Diplomatic Conference on the Patent Cooperation Treaty and was ambassador and head of the U.S. delegation to the second session at the Diplomatic Conference for the Revision of the Paris Convention in Nairobi. He has been chairman of the Section on Patent, Trademark, and Copyright Law and delegate from the Section of Patent, Trademark, and Copyright Law to the House of Delegates of the American Bar Association. Mr. Schuyler received the B.S. in engineering from Catholic University and the law degree from Georgetown University.

Albert Shapero received the B.S. in engineering and the M.S. in industrial engineering from the University of California at Berkeley. He currently holds the Davis Chair in the Management Sciences Department at The Ohio State University. Previously he was professor of management at the University of Texas at Austin. Professor Shapero's research interests are innovation, technology transfer, and entrepreneurship. He frequently gives expert testimony before legislative bodies and the United States Senate and House, and has published over a hundred articles, monographs, chapters, and technical reports.

About the Editor

Calvin A. Kent is Herman W. Lay Professor of Private Enterprise and director of the Center for Private Enterprise and Entrepreneurship at Baylor University. Before coming to Baylor he was chief economist to the South Dakota legislature and served as a consultant to the Internal Revenue Service and the U.S. Senate Finance Committee. Among the thirteen books which he has either authored or edited is *The Encyclopedia of Entrepreneurship* (1982). He was president of the National Association of Economic Educators and is secretary/treasurer of the Association for Private Enterprise Education. He received the B.A. from Baylor University and the Ph.D. from the University of Missouri/Columbia.